24.95

D0811998

People, States and Fear

People, States, and Fear

The National Security
Problem in International
Relations

by

Barry Buzan

The University of North Carolina Press
Chapel Hill

Published in the United States of America 1983
by The University of North Carolina Press

Library of Congress Cataloging in Publication Data

Buzan, Barry.
  People, states, and fear.

  1. National security. 2. International relations.
I. Title
UA10.5.B89   1983   355′.03   83–3559
ISBN 0–8078–1572–1
ISBN 0–8078–4113–7 pbk

Published in Great Britain 1983
by The Harvester Press Ltd.
16 Ship Street, Brighton, Sussex, England

Printed and bound in Great Britain

Contents

72000

Contents

To my brother Tony.
May he be right in thinking
that humanity can develop the
intelligence necessary to solve
the national security problem.

Preface

This book has had a long gestation. The idea of it took root in my mind during 1976, and in the intervening period the work of many people has influenced its development. As the idea grew, it increasingly conditioned my reading, pushing me into unfamiliar areas and establishing the relevance of literatures which previously lay at the periphery of my thinking. Partly because the sources became so diverse, I have used bibliographical footnotes, rather than a single bibliography, to acknowledge my debts. Since the references do not constitute a coherent literature, it seemed more useful to concentrate them at their point of relevance in the text rather than to cluster them at the end.

Many people have helped in ways more direct than my encounters with their writing. The late Fred Hirsch told me I would have to learn some political economy, and on that point, as on many others, he proved correct. My participation in a colloquium organised by John Ruggie on 'alternative conceptions of international order' provided an ideal context in which to pursue Fred's advice, and set me to thinking on a scale appropriate to this book. Dialogues with H.O. Nazareth have enriched my mind more than he might suspect, and although they have been in a completely different context from this project, the cross-fertilisation has been considerable. The International Relations Group chaired by R.J. Barry Jones has stimulated me to think about several questions which I would otherwise probably have ignored, and important parts of this book have grown from seeds planted during its discussions.

I am deeply grateful to the following friends and colleagues for their comments on the penultimate draft: Ken Booth, Hedley Bull, Deborah Buzan, Tony Buzan, Joseph Frankel, Roger Harrison, Kal Holsti, Peter Mangold, Peter Murray, Gonzalo Ramos, Gowher Rizvi, John Ruggie and Kenneth Waltz. Richard Little did me the immense service of commenting on a first draft, and Charles Jones and Robert Skidelsky contributed detailed criticisms of chapter 5. The book would not be what it is without their assistance, and even where I have not agreed with them, they have prodded me to express my own views more clearly. The published result is, of course, my responsibility, but I can carry that responsibility more confidently for having taken some of my beatings in earlier rounds of criticism.

I would like also to thank the University of Warwick for allowing me two terms of sabbatical leave during 1981. Without that uninterrupted stretch of time I could not have written the complete first draft which was the distant ancestor of this book. Finally, I take pleasure in acknowledging the very able assistance of Mrs Joy Gardner, who does more than her share to make our Department an efficient and pleasant place in which to work, and who produced all the typescripts neatly and on time.

Barry Buzan
London
August 1982

Introduction

The National Security Problem in International Relations

Few people would deny that national security ranks prominently among the problems facing humanity. States, which are the highest form of political order that we have so far been able to develop and sustain, seem unable to coexist with each other in harmony. Throughout the history of states, each has been made insecure by the existence of others, and the actions of each in pursuit of its own national security have frequently combined with those of others to produce war. Given the power of our military technology, war is now the most prominant and, arguably, the most likely threat to the continuity of our species. Since the national security problem lies at the root of war, addressing it is a matter of acknowledged importance.

The principal contentions of this book are first, that one needs to understand the concept of security in order to have a proper understanding of the national security problem, and secondly, that in its prevailing usage the concept is so weakly developed as to be inadequate for the task. We shall seek to demonstrate that an underdeveloped concept of security constitutes such a substantial barrier to progress that it might almost be counted as part of the problem. Conversely, we shall try to show how a more fully developed and expanded concept can lead to constructive redefinitions of the problem.

Security is not the only concept through which the national security problem can be approached. Most of the literature which attempts analysis or prescription is based on the concepts of power and peace. Those who favour the approach through power derive their thinking from the traditional Realist school of International Relations pioneered by E.H. Carr and Hans Morgenthau.[1] They can

1

argue that their concept leads them not only to the basic pattern of capabilities in the international system, but also to a prime motive for the behaviour of actors. They gain, in addition, the wealth of insights associated with the long-standing study of power in the discipline of Politics. Those who favour the approach through peace are more loosely associated into the idealist school. They can argue that their concept leads them not only to see the problem in holistic terms, as opposed to the necessarily fragmented view of the Realists, but also that it focuses attention directly on the essential matter of war. Since war is the major threat arising from the national security problem, a solution to it would largely eliminate the problem from the international agenda.

These two approaches dominate thinking about the national security problem and have done so for decades, if not centuries. They often lead, as we shall see, to highly polarised and conflicting prescriptions. Within this universe of debate the concept of security plays a subsidiary role. It tends to be seen either as a derivative of power, in the sense that an actor with enough power to reach a dominating position will acquire security as a result, or as a consequence of peace, in the sense that a lasting peace would provide security for all. We shall argue that the concept of security is much more powerful and useful than its current status would suggest, and that it deserves elevation to equal rank with power and peace as an approach to the problem. By itself, it leads us to a prime motive for behaviour which is different from, but no less significant than that provided by power, and to a holistic perspective which is likewise different from, but no less useful than that provided by peace. In combination, these add up to an analytical framework which stands comparison with anything available from the more established concepts. In addition, a more fully developed concept of security can be seen to lie between the extremes of power and peace, and to enrich both of them. It provides many ideas which link the established conventions of the other two schools and help to bridge the gulf which normally, and to their mutual detriment, separates them. We shall argue that security is more usefully viewed as a companion to, rather than a derivative of, power, and that it is more usefully viewed as a prior condition of peace than a consequence of it.

Our task is to habilitate the concept of security – we cannot rehabilitate it because it has never been in proper working order. We shall begin in this Introduction by looking at the evidence that the concept is underdeveloped, and by exploring the reasons for that condition. We shall then introduce the approach of the book, outline its objectives in more detail, and explain the logic of its organisation.

Security as an Underdeveloped Concept

The principal evidence for the underdevelopment of security as a concept in International Relations is to be found in its use in the literature. By way of comparison, the literature on power contains not only a mass of empirical work, but also a well-developed body of theoretical writing. We might reasonably expect to find a similar balance for any major academic concept.

When we turn to security, however, a rather different situation obtains. While the term itself is in wide use, and appears to be accepted as a central organising concept by both practitioners and academics, the literature on it is very unbalanced. A large and flourishing literature exists on the empirical side dealing with contemporary security problems and issues. Most of this comes out of the sub-field of Strategic Studies, for which security is the core concept. The foreign, military and economic policies of states, the intersection of these policies in areas of change or dispute, and the general structure of relations which they create, are all analysed in terms of national and international security. But the concept of security is seldom addressed in terms other than the policy interests of particular actors or groups, and the discussion has a heavy military emphasis. Endless disputes rage about the particularities of security policy both within and between states. The discussion is normally set within very limited temporal and conceptual frameworks, and general notions like 'dominance' and 'stability' mark the limits of attempts to give enduring meaning to the idea of security.

But when we search for a matching conceptual literature on security relatively little comes to hand, and there is certainly nothing equivalent to a coherent school of thought like the Realists on power. The enthusiasm for collective security after the First World War had some promise in this direction, but the failure of both the League of Nations and the United Nations to measure up to the task has not surprisingly truncated interest in this whole approach.[2] John Herz introduced the idea of the security dilemma in the early 1950s,[3] a structural notion in which the self-help attempts of states to look after their security needs tend automatically (i.e. regardless of intention) to lead to rising insecurity for others as each interprets its own measures as defensive, and the measures of others as potentially threatening. The security dilemma idea is widely acknowledged in the literature, but aside from some notable recent work by Robert Jervis, there has been almost no attempt to build on it.[4] This is surprising because, as we shall see, the idea offers a weighty and sophisticated alternative to the power struggle model of the Realists as a way of interpreting the basic dynamics of international politics.

Probably the best known conceptual piece on security is Arnold Wolfers' chapter on national security in his book *Discord and Collaboration*.[5] Wolfers' emphasis on *national* security certainly reflected the dominant orientation in the empirical literature, and his essay is a masterly introduction to the many-dimensioned complexities of the concept. His characterisation of security as an 'ambiguous symbol' – at one point he argues that it 'may not have any precise meaning at all' – would seem, unfortunately, to have killed off further interest in developing security as a major approach to understanding international relations. This was almost certainly not his intention, since the principal burden of the essay was to point out the potential mischief of ambiguity in a symbol of such great potency in national politics.

In addition to these core works, one can find only a few other conceptual discussions of security. Hedley Bull, Bernard Brodie, Frank Trager and Frank Simonie make brief, but useful contributions on the difficulties of applying it.[6] Hugh Macdonald attempts to tackle the ambiguity of the concept, but ends up defeated by his own categories, and withdraws from the struggle by dismissing security as an 'inadequate' concept.[7] Robert Jervis introduces the interesting idea of security regimes, which draws attention from the state to the system level of analysis.[8] And Gert Krell attempts a broad critique of excessively military conceptions of security from a peace research perspective.[9] More peripherally, we can find general discussions of security in the context of American policy choices.[10] We might also include the large and well-known critical literature on Strategic Studies which often contains comments relevant to the use of security as a concept.[11] But these works, whatever their individual merits, do not even begin to add up to a coherent investigation of the concept, and their impact on the study of international relations has been marginal. At best, like Herz, Jervis and Bull, they have generated useful ways of looking at particular problems, but they have not tapped the full potential of the concept as a lens through which to view the subject as a whole.

The hazards of a weakly conceptualised, ambiguously defined, but politically powerful concept like national security have not gone unnoticed. The concept has come to be dominated in use by the idea of national security, and many authors have criticised the excessively narrow, hollow and militarised interpretation of security to which this approach can easily, though not necessarily, give rise. Wolfers' article cited above, written during the thick of the Cold War (1952) was pointing in this direction. Richard Ashley mounts an extensive critique of reductionist, actor-oriented, narrowly focused approaches to security analysis (what he calls 'technical rationality'), urging instead a more holistic, linkage-oriented, systemic view ('rationality proper').[12] He argues that technical rationality is itself a principal factor exacerbating the security dilemma. Ken Booth argues convincingly that the state-bound, ethnocentric confines within which Strategic Studies pursues its analysis is not only seriously deficient in relation to the character of the problem, but also dangerous in that the resultant skewed diagnosis, as applied through state policy, makes the problem worse. Despite their wholly different starting points, both Ashley and Booth come to similar conclusions, in Booth's words: 'those strategists who do not attempt to be part of the solution will undoubtedly become an increasingly important part of the problem'.[13]

Leonard Beaton has similarly argued for the need to expand conceptions of security outward from the limits of parochial national security to include a range of systemic considerations.[14] Likewise, but again from a different perspective, Stanley Hoffmann argues for the need to begin 'turning national security into an aspect of world order policy'.[15] Hedley Bull argues against excessive self-interest in approaches to national security, and for a broader view in which common interests and linkage among national securities receive greater attention.[16] More generally, L.B. Krause and Joseph Nye have observed that 'neither economists nor political scientists have paid enough attention to the complexity of the concept of security, including its *instrumental role* in the enhancement of other values'.[17] Even the Brandt Commission has called for a new concept of security which would transcend the narrow notions of military defence and look more towards conditions conducive to peaceful relations.[18]

The common theme underlying these voices is that a notion of security bound to the level of individual states is inherently inadequate. At best, such a notion produces the dangerously ambiguous symbol outlined by Wolfers which 'while appearing to offer guidance and a basis for broad consensus, . . . may be permitting everyone to label whatever policy he favours with an attractive and possibly deceptive name'.[19] At worst, it drives the security dilemma to such a pitch of intensity that it begins to resemble the model of those who see international relations as an unending struggle for power. *National* security, these authors argue, might well be a self-defeating contradiction in terms.

Because security is seen primarily in national terms by both policymakers and strategists, there exists a problem here of considerable importance. That section of academia which is most concerned with security is largely locked into a narrow view of it. National policy-makers are virtually required, because of their position and because of the nature of their powers and responsibilities, to take a national view. And no policy-makers exist above the national level. Thus, we are faced with a situation in which the primary thrusts of both effort and analysis are pushing in a destructive direction, and in which the main actors, both academics and practitioners, are locked into their roles by deeply-rooted and heavily institutionalised traditions.

Since security is a widely-used core concept in the study of international relations, and since the empirical literature confirms Wolfers' analysis that there is much dispute about its meaning, we must ask why the idea has remained relatively unexplored. This question becomes especially important in as much as the disputes at the empirical level derive much of their force and persistence from the lack of any deeper and more general understanding of the concept. At least five lines of explanation apply.

The first is simply that the idea has proved too complex to attract analysts, and therefore has been neglected in favour of more tractable concepts. This explanation has some weight, for security clearly is a difficult concept. But security is no more difficult than other core concepts in the social sciences. Like power, justice, peace, equality and freedom, it is what W.B. Gallie has called an 'essentially contested concept'.[20] Such concepts necessarily generate unsolvable debates about their meaning and application because, as Richard Little points out, they 'contain an ideological element which renders empirical evidence irrelevant as a means of resolving the dispute'.[21] Even an apparently concrete concept like the state virtually defies precise, generally accepted definition because of its essentially contested nature.[22] The utility of these concepts stems in some paradoxical way from whatever it is that makes them inherently ambiguous, and it is their ambiguity which normally stimulates theoretical discussion about them. They encompass a whole domain, rather than just a fixed point, within the landscape of social science. For this reason, they cannot be defined in any general sense, but only in relation to specific cases. They indicate an area of concern rather than a precise condition, and consequently require theoretical analysis in order to identify the boundaries of their application, the contradictions which occur within them, and the significance for them of new developments. The domain and contradictions of security have not been adequately explored, and the reason cannot be found in the inherent difficulty of the task.

A second, and more convincing explanation for the neglect of security lies in the scope for overlap between it and the concept of power. The Realist model of international politics as a struggle for power had an obvious relevance in the highly polarised environment of the Second World War, and almost immediately thereafter of the Cold War. States were seen as locked into a power struggle, and security easily slipped into the subordinate role in which it was seen as a derivative of power. In the Realist orthodoxy, power dominated both as end and as means. Security necessarily shrank conceptually to being a way of saying either how well any particular state or allied group of states was doing in the struggle for power, or how stable the balance of power overall appeared to be. Reduced to little more than a synonym for power, security could have little independent relevance in wider systemic terms, and therefore the security dilemma approach could function at best as a minor adjunct to the power model of international relations. The point here is not that power and security *are* interchangeable, but merely that they *appeared* to be so at the time, and that appearance was sufficiently convincing to stifle further inquiry into security as a separate concept. Power may become the essence of security in situations of intense confrontation or conflict, but to assume that such an identity always holds, creates, as we shall see, a self-fulfilling prophecy.

A third reason for the conceptual underdevelopment of security lies in the nature of the various revolts against the Realist orthodoxy, none of which was sympathetic to the idea. Those of an idealist bent rejected the Realist model as dangerously self-fulfilling, and far too war-prone for a nuclear-armed world. They could have organised themselves around the concept of security, as many of like mind did during the interwar years, but they did not, the idea of collective security having been emasculated by the experiences of the 1930s. Idealists turned instead to the even grander, essentially contested concept of peace. The policies for peace – arms control and disarmament, and international co-operation – echoed those of the interwar years, and in the shadow of nuclear obliteration clearly provided a more inspirational base than the complexities of security, which played only a marginal role in their analyses. Security was, in any case, already sullied by its association with the power model.

A later reaction against Realism centred on the concept of interdependence, which potentially offered an intellectual orientation highly appropriate to the development of security along the paths opened up by Herz. But the primary motivation for this movement stemmed from the deepening of economic troubles in the early 1970s, and its practitioners understandably concerned themselves mainly with the impact of economic issues on world politics. Their inclination was to push the traditional, military power-oriented Realist model into the background, seeing its competitive, fragmented, force-based approach as increasingly irrelevant to the interwoven network world of international political economy. This attitude tended to produce a two-tiered framework. Military considerations were seen as largely marginal to outcomes involving interdependence issues. They were left to be considered as an almost separate sector, important as an underlying condition for interdependence, but operating in a more or less self-contained fashion, largely paralysed by the nuclear stalemate, and no longer at the undisputed centre of high politics. Economic issues crept into Strategic Studies in the form of worries over supplies of strategic resources, and power models infiltrated interdependence thinking as it became apparent that interdependence was distributed unevenly.[23] But little attempt was made to integrate the two by applying interdependence logic, via the more interconnective concept of security, to the problem of military power in an international anarchy. Part of the purpose of subsequent chapters is to suggest how such an integration might be pursued.

Security also suffered neglect because of the great methodological upheaval which consumed the field of International Relations from the late 1950s through to the mid-1970s. Behaviouralism, with its scientific, value-free, and quantitative concerns, was by definition not suited to the universe of essentially contested concepts. Indeed, it was an explicit revolt against the dominance of such an ambiguous and non-cumulative mode of thought. Behaviouralists had to deal with power, because it represented the dominant orthodoxy. The prospect of yet another operational quagmire like security could hardly be expected to arouse them to enthusiasm.

A fourth reason for the conceptual underdevelopment of security can be found in the nature of Strategic Studies, which as a sub-field produced a large volume of empirical literature on problems of military policy. Why then has this not served as a base for development of security's more conceptual side? As I have argued at length elsewhere, there are three reasons.[24] First is that Strategic Studies has to spend a very high proportion of its energies on keeping up with new developments. The shifting patterns of international amity and enmity, plus the ceaseless interplay of developments in weapons technology and deployment, require constant monitoring and evaluation. The vastness of this task has largely confined Strategic Studies to short-term perspectives, leaving neither much capacity nor much inclination to move beyond empirical and policy-oriented horizons.

Second, Strategic Studies is for the most part an offspring of Anglo-American defence policy needs, and as such it bears conspicuous signs of its parentage. Its attachment to security is heavily conditioned by the status quo orientations of hegemonic countries safely removed from the pressure of large attached neighbours.

Strategic Studies is policy-oriented, and therefore both empirically bound and constrained not to wander much beyond the imperatives of the national policy level. In this sense, Strategic Studies still exists largely within the confines of the classical Realist model of the struggle for power.[25] Third, Strategic Studies has a fundamentally military orientation inherited from its roots in military strategy and defence studies. Security is about much more than military capability and relations, and this, along with the other two factors just outlined, has made Strategic Studies an infertile seedbed for the further growth of the concept.

A fifth, and final reason for the neglect of security hinges on the argument that, for the practitioners of state policy, compelling reasons exist for maintaining its symbolic ambiguity. The appeal to national security as a justification for actions and policies which would otherwise have to be explained is a political tool of immense convenience for a large variety of sectional interests. An undefined notion of national security offers scope for power-maximising strategies to political and military elites, because of the considerable leverage over domestic affairs which can be obtained by invoking it. While such leverage may sometimes be justified, as in the case of Britain's mobilisation during the Second World War, the natural ambiguity of foreign threats during peacetime makes it easy to disguise more sinister intentions in the cloak of national security. It hardly needs to be pointed out, for example, that many interests in the United States and the Soviet Union benefit from exaggerating the level of threat which each poses to the other. Cultivation of hostile images abroad can justify intensified political surveillance, shifts of resources to the military, and other such policies with deep implications for the conduct of domestic political life. At an extreme, the need for national security can even be evoked as a reason for not discussing it. One has only to think of the dying days of the Nixon White House to feel the implications of this state of affairs. This line of reasoning points back to the notion of essentially contested concepts, whose ideological cores take us to the heart of politics. Security is an intensely political concept, and exploration of this aspect will be a main theme of subsequent chapters.

The Approach of this Book

If our criticism of the prevailing conception of security is that it is too narrowly founded, then not only must the inadequacies of the prevailing view be fully analysed, but also the grounds for a broader view (which is implicit in the criticism) must be explored and laid out. In other words, we must try to map the domain of security as an essentially contested concept. This cartographic exercise is necessarily more abstract than empirical, because its purpose is to draw the conceptual framework on which the mass of empirical studies by strategists and others rests. Since we are trying to transcend the criticisms aimed at the excessively narrow focus on national security, we must detach ourselves somewhat from the pressures of day-to-day policy issues and the conventional modes of thought that have grown up around them. The approach in this book will thus be in complete, though complementary, contrast to that taken by Neville Brown in *The Future Global Challenge: A predictive study of world security 1977–1990.*[26] Both books aim to encourage a wider perspective on security than that encompassed by the traditional focus on national military policy. Brown argues specifically from the multi-faceted trends and developments in world affairs, which he surveys exhaustively, and concludes that the changing character of the international environment necessitates a broader view of security. The limits to his highly empirical approach come from the rapidly decreasing reliability of projections into the future as they move away from the known facts of any specified present.

In what follows, we shall look more at the idea of security than at the contemporary empirical conditions in which security policy has to be formulated. What does security mean, in a general sense? And how is this general meaning transferred to the specific entities like states in which we are interested? What exactly is the referent object of security when we refer to national security? If it is the state, what does that mean? Are we to take the state as meaning the sum of the individuals within it? Or is it in some sense more than the sum of its parts? In either case, how do individuals relate to an idea like national security in terms of their own interests? At the other extreme, what does international security mean? Does it apply to some entity higher than states, or is there some sense in which security among states is an indivisible phenomenon?

The limits to such an exercise are more philosophical than empirical. Because security is an essentially contested concept it naturally generates questions as well as answers. It encompasses several important contradictions and a host of nuances all of which can cause confusion if not understood. Major contradictions include that between defence and security, that between individual security and national security, that between national security and international security, and that between violent means and peaceful ends. Add to these the difficulties of determining the referent object of security (i.e. what it is that is to made secure), and the pitfalls of applying the idea across a range of sectors (military, political, economic and social), and the scope of the task becomes clear. The object of the exercise is not to try to resolve these conundrums, but rather to explore them, and to clarify the problems they pose for any attempt to apply the concept to real problems. The easy part of the exercise is using these insights to demolish the logic of conventional applications of security which ignore some of the contradictions they contain. The hard part is finding derived concepts which enable the concept of security to be applied to practical situations in the full knowledge of the contradictions involved.

As argued above, the character of security as an essentially contested concept defies the pursuit of an agreed general definition, and we shall not pursue this phantom here. Years of effort have failed to produce a generally accepted definition or measure for power, and the concept of justice is traditionally notorious for the way in which it divides opinion. There is no reason to think that security would be any easier to crack, and there is not much point in trying. As with power and justice, the general sense of what we are talking about is clear: the political effects of physical capabilities in the case of power, the pursuit of fair outcomes when behaviour is contested in the case of justice, and the pursuit of freedom from threat in the case of security. Lack of an overall definition does not inhibit discussion, and the attempt at precise definition is much more suitably confined to empirical cases where the particular factors in play can be identified. Since we shall not be working at the level of case-studies in this book, our task is pre-definitional. The objective is to develop a holistic concept of security which can serve as a framework for those wishing to apply the concept to particular cases. Such a framework is broader than a definition, because it encompasses the contraditions rather than trying to resolve them. Its purpose is to map the terrain of the concept, identifying both its general features and its conspicuous hazards. Such a map will reveal not only the costs of working with a narrow conception of security, but also the advantages to be gained by attempting to apply a broader view.

The objective of this intellectual trek is not to arrive somewhere new, but, in the words of T.S. Eliot, 'to arrive where we started and know the place for the first time'.[27] As Michael Howard has pointed out, discussion about security affairs is frequently marked by appallingly crude conceptual standards: 'pronouncements about military power and disarmament are still made by public figures of apparent intelligence and considerable authority with a naive dogmatism of a kind such as one finds in virtually no other area of social studies or public affairs'.[28] The result of the present exercise might serve to raise the conceptual sophistication with which people discuss security. It might also reduce the political potency of national security by exposing its limits and contradictions, and thereby mitigate some of the dangers pointed out three decades ago by Wolfers.

An improved understanding of security serves two other academic purposes. First, it opens up a new perspective on the field of International Relations. Because security is a core concept in the field, the process of mapping it inevitably takes us on a grand tour of international relations. We visit much familiar ground, but see it through the perceptual lens of security rather than through more familiar lenses like power and peace. As a result, newly derived concepts emerge to fit the patterns which the security lens reveals, in the same way that derived concepts like the balance of power emerge from looking at international relations through the power lens. By the end of our tour, we find that our search for a more effective approach to the national security problem has produced an alternative framework for International Relations as a whole. The concept of security yields a perspective which complements those already well-established, and yet which is sufficiently powerful in its own right to provide an ideal model of international relations derived from Waltz's observation that 'in anarchy, security is the highest end'.[29] New light is cast on old concepts like system structure and arms racing, and new concepts are cast on the old problem of national security policy-making.[30]

Secondly, it provides a conceptual introduction to Strategic Studies. A primary motive for writing this book arose from the problems of trying to teach Strategic Studies without being able to offer students a basic introduction to the underlying concept of the field. One is forced to push students straight into the deep end of a fast moving and complex stream of empirical literature. The idea of security weaves all through this literature, and some sense of what it means is necessary in order to interpret and evaluate much of the argument. Without some guidelines, students can easily find that the natural ambiguity of the concept confuses them even more than either the formidable mass of technical material or the political fog which inevitably surrounds any security issue. A relatively stable conceptual framework within which to think about the great press of contemporary strategic problems would not only help them to avoid being swept away by the hectic empiricism of the field, but would also provide them with some useful tools for analysing the problems with which they are confronted.

A primarily abstract approach of this sort is, it seems to me, almost the only way to evade the intense pressure for short-term analysis that is such a strong feature of Strategic Studies. Only by stepping away from the front line of new developments for a while can one obtain a broader and perhaps more stable perspective. The advantage of an abstract as opposed to an historical view is that the latter suffers from the uniqueness of all phenomena as conditioned by their own time and context. While broad outlines of phenomena like arms races, balances of power and war are discernible, the particularities are always sufficiently different to make parallels, and the inferences drawn from them an exceedingly uncertain business. The abstract approach of course has its own pitfalls, but it is the preferred one here in good measure because it has been so little explored in the contemporary literature.

The Structure of this Book

Although the subject here is security, the reader will find that what follows is not organised around the conventional subject categories of Strategic Studies. While topics such as deterrence, arms control and disarmament, crisis management, alliances, military technology, strategy, arms racing and contemporary national security problems and policies will play a part in our discussion, they do not constitute its principal focus. Instead, our inquiry will be centred on two questions: What is the referent object for security? And what are the necessary conditions for security? Security as a concept clearly requires a referent object, for without an answer to the question 'The security of what?', the idea makes no sense. To answer simply 'the state', does not solve the problem. Not only is the state an amorphous, multi-faceted, collective object to which security could be applied in many different ways, but also there are many states, and the security of one cannot be discussed without reference to the others. The search for a referent object of security goes hand-in-hand with that for its necessary conditions, a link which becomes stronger as we discover that security has many referent objects. These objects of security multiply not only as the membership of the society of states increases, but also as we move down through the state to the level of individuals, and up beyond it to the level of the international system as a whole. Since the security of any one referent object or level cannot be achieved in isolation from the others, the security of each becomes, in part, a condition for the security of all.

The need to explore the referent objects of security on several different levels is what determines the structure of this book. I have taken from Waltz the idea of three levels of analysis centred on individuals, states and the international system.[31] These will be referred to respectively as levels 1, 2 and 3, and they provide the framework around which the chapters are organised. These levels should be treated only as a convenient sorting device, and not as strict categorisations. Extensive grey areas exist in the universe of sub-state and transnational organisations which lie between the individual and the states, and in the universe of multi-state and non-state collectivities which lie between states and the international system as a whole. Although these levels form the major ordering principle of the book, no inference should be drawn that security can be isolated for treatment at any single level. Rationalisations for single-level security policies are quite common, as in the case of individuals who arm themselves before going out onto the streets, and states which pursue policies of national security by cultivating military power. The burden of the argument here is precisely to refute such notions by illustrating the extent to which security connects across all levels. The academic disaggregation is undertaken only in order to make the reassembled whole easier to understand.

Chapter 1 begins at level 1 by looking at individuals and security. To what extent are individuals the basic referent object of security, and how does individual security relate to the state? Chapter 2 follows this line of inquiry up to level 2, concentrating on the nature of the state as an object of security. Extensive investigation is made into the different components of the state to which security might apply, and conclusions appropriate to this level are drawn about the limitations of a concept of national security. These first two chapters introduce the contradiction between individual and national security. Chapter 3 is a bridge between levels 2 and 3, linking state and system in a survey of the threats and vulnerabilities which define national insecurity. Part of security as a policy problem is revealed here in the unresolvable ambiguity of threats.

Chapters 4 and 5 move up to level 3, looking at the structure of the international system and the nature of international security. Both the political and economic structures are surveyed in relation to the national security problem, and the system itself is addressed as an object of security. The emphasis of these two chapters is on the systemic conditions for national security. Chapters 6 and 7 continue at level 3, but concentrate on the dynamics of security interactions among states, and the contradictions they produce between national and international security. Two dilemmas are explored: the defence dilemma, which stems from the contradiction between defence and security; and the power-security dilemma, which is generated both by the tension between status quo and revisionist actors, and by relentless advances in military technology. Chapter 8 draws the arguments from the three levels together in the context of national security policy-making, and addresses the contradiction between ends and means. The logical, perceptual and political problems facing national security policy-makers are explored, and the domestic policy process is identified as an independent factor in the national security problem. Chapter 9 draws conclusions about the folly of trying to separate individual, national and international security as approaches to the problem. It explores the weaknesses of policy prescriptions based excessively on level 2 or on level 3, and outlines a more holistic concept, arguing that this serves not only as a sounder approach to policy, but also as a major integrating concept for the field of International Relations.

Notes

1 E.H. Carr, *The Twenty Years Crisis* (London, Macmillan, 1946, 2nd edn); Hans Morgenthau, *Politics Among Nations* (New York, Knopf, 1973, 5th edn). See also, for a more recent and sophisticated Realist view, Kenneth N. Waltz, *Theory of International Politics* (Reading, Mass., Addison–Wesley, 1979). Realism in this context should not be confused with the philosophical school of thought of the same name.

2 See, for example, Otto Pick and Julian Critchley, *Collective Security* (London, Macmillan, 1974); Roland N. Stromberg, *Collective Security and American Foreign Policy* (New York, Praeger, 1963); and M.V. Naidu, *Collective Security and the United Nations* (Delhi, Macmillan, 1974).

3 John H. Herz, 'Idealist Internationalism and the Security Dilemma', *World Politics*, vol. 2. (1950), pp. 157–80; John H. Herz, *Political Realism and Political Idealism* (Chicago, University of Chicago Press, 1951); and John H. Herz, *International Politics in the Atomic Age* (New York, Columbia University Press, 1959), pp. 231–43.

4 Robert Jervis, *Perception and Misperception in International Politics* (Princeton, Princeton University Press, 1976), esp. ch. 3; 'Security Regimes', *International Organization*, 36 : 2 (1982); and 'Cooperation Under the Security Dilemma', *World Politics*, 30 : 2 (1978), pp. 167–214. See also Richard K. Ashley, *The Political Economy of War and Peace: the Sino-Soviet-American Triangle and the Modern Security Problematique* (London, Frances Pinter, 1980).

5 Arnold Wolfers, 'National Security as an Ambiguous Symbol', *Discord and Collaboration* (Baltimore, Johns Hopkins University Press, 1962), ch. 10.

6 Hedley Bull, *The Control of the Arms Race* (London, Weidenfeld & Nicolson, 1961), pp. 25–9; Bernard Brodie, *War and Politics* (London, Cassell, 1973), ch. 8; Frank N. Trager and Frank L. Simonie, 'An Introduction to the Study of National Security', in F.N. Trager and P.S. Kronenberg (eds), *National Security and American Society* (Lawrence, Kansas University Press, 1973).

7 Hugh Macdonald, 'The Place of Strategy and the Idea of Security', *Millennium*, 10:3 (1981).

8 Jervis, *op. cit.* (note 4) (1982).

9 Gert Krell, 'The Development of the Concept of Security', *Arbeitspapier* 3/1979, Peace Research Institute, Frankfurt.

10 For example, Richard J. Barnet, 'The Illusion of Security', in Charles R. Beitz and Theodore Herman (eds), *Peace and War* (San Francisco, W.H. Freeman, 1973); and Maxwell D. Taylor, 'The Legitimate Claims of National Security', *Foreign Affairs*, 52:3 (1974).

11 For example, Anatol Rapoport, 'Critique of Strategic Thinking', in Roger Fisher (ed.), *International Conflict and Behavioural Science* (New York, Basic Books, 1964), ch. 11.

12 Ashley, *op. cit.* (note 4), esp. ch. 10.

13 Ken Booth, *Strategy and Ethnocentrism* (London, Croom Helm, 1979).

14 Leonard Beaton, *The Reform of Power: A Proposal for an International Security System*, (London, Chatto & Windus, 1972).

15 Stanley Hoffmann, *Primacy or World Order* (New York, McGraw-Hill, 1978), p. 252.

16 Bull, *op. cit.* (note 6), pp. 28–9.

17 L.B. Krause and J.S. Nye, 'Reflections on the Economics and Politics of International Economic Organisations', in C.F. Bergsten and L.B. Krause (eds), *World Politics and International Economics* (Washington, DC, Brookings Institution, 1975), p. 329 (emphasis original).

18 *North-South: A Programme for Survival*, Report of the Brandt Commission (London, Pan, 1980), pp. 124–5.

19 Wolfers, *op. cit.* (note 5), p. 147.

20 W.B. Gallie, 'Essentially Contested Concepts', in Max Black (ed.), *The Importance of Language* (New Jersey, Prentice-Hall, 1962), pp. 121–46. See also T.D. Weldon, *The Vocabulary of Politics* (Harmondsworth, Penguin, 1953), esp. ch. 2.

21 Richard Little, 'Ideology and Change', in Barry Buzan and R.J. Barry Jones (eds), *Change and the Study of International Relations* (London, Frances Pinter, 1981), p. 35.

22 Kenneth H.F. Dyson, *The State Tradition in Western Europe* (Oxford, Martin Robertson, 1980), pp. 205–6.

23 For the latter phenomenon, see Robert O. Keohane and Joseph S. Nye, *Power and Interdependence* (Boston, Little Brown, 1977). Chapter 2 makes the case for pushing military factors into the background, thereby throwing out the security baby with the Realist bathwater.

24 Barry Buzan, 'Change and Insecurity: a Critique of Strategic Studies', in Buzan and Jones, *op. cit.* (note 21), ch. 9.

25 For an excellent critique of Strategic Studies from this perspective, see Booth, *op. cit.* (note 13).

26 Neville Brown, *The Future Global Challenge: A Predictive Study of World Security 1977–1990* (London, RUSI, 1977).

27 T.S. Eliot, *Collected Poems 1902–1962* (London, Faber & Faber, 1963), 'Little Gidding', p. 222.

28 Michael Howard, 'Military Power and International Order', *International Affairs*, 40:3 (1964), pp. 407–8.

29 Waltz, *op. cit.* (note 1), p. 126.
30 Although our tour will touch on most aspects of International Relations we shall not go into the subject of war. Under conditions of war, security assumes a largely military identity which bears little relation to its character in the absence of war. In war, security hinges on a much narrower, and on the whole well-understood, set of factors than is the case during peace. The whole issue of security during war has declined in salience because of deterrence and the nuclear stalemate, but at the same time the general concern about security has not diminished. The national security problem is a constant feature of international relations regardless of war: it could exist, for example, within the framework of a political-economy struggle such as that envisaged within the Soviet idea of peaceful coexistence. For these reasons, and for considerations of space, we shall treat war as part of the national security problem without examining in any depth the special case of security in war conditions.
31 Kenneth N. Waltz, *Man, the State, and War* (New York, Columbia University Press, 1959). For other approaches using variations on the idea of a three-level analysis, see Arnold Wolfers, 'Nation-State', in Fred A. Sonderman, W.C. Olson and D.S. McLellan (eds), *The Theory and Practice of International Relations* (New Jersey, Prentice Hall, 1970), pp. 16–22; R.W. Cox, 'Social Forces, States and World Orders', *Millennium*, 10:2 (1981); and Andrew Linklater, 'Men and Citizens in International Relations', *Review of International Studies*, 7:1 (1981).

1 Individual Security and National Security

We start our analysis with the individual, because people represent, in one sense, the irreducible basic unit to which the concept of security can be applied. Although the traditional emphasis in International Relations has been on the security of collective units, particularly states, individuals can be analysed in the same way. If we pursued this as a subject for its own sake, it would take us deeply into the realms of politics, psychology and sociology. Such an analysis is beyond the scope of this book. The relevance of individual security to our present task lies in the important connections between personal security and the security of entities at level 2 like the state. Level 2 entities act as a source of both threats to and security for individuals, while individuals provide much of the reason for, and some of the limits to, the security-seeking activities of collective units. It is these connections that we shall explore here.

Individual Security as a Social Problem

Security, as indicated in the Introduction, is a relative concept. It is usually much easier to apply to things than to people. The level of security of money in a bank is quite amenable to calculation in relation to specified threats of unauthorised removal or likelihood of *in situ* deflation in value. Since material goods are often replaceable with like items, their security (that is, the owner's security in possession of them) can usually be enhanced further by insuring them against loss, the insurance itself being based on actuarial statistics of risk. Security for individuals, however, cannot be defined so easily. The factors involved – life, health, status, wealth, freedom – are far more complicated, not infrequently contradictory, and plagued by the distinction between objective and subjective evaluation. Many of them cannot be replaced if lost (life, limbs, status), and cause-effect relationships with regard to threats are often obscure.

Dictionary definitions give the flavour of this ambiguity with their reference to notions like being protected from danger, feeling safe, and being free from doubt. The referent threats (danger and doubt) are very vague, and the subjective feeling of safety has no necessary connection with actually being safe. Even if we take as an illustration a well-off individual in a well-off country, the resultant image of day-to-day life leaves no doubt that security in any comprehensive sense is beyond reasonable possibility of attainment. An enormous array of threats, dangers and doubts loom over everyone, and although the better-off can distance themselves from some of these (starvation, preventable/curable disease, physical exposure, criminal violence, economic exploitation, and such like), they share others equally with the poor (incurable disease, natural disasters, nuclear war), and create some new ones for themselves because of their advantages (air crashes, kidnapping, diseases of excessive consumption, and so forth). Security cannot be complete for any individual and indeed few would relish for more than a short time the flatness and predictability of life in which it was so.

It is useful to discuss security in relation to specific threats. Against some threats, such as preventable diseases or poverty, some individuals can achieve very high levels of security. Against others, especially where cause-effect relationships are obscure (cancer, crime, unemployment), security measures may be chancy at best. Given limits on resources, decisions will also have to be made as to where to allocate them in relation to an impossibly large number of threats. Efforts to achieve security can become self-defeating, even if objectively successful, if their effect is to raise awareness of threats to such a pitch that felt insecurity is greater than before the measures were undertaken. The urban householder's efforts to burglar-proof his house can have this effect. As locks, alarms and bars proliferate, their daily presence amplifies the magnitude of the threat by, among other things, advertising to burglars that he thinks his possessions are valuable, thereby leading to a net loss of tranquility for the fortified householder. Paranoia is the logical, self-defeating extreme of obsession with security, and there is thus a cruel irony in one meaning of secure which is 'unable to escape'.

The aspect of individual security which we need to pursue here relates to what might be called social threats: those arising from the fact that people find themselves embedded in a human environment with unavoidable social, economic and political consequences. It is in this area that we find the important links between security at levels 1 and 2. Social threats come in a wide variety of forms, but there are four obvious basic types: physical threats (pain, injury, death), economic threats (seizure or destruction of property, denial of access to work or resources), threats to rights (imprisonment denial of normal civil liberties), and threats to position or status (demotion, public humiliation). These types of threat are not mutually exclusive in that the application of one (injury) may well carry penalties in another (loss of job). The existence of these threats to individuals within the context of human society points to the great dilemma which lies at the root of much political philosophy. That is, how to balance freedom of action for the individual against the potential and actual threats which such freedom poses to others, or, put another way, how to enhance the liberation of community without amplifying oppression by authority. The great potency of Hobbes' image of the state of nature derives precisely from the fact that it expresses this dilemma with such clarity. Individuals, or collective human behavioural units, existing with others of their kind in an anarchical relationship, find their freedom maximised at the expense of their security. As Waltz puts it, 'States, like people, are insecure in proportion to the extent of their freedom. If freedom is wanted, insecurity must be accepted.'[1]

The state of nature image postulates a primal anarchy in which the conditions for the individuals involved are marked by unacceptably high levels of social threat, in a word, chaos. Unacceptable chaos becomes the motive for sacrificing some freedom in order to improve levels of security, and, in this process, government and the state are born. In the words of Hobbes, people found states in order to 'defend them from the invasion of foreigners and the injuries of one another, and thereby to secure them in such sort as that by their own industry, and by the fruits of the earth, they may nourish themselves and live contentedly'.[2] Similarly, John Locke: 'The great and chief end . . . of men's . . . putting themselves under government is the preservation of their property' (meaning here their 'lives, liberties and estates') which in the state of nature is 'very unsafe, very unsecure'.[3] The state becomes the mechanism by which people seek to achieve adequate levels of security against social threats.

The paradox, of course, is that the state also becomes a source of social threat against the individual. The stability of the state derives from the assumption that it is the lesser of two evils (that is, that whatever threats come from the state will be of a lower order of magnitude than those which would arise in its absence). This assumption grows in force as society develops around the state, becoming increasingly dependent on it as a lynchpin for other social and economic structures. As the symbiosis of society and state develops along more complex, sophisticated and economically productive lines, the state of nature image becomes more and more unappealing as an alternative, regardless of its historical validity. As the historical distance grows between the state and the state of nature, the enormous costs of the reversion have to be added to the dubious benefits of existence in a state of nature. If the state of nature was unacceptable to thinly scattered and primitive peoples, how much more unacceptable would it be to the huge, densely-packed and sophisticated populations of today? The state, then, is irreversible. There is no real option of going back, and the security of individuals is inseparably entangled with that of the state.

Individual Security and the Two Faces of the State

But if the security of individuals is irreversibly connected to the state, so, as state and society have become increasingly indistinguishable, is their insecurity. This is not only a question of the efficiency, or lack thereof, with which the state performs its internal (social order) and external (group defence) functions, but also a matter of the state itself becoming a source of controversy and threat. We are led by these questions to inquire into the nature of the state itself for, if the state becomes a major source of threat to its citizens, does it not thereby undermine the prime justification for its existence? Different views of the state exist. For our purposes, we can divide these views into two general models: the *minimal* and the *maximal* conceptions of the state.

The minimal state arises out of John Locke's concept of a social contract which provides us with a view of the state very much oriented towards the individuals who make it up. The foundations of the state rest on the consent of its citizens to be governed, and therefore the actions of the state can be judged according to their impact on the interests of its citizens. In this view, the state should not be much more than the sum of its parts, and serious clashes between citizens and state should be avoided. P.A. Reynolds argues explicitly that individual values are, or should be, the prime referent by which state behaviour is judged, and similar sentiments underlie Robert Tucker's thoughtful essay on this subject. Robert Nozick offers a deep, and wide-ranging defence of the minimal state in which the acknowledged need for collective structures is subordinated to the prime value of individual rights.[4] If one accepts this view, it clearly leads upwards to an interpretation of national security at level 2 which places great emphasis on values derived directly from the interests of the citizens. It also requires a form of government in which the consent of the governed plays such an active part that clashes of interest between state and citizens do not assume major proportions.

The opposed, maximal state view grows from the assumption that the state is, or should be, either considerably more than the sum of its parts, or something different from them, and that it therefore has interests of its own. These interests might derive from a number of sources. Marxists interpret them as the interests of a dominant élite who use the state to advance their own cause.[5] Realists have the makings of a transcendent state purpose in the imperative of the struggle for power. One version of this is the position taken by Heinrick von Treitschke. Building on Hegel's 'deification' of the state, he argues forcefully that the state is 'primordial and necessary', that it exists as 'an independent force', and that 'it does not ask primarily for opinion, but demands obedience'.[6] In his view, the state as a collective entity encompassing the nation stands above the individuals comprising it, and cannot even be seen as something created by individuals, as implied in notions of social contract. If we invert this perspective, it can even be argued, as an extension of the social contract view, that the state acquires independent status because of its essential role in the realisation of individual interests. In the state of nature, chaotic conditions prevent the effective pursuit of individual values, which therefore cannot be said to have meaning outside the framework of the state. Since the state has to be viewed either as the source of all value, or, at a minimum, as the necessary condition for the realisation of any value, the preservation of the state, and the consequent pursuit of state interest, supersede the individual values from which they notionally derive.[7] This view, in whatever version, clearly results in a different interpretation of the relationship between individual security and national security from the alternative outlined above. If the state has its own purposes, then it is much more detached from, and unresponsive to, individual security needs than in the previous model.[8]

These minimal and maximal views of the state are based on their distance from the notion that the state is, or ideally should be, merely the sum of its parts, and simply instrumental to their ends. While the two models give us a useful conceptual handle on different interpretations of the relationship between the citizen and the state, the two types are not easy to distinguish in practice. This difficulty arises from another traditional puzzle of political philosophy, the linked problems of how to determine the general will, and how to calculate what level of state intervention in the lives of the citizens will be necessary to fulfil the Hobbesian tasks of defending them from the 'invasion of foreigners and the injuries of one another'. If one assumes the citizens to be naturally fractious, and the international environment to be unremittingly hostile, then even a minimal state will be a large intervening force in the lives of its citizens. This uncertainty makes it impossible in practice to draw a clear boundary between minimal and maximal states. How far can maintenance of civil order and provision for external defence go before the immensity of the task creates in the state a purpose and momentum of its own?

Two factors suggest themselves as possible boundary-markers between minimal and maximal states. First is the existence of extensive civil disorder such as that in Russia in 1905, in Hungary in 1956, in Lebanon after 1976, in Nicaragua during the late 1970s, in Iran after 1979, in El Salvador during the early 1980s, and in numerous other places where popular unrest has dominated the news over the years. Such disorder could well indicate a degree of falling out between citizens and government arising where a maximal state had pursued its own interests to the excessive detriment of the mass of individual interests within it. Unfortunately, it could also indicate the failure of a minimal state to contain the contradictions among its citizens. Second is the existence of a disproportionate internal security apparatus although, again, considerable difficulties occur in finding a measure for this. The argument is that a minimal state should not require a massive police force, and that the presence of one is symptomatic of the distance between a maximal state and its people. A minimal police state might just be possible in conditions of severe external threats of penetration, as in Israel, but the kind of police machinery associated with totalitarian states, or the kind of independent police powers exemplified in South Africa, might normally be taken to indicate a maximal state. One problem here is that opinions differ markedly on where normal policing ends and the police state begins. Britain would be far removed from most lists of police states, but many black citizens in Bristol, Brixton and Notting Hill cite excessive policing as a major grievance underlying riots there. Similar views could easily be found in many American cities, and in the United States one has, in addition, recurrent bouts of concern about the domestic activities of the CIA and the FBI. Even these rather extreme boundary-markers do not, in the end, provide us with a reliable distinction between the minimal and maximal states, because it could still be argued that both conditions might simply reflect the difficulty of maintaining a minimal state given the nature of particular historical circumstances. If the Russians have too many police, and the Argentines too much disorder, that could reflect the severe domestic problems of establishing a minimal state in these areas.

This line of argument pushes increasingly towards the conclusion that in practice the maximal state, or something very like it, rules. For purposes of analysis, the maximal state model would seem to offer a better correspondence with what we actually find in the real world, the main utility of the minimal state view being a standard for judgement and criticism. This conclusion has important implications for our inquiry into the relationship between individual security and the state. In the minimal state model, we assumed a low level of disharmony between state and individual interests, in the context of a state structure responsive to individual interests except for the restraints imposed in pursuit of civil order and external defence. Although we would expect to find some tension between state and citizen in such an arrangement, we would not expect there to be either a major domestic side to state security, or a substantial individual security problem stemming from the state.

In the maximal state model, by contrast, internal security becomes a natural and expected dimension, and there is no necessary striving to harmonise state and individual interests. Limits to the disharmony between state and citizen do, of course, exist, and constraints of efficiency require that even extreme maximal states pay some attention to the needs of their people. These limits, however, appear to be wide, for states of almost any type all benefit from the nearly universal feeling that anything is better than reversion to the state of nature. So long as the state performs its Hobbesian tasks of keeping chaos at bay, this service will be seen by many to offset the costs of other state purposes, whatever they may be. Thus what might be judged appalling regimes by outside observers (the Duvaliers in Haiti, Boukassa in Central Africa, Stalin, Hitler, and others) keep themselves in power by a combination of heavy, but by no means cripplingly expensive, police presence, and a reliance on the formidable ballast of political inertia in the population. Under these conditions, the clash between individual and state interests might normally be quite extensive. It need be neither unusual nor paradoxical to find individuals dependent on the state for maintenance of their general security environment, while at the same time seeing the state as a significant source of threats to their personal security.

The State as a Source of Threat

Now that we have clarified this two-edged relationship between state and individual security, we can explore its features in more detail. The individual citizen faces many threats which emanate either directly or indirectly from the state, and which not uncommonly may occupy an important place in the person's life. Such threats can be grouped into four general categories: those arising from domestic law-making and enforcement; those arising from direct political action by the state against individuals or groups; those arising from struggles over control of the state machinery; and those arising from the state's external security policies.

Threats to the individual from the process of domestic law can occur as a result of inadequate or excessive policing and prosecution practices. Miscarried or deficient justice can have an immense impact on the life of the individual concerned, and cases of both types are an inevitable cost of any attempt to balance effective law enforcement with protection of broad civil liberties. This problem, however, is not generally relevant to our line of analysis unless disaffection with law enforcement becomes very widespread and politicised. Such threats can also take ecological forms. Widespread contemporary concern over chemical and nuclear pollution reflects individual fears of both inadequacies in state regulation and misplaced priorities in what activities the state promotes. Again, impacts at the individual level can be catastrophic.

A rather more serious level of threat can come to individuals directly from the institutions of the state. The late-night knock on the door of police states is still the most striking image of this threat, but it comes in many lesser forms as well. The modern bureaucratic state possesses an enormous range of legal powers which it can exercise against its citizens in the name of the common good. Property owners can be expropriated to make way for motorways, the children of unstable families can be taken into care, manipulations of the economy can throw millions out of work. All of this has to be balanced against the services and social security provided by the state. But, none the less, it is clear that the powers and actions of the state constitute significant threats to many individuals.

In part, this is what Galtung has characterised as 'structural violence',[9] but much of it is direct as well. The ruining of people's careers in the McCarthy hearings in the United States, the incarceration of Soviet dissidents in psychiatric hospitals, the removal of the right to worship for Huguenots in France by the revocation of the Edict of Nantes in 1685, the persecution of Jews in Nazi Germany, legal discrimination against blacks in South Africa, maiming of suspects by police in India, assassinations by police 'death squads' in Argentina, ruthless relocation, liquidation and enforced labour in Pol Pot's Kampuchea, and an endless catalogue of similar items, are all examples of the kinds of threat which the state can pose to its citizens. These threats can arise as part of explicit state policy against certain groups, such as the purges against leftists in Chile after the fall of Allende in 1973, or Stalin's purges against a wide variety of opponents during the 1930s. Or they can arise simply as a matter of normal policy procedure in which the state sacrifies the interests of some for what is seen to be a higher collective interest, as in the case of those condemned to unemployment because of the need to control the money supply. For perhaps a majority of the world's people threats from the state are among the major sources of insecurity in their lives. The ultimate form of this is the theory that the rights, comforts and welfare of the present generation must be sacrified for the development of a better life for those to come, a thesis critically examined by Peter Berger in *Pyramids of Sacrifice*[10] in both its capitalist and socialist variants.

The other side of the coin of threat from the state is threat arising from political disorder – the struggle for control over the state's institutions. Only a minority of states have developed stable mechanisms for the transfer of political power. In the rest, violent conflicts over the reins of office pose an intermittent, and frequently serious threat to large sections of the population. The archetypes for this situation are countries like Argentina and Bolivia where military factions play an endless game of push-and-shove around the high offices of the state, while at the same time fighting an interminable, and often savage internal war against a variety of mostly left-wing revolutionary groups. Remarkably, the state is a sufficiently durable institution to withstand quite astonishing amounts of disarray in domestic political life but, on the individual level, such disarray becomes a central source of personal insecurity for many. Participation in what passes for the national political process can bring threats of death or worse, and even opting for the role of innocent bystander is no guarantee of safety. Society as a whole stands in fear of political violence, and those (temporarily) in control of the state apparatus use it in the ways outlined in the previous paragraph to support their own political ends. Political violence can become endemic, as it did in Turkey in the late 1970s, with factional gun battles and assassinations producing casualties on a war-like scale, and eventually leading in 1978 to extensive imposition of martial law. It can lead to the nightmare of civil war, as in Spain during the early and mid-1930s, or to the political limbo and institutionalised violence of a state in dissolution, as in the Lebanon since 1976. Domestic political violence frequently opens the door to the further threat of external intervention, either as participant on one side or the other (the Syrians and the Israelis in Lebanon, the Indians in Bangladesh), or as invaders taking advantage of a state weakened by internal dispute (the Japanese in China during the 1930s). One has only to recall the catastrophic effects of American intervention on the people of Vietnam and Cambodia to sense the full dimension of this threat.

Political terrorism also fits under this heading, regardless of whether or not the terrorists see themselves as contending for political power. The use of terror, such as bombings or hijackings, to pressure, weaken or discredit a government explicitly poses threats to the citizen as its prime instrument. Individuals face random risks of victimisation because of others' disputes about the nature or control of state policy. Those varieties of terrorism which take the state apparatus as their direct target also threaten individuals although, innocent bystanders excepted, these come from a much more select group than the mass victims of hijackers and public bombings. Terrorism, like other forms of political violence, not only undermines the individual's security directly, it is likely also to increase the threats to individual security offered by the state itself, as well as those coming from other states. By undermining trust in the state's capacity to provide domestic security, terrorists can force the state to make its security measures more obtrusive. This process has been much enhanced by the actual and potential danger of terrorists acquiring high technology weapons. The extreme fear here is that of terrorists armed with a nuclear weapon. The combination of ruthless, or mindless, determination, and a capacity for mass destruction, would pose an unprecedented challenge to the balance between individual rights and public order. In responding to such threats even a minimal state would necessarily begin to adopt a maximal hue.

The final dimension in which state and individual security link together is foreign policy. Just as we revealed a very mixed set of costs and benefits to individual security in relation to the state's civil order functions, so can we for its external security functions. The state is supposed to provide a measure of protection to its citizens from foreign interference, attack and invasion, but obviously it cannot do so without imposing risks and costs on them. In its essence, this arrangement does not normally raise extensive controversy. As with the risks of a certain level of miscarried justice and unpunished crime, the risk of war service is usually accepted by citizens as a fair trade-off for the broader measure of security provided by the state. While the principle may be firmly rooted, however, the practice which develops around it can easily become an intense source of dispute on the grounds of individual versus state security. This process is much stronger and more visible in democracies, because the expression and mobilisation of public opinion is easier and more influential in the democratic context. Modern war is known to produce high risks and high casualties, and this makes decisions about what constitutes a threat to the security of the state a matter of considerable public concern.

While the state can usually count on mass support in an obvious and imminent crisis, as, say, in Britain after 1938, more remote and ambiguous entanglements can easily run the risk of being seen as insufficient cause for placing citizens at risk, as the Americans discovered in Vietnam. Especially where armed forces are raised by conscription, policies requiring citizens to place themselves at risk in the service of the state will naturally tend to raise political questions about the value of the trade-offs involved between individual and state security. This is not nearly so much the case where professional soldiers are involved, because they are seen as having already made their decision to place other values higher than their own lives.

Indeed, it is a point too easily forgotten that individuals frequently choose to place their lives at risk in pursuit of other values. The early American pioneers accepted substantial risks on the frontier in order to pursue freedom and wealth. Enthusiasts for dangerous sports like hang-gliding and potholing balance the risks against the thrills of achievement. American teenagers, playing 'chicken' in their cars (to take one of the famous metaphors of Strategic Studies), gamble injury or death against status in the eyes of their group. Policemen, soldiers and mercenaries accept the risk of injury and death for a great variety of reasons, amongst which, for some, is the pleasure of being authorised to inflict injury and death on others. Life for its own sake is frequently not ranked first among individual values, and it is useful to keep this in mind when trying to judge the morality of state policies against values derived from the interests of the citizens (that is, when using standards based on the minimal model of the state). Maximal states do not have this problem to the same extent because they are by definition less bound, or not bound at all in some cases, to the notion that individual values have any relation to state policy in the short term.

A different, but no less interesting, variant of the conflict potential between individual and state security arises in relation to nuclear weapons and the kinds of national security policies based on them. The whole idea of a national security policy based on threats of exchanged nuclear salvoes strikes many people as being the *reductio ad absurdum* of arguments for collective defence. If the minimal state point of view is taken, then any policy which envisages the possibility of the population being obliterated is unacceptable almost by definition. Even with a maximal state view, it becomes hard to find ends which justify such risks. The fine logic of deterrence theory appears to be an exceedingly thin thread on which to hang national security, insult being added to prospective injury by the notion of mutually assured destruction, which aims to ensure deterrence stability by deliberately keeping populations vulnerable to nuclear attack. The merits of nuclear deterrence have been powerfully argued both ways, and there is no need to repeat the exercise in these pages.[11] The point of interest here is that deterrence policy displays the divorce between individual and state security at the highest and most visible level. The apparent end of a long tradition of national defence is a situation in which states seek to preserve themselves by offering each other their citizens as hostages. Obviously, there is a strong logic in deterrence which connects the interests of the individual to those of the state. But no matter how impeccable this logic is, it remains a political fact that large numbers of people think that a threat of societal obliteration is too high a price to pay for national security.

The European Nuclear Disarmament Campaign (END) is the latest and most prominent manifestation of the sentiment that the price of national security has gone too high, the means having made a nonsense of the ends. Given the record of the two world wars, it is hardly surprising that such opinions should be most advanced in Europe. Nearly all the western European countries have accepted that by themselves they are incapable of mounting effective defence policies, an acceptance symbolised by membership in, or dependence on, the NATO alliance. Any kind of large-scale modern war in Europe, whether nuclear or conventional, would have catastrophic social effects, and in combination these factors make Europe a rich case for studying the interlinked levels and dimensions of security.

The conventional wisdom rests on a NATO-type approach in which the prime threat is seen to come from the Soviet Union, and in which security policy is oriented to the preservation of the western European state system. Given the nature of the threat and the objective of the policy, security is achieved by cultivating military power, nuclear deterrence, and the American connection on which these rest. The opposing view is slightly less well-defined, but stems from the conviction that the primary threat comes from war itself, particularly nuclear war, and that the main objective of security policy is the preservation of European society and civilisation. From this perspective, the Americans are as much of a threat as are the Soviets, or perhaps more so, when tough-taking administrations take office in the United States, as happened in 1981. As a correspondent for the *Washington Post* put the European view: 'The Soviets, although the enemy, are seen as somehow capable of being dealt with because they are part of Europe and understand the continent's fear of war. But the Americans, an ocean away, are regarded as perhaps more inclined to turn Europe into a battlefield.'[12] If war is seen as the prime threat, then a logical approach to security consists of policies like disengagement from the super-power rivalry, creation of a European Nuclear Weapon Free Zone, and adoption of some form of low-profile military defence.[13] We shall return to the European case in more detail in later chapters. For the moment, it serves to illustrate not only the alarming ambiguity of security as a concept, but also the wide range of policy conclusions which result from different value choices. The NATO approach represents a logical extension of national security thinking, whereas the more radical END view places values derived from individual security much more to the fore. The two views are probably impossible to reconcile, and yet each seeks to fulfil the common craving to realise security as a value in its own right.

Conclusions: Individual Security and National Security

This argument about individual and state security leads to the conclusion that there is no necessary harmony between the two. A gruesome symbol of this contradiction is provided by 'Baby Doc' Duvalier, who recently renamed as the 'Volunteers for National Security' his father's notorious private police, the Ton Ton Macoutes.[14] A quite different indicator of it is the facility for individuals to appeal against their governments under the European Convention on Human Rights. While the state provides some security to the individual, it can only do so by imposing threats. These threats, whether from the state itself, or arising indirectly either as a side-effect of state actions aimed at serving the common good, or as a result of the state becoming an object of social conflict, are frequently serious enough to dominate the relatively small and fragile universe of individual security. Although they are balanced to some extent by the domestic and external security which the state provides, these threats make it mistaken to assume, as for example John Herz did, that political authority will only accrue to units able to provide both pacification of, and control over, internal relations, and protection from outside interference.[15] The record indicates that viable states need only provide some security in these directions, and that they can get away with being a considerable source of threat themselves. The state already enjoys a wide tolerance for its inefficiencies and perversities in relation to security, and therefore a decline in its defensive impermeability brought about by the development of strategic bombing and nuclear weapons, is unlikely to undercut its authority significantly. The link between individual and state security is anyway so partial that variations in the latter should not be expected to produce immediate or drastic variations in the political stability of the state as a whole.

The unavoidability of this contradiction between individual and state security must be emphasised. The contradiction is rooted in the nature of political collectives. In the real world, it can be neither resolved nor evaded. Consequently, our task in the succeeding chapters will not be to reduce the other levels down to some basic common denominator of individual security. To attempt this, would in my view simply avoid the reality of a permanent tension between the individual and the collective. Instead, our task will be to register this contradiction as a central dilemma in the concept of security, and to observe its effects on the other levels of the problem.

We have examined in some detail the range of threats posed by the state to individuals, and drawn the conclusion that significant disharmonies exist between the two levels of security. How might the actions of individuals motivated by their own security needs have feedback effects up to the national security level? Individuals can do many things to enhance their security both against threats from the state and against threats which the state has failed to alleviate, though of course their range of options will be much narrower in a tightly run maximal state than in a relatively open democracy. Much can be done by way of self-help in terms of individual security strategies for both person and property. In the United States and in many other western countries, a considerable industry caters to this demand.

Beyond the personal level, it is possible for individuals to set up or join organisations of many kinds aimed at improving their security. These can be of a direct defence kind, such as the Catholic and Protestant militant groups in Northern Ireland, vigilante groups set up by Asians in British cities to defend themselves against 'Paki-bashing' racists, militant nationalist groups in Spain (Basques), France (Bretons), Iran and Iraq (Kurds), and elsewhere, militant political groups such as the Ku Klux Klan in the United States, or the Chinese secret societies of pre-communist days. Or they can be more indirect and political in nature, working as pressure groups on governments and trying to turn state policy in directions more conducive to the security needs of the individuals involved. These organisations might include minority rights groups, peace organisations like END, or the various campaigns against the Vietnam war, political parties, local community groups, indeed almost the whole array of sub-state organisations encompassed by the notion of pluralist politics. In states where the structure of government is weak, and the state itself is not pervasive in society, pre-state social structures like families, clans, tribes and religious organisations might also play a central role in relation to individual security needs. When the organisational approach to individual security is taken, of course, an additional level of collective interest is likely to interpose

itself between individual and state, making the domestic model of
security richer and more complex than the simple polarisation
between individual and state.

This considerable range of individually-oriented security concerns
and policies can have very substantial implications for national
security in at least four ways. First, individuals or sub-state groups
can become a national security problem in their own right. Assassins,
terrorists, separatists, *coup*-makers and revolutionaries all pose
threats to the state. The United States has to weigh the safety of its
leaders against the right of its citizens to bear arms. Western
European states have to weigh anti-terrorist police measures against
civil liberties. Military resources have to be allocated against
separatist movements in Britain, Spain, Pakistan, Iran, Yugoslavia,
Indonesia, Nigeria, and elsewhere. Spanish, Latin American and
many other governments must guard themselves against *coup*-
makers, and governments everywhere devote resources to preventing
revolutions against their own authority, sometimes covertly, as in
most western states, sometimes with more obvious repression, as in
the communist states, and sometimes by all-out internal warfare, as
in China before 1949, and Indonesia in 1965-6. A highly divided state
with rather narrow political views of propriety might have to treat
virtually its whole population as a security problem, largely determining its own character and pattern of resource allocation in the
process.

Second, and related to the direct domestic security problem, is the
role that citizens can play as a fifth column in support of some other
state's interests. Nazis in France during the 1930s, Moscow-oriented
communists in many countries, Japanese in the United States and
Canada during the Second World War, western-oriented dissidents
in the Soviet Union, Chinese in Malaya during the 1950s, Palestinians
in Israel, and such-like, have all either played, or been cast in, this
role. The permeability of states to both ideas and peoples associated
with other states blurs the boundary between domestic and international security. Where this happens, neat distinctions between
citizens and foreigners, state and government, and domestic and
international policy, begin to break down, and the meaning of
national security becomes even more ambiguous than usual.

The third implication of individual security for national security
lies in the stimuli and constraints which bear upwards from level 1 to
level 2. We shall examine these in more detail in subsequent chapters,
but their essence stems not from direct threats to the state or
government, but from the influence which public opinion exerts on
state policy, or, to put it another way, from the limits to the state's
ability to mould public opinion to its own ends. Examples of the

phenomenon include: Woodrow Wilson's and Franklin Roosevelt's struggles against isolationist opinion in the United States respectively after the First World War and before the Second World War; the Jewish lobby's influence on American middle-east policy; French-Canadian objections to conscription in Canada; electorally significant anti-nuclear weapon sentiments in Britain, the Netherlands, Japan and elsewhere; Soviet concerns about the politicisation of troops used to quell reformist movements in eastern Europe; popular opposition to particular wars or actions, as in Britain over Suez, America over Vietnam, and France over Algeria; and the restraint on state war-making capabilities arising from the need to justify the enormous costs and sacrifices of mobilising for modern war, as illustrated by British and French hesitancy during the 1930s, and by the American dilemma during Vietnam. Such influence may also come from élite groups like the armed forces, rather than direct from the public at large, as is the case in countries like Spain, Pakistan, South Korea, Egypt, Nigeria, Bolvia, Peru, Brazil, Chile, Argentina, and others in which the military play a central role in politics.

Fourth is the role that individuals play as leaders of the state. The abstract distinction between individual and state dissolves when we reach the level at which individuals make a reality of the concept we refer to as the state. Each of these individuals has his or her own universe of security concerns and perceptions, and it is part of the work of historians, journalists and pundits to assess the influence of this on state policy. Chamberlian and Churchill demonstrated markedly different styles and degrees of security consciousness, and the gulf between them indicates the potential impact of this variable on national security policy-making. At the extreme of centralised dictatorship, as in Germany under Hitler, or the Soviet Union under Stalin, individual and state merge to the point of indistinguishability, whereas at the extremes of democracy, as in the United States, the intricate divisions of power make it difficult for any individual to have much impact on the totality of national policy.

The whole subject of the relationship between individuals, whether as leaders, or aggregated as interest groups or public opinion, has been well explored in the literature on foreign policy analysis, and there is no need for us to repeat that effort here.[16] The purpose of this chapter is served by the following conclusions:

1 that security has a meaning independent of the state at the level of the individual;
2 that individual security is affected both positively and negatively by the state, and that the grounds for disharmony between individual and national security represent a permanent contradiction; and

3   that individual pursuit of security has a variety of influences on national security, both as problem and as stimulus and constraint.

This third conclusion can be elaborated along two lines which relate to the internal and the external dimensions of the state's Hobbesian security functions. Along one line, we are led into the whole dimension of domestic conflict between the state and its citizens over the general process of government. In one sense, this can be seen as part of the national security problem, but in another, as we shall see, it both raises awkward questions about the definition of the state, and brings the idea of national security to the boundary of meaninglessness. Along the other line, we are led to the more particular question of the links between individual security on the one hand, and the national security policy of the state in its external dimension on the other. As suggested by the case of END and nuclear deterrence policy, significant grounds for contradiction can be found here, and we shall explore these more fully in chapter 6.

Notes

1   Kenneth N. Waltz, *Theory of International Politics* (Reading, Mass., Addison–Wesley, 1979), p. 112.
2   Thomas Hobbes, *Leviathan*, reprinted in Carl Cohen (ed.), *Communism, Fascism and Democracy: The Theoretical Foundations* (New York, Random House, 1972, 2nd edn), p. 275.
3   John Locke, *Second Treaties of Government*, reprinted *ibid.*, pp. 406–7.
4   P.A. Reynolds, *An Introduction to International Relations* (London, Longman, 1980), pp. 47–8; Part II, 'The Rationale of Force', in Robert E. Osgood and Robert W. Tucker, *Force, Order and Justice* (Baltimore Johns Hopkins University Press, 1967); and Robert Nozick, *Anarchy State and Utopia* (Oxford, Blackwell, 1974). For a critique of the liberal view of the relationship between individual and state, see Vernon Van Dyke, 'The Individual, the State and Ethnic Communities in Political Theory', *World Politics*, 29:3 (1977).
5   See, for example, Fred Block, 'Marxist Theories of the State in World Systems Analysis', in Barbara H. Kaplan (ed.), *Social Change in the Capitalist World Economy* (Beverly Hills, Sage, 1978), p. 27; and Ralph Miliband, *The State in Capitalist Society* (London, Quartet Books, 1973).
6   Heinrich von Treitschke, *Politics*, reprinted in Cohen (ed.), *op. cit.* (note 2), pp. 289–96.
7   This line of argument is explored in more depth by Tucker, *op. cit.* (note 4), pp. 282–4.
8   See Ralph Pettman, *State and Class: A Sociology of International Affairs* (London, Croom Helm, 1979), ch. 4, for a useful review and assessment

of theories of the state. This view of the primacy of state over individual interests can reflect two lines of thought: one in the mould of Treitschke, that state interests in some holistic sense are transcendent over individual ones; the other, in the Marxist mould, that sectional interests dominate the state and use it to serve their own ends. An interesting contemporary manifestation of the former view is explained and attacked in Roberto Calvo, 'The Church and the Doctrine of National Security', *Journal of Inter-American Studies and World Affairs*, 21:1 (1979).

9   Johan Galtung, 'Violence, Peace and Peace Research', *Journal of Peace Research*, vol. 2 (1969), pp. 166–91.

10 Peter L. Berger, *Pyramids of Sacrifice: Political Ethics and Social Change* (Harmondsworth, Penguin, 1974).

11 See, for example, Thomas C. Schelling, *Arms and Influence* (New Haven, Yale University Press, 1973); Philip Green, *Deadly Logic* (New York, Schocken Books, 1968); Richard Rosecrance, 'Strategic Deterrence Reconsidered', *Adelphi Papers*, no. 116 (London, IISS, 1975); Patrick M. Morgan, *Deterrence: A Conceptual Analysis* (Beverly Hills, Sage, 1977); Robert Jervis, 'Why Nuclear Superiority Doesn't matter', *Political Science Quarterly*, 94 (1979–80); Hedley Bull, *The Anarchical Society* (London, Macmillan, 1977), pp. 112–26.

12 Washington Post Foreign Service, 'German Heartland Uneasy', *The Guardian Weekly* (6 December 1981), p. 16.

13 There is no definitive statement of the radical view, but see, for example, E.P. Thompson and Dan Smith, *Protest and Survive* (Harmondsworth, Penguin, 1980); Mary Kaldor, 'Why We Need European Nuclear Disarmament', *ADIU Report*, 3:1 January/February 1981), pp. 1–4; and Tony Benn, 'Vision of Europe Free of Nuclear Threat', *Guardian Weekly* (29 March 1981).

14 *The Guardian Weekly* (24 January 1982), p. 17.

15 John Herz, *International Politics in the Atomic Age* (New York, Columbia University Press, 1959), pp. 40–2; and 'The Rise and Demise of the Territorial State', *World Politics*, 9 (1957). Herz later qualified his view when it became apparent that nuclear weapons had created a substantial paralysis of large-scale use of force: 'The Territorial State Revisited', *Polity*, 1:1 (1968).

16 See, for example, Kenneth N. Waltz, *Foreign Policy and Democratic Politics* (Boston, Little Brown, 1967); J.N. Rosenau (ed.), *Domestic Sources of Foreign Policy* (New York, Free Press, 1967); J.N. Rosenau, 'Pre-Theories and Theories of Foreign Policy', in R. Barry Farrell (ed.), *Approaches to Comparative and International Politics*, (Evanston, Northwestern University Press, 1966); Henry Kissinger, 'Domestic Structure and Foreign Policy', *Daedalus*, 95 (1966); Gregory Flynn (ed.), *The Internal Frabric of Western Security* (Totowa, NJ, Allanheld Osmun, 1981).

2 National Security and the Nature of the State

Identifying the State as an Object of Security

In this chapter, we shall examine the state as the referent object of the term national security. What is it within the multi-faceted phenomenon which we call a state, that policy-makers are trying to make secure? In the previous chapter we found security at the individual level to be both complex and contradictory in character. Since the state is composed of individuals bound together into a collective political unit, we might expect these difficulties to be compounded when we try to make sense of security at level 2. Not only are the units at level 2 larger and more complicated than those at level 1, but they are also more amorphous in character. While we can identify individuals with ease, and be fairly certain about the meaning of threats and injuries to them, the same exercise cannot as easily be applied to collective units like nations and states. Can such units die? And if so, what are the criteria for mortality? What constitutes a threat to the state, and where are its physical boundaries so that we may observe when it is touched by the actions of other units? Simple answers to these questions do not take us far in the real world of international relations. States have boundaries other than their territorial ones, as can be seen from the way they define threats, for example, in the ideological realm. Republicanism did not threaten state territorial boundaries in the eighteenth and nineteenth centuries, just as communism (or capitalism) does not threaten them now. Did Poland, France, Germany, Japan and others cease to exist in some sense during periods of foreign occupation? And how do we reconcile such discontinuities with the obvious continuities which those units have in historical terms? Was the outcome of the Second World War good or bad for Japan in national security terms? And what is the time-scale by which the actions, reactions, injuries and advances of collective units should be assessed?

These questions reveal the pervasive ambiguity which attends the idea of the state. Whereas individuals are relatively coherent systems whose behaviour, welfare and survival can be analysed in fairly precise terms, states are looser and less coherent systems, offering much less scope for analytical rigour. No agreement exists as to what the state is as a behavioural unit, let alone whether or not such anthropomorphic notions as life-cycle, growth, development, purpose, progress, will, and such-like are relevant to it. Despite the elusive character of the state as a behavioural unit, we are stuck with the fact that both International Relations and Strategic Studies make it the central focus of their analyses. Sound reasons justify this priority. Not only is the state by far the most powerful type of unit in terms of political allegiance and authority, but also it is normally dominant everywhere in terms of its command over instruments of force, particularly the major military machines required for modern warfare. Most of the non-state units that also command political and military power see themselves as aspirant states or state-makers, such as the Palestine Liberation Organisation, the Irish Republican Army, Kurdish nationalist organisations, and many others. Political centrality and military power make the state the dominant type of unit at level 2, despite its lack of anthropomorphic coherence. Consequently, we face the difficult task of unraveling the complex interplay between the ambiguous symbol of security, and the ambiguous structure of the state.

As argued above, the state is not the same sort of object as an individual, and therefore analogies between the two in relation to security must be undertaken with caution. The tendency to draw analogies has its roots in a number of similarities between individuals and states. Both are sentient, self-regarding, behavioural units with definable physical attributes. Both exist in a social environment with units of the same type, and therefore face similar sets of problems in working out satisfactory conditions for coexistence. And both share what might be called a human essence, the individual by definition, and the state because it is composed of, and run by, individuals. These similarities must be balanced against some formidable differences. Physical dissimilarities are particularly striking. States are much larger, their territorial 'bodies' bear little resemblance to the human organism, they are largely fixed in one position, they have no standard life-cycle which progresses from birth to death, their demise does not necessarily, or even usually, result in the death of their component parts.

The great size of states compared to individuals correlates with a much looser structure. For all their mental confusion and imprecise physical control, individuals are simply on a different plane of coherence than are states. This makes them far swifter, more agile, and more oriented towards detail in their behaviour than are states, but it also leaves them less powerful, and much more physically fragile and vulnerable. The state may be lumbering, incoherent and generally Brontosaurus-like in its behaviour, but it has no fear of certain death, can defend itself much more efficiently than a sleep-betrayed and easily killed, individual, and can command an enor-mous range of resources to its support.[1] Furthermore, while the state may reflect its human components to some extent, it may also become more than the sum of its parts, and therefore develop non-human modes of behaviour. This phenomenon underlies the 'idiosyncratic' versus 'role' variables used in analysing the actions of individuals holding state offices. Do the people concerned do what they do because of factors unique to them as individuals, or because of factors stemming from their position as office-holders?[2] Taken together, these factors make the state a significantly different type of actor, within a quite different kind of society, from the individual.

If the analogy between individual and state carries too many flaws to be used safely, particularly in regard to the central questions of death and injury, how can we best approach the question of what is being referred to when we talk of national security? What is the essence of the state to which the idea of security applies? There is no easy answer to this question. Ralph Miliband captured this basic ambiguity of the state when he observed that '"the state" is not a thing . . . it does not, as such, exist'.[3] We can, however, explore the concept of the state with a view to identifying which of its features and contradictions seem most relevant to the idea of security.

The contrasts between individual and state discussed above provide us with one interesting lead. If, as Miliband suggests, the state is not primarily a physical thing, where do we look for the referent object of national security? States are vulnerable to physical damage and deprivation, but the state appears to be much less intimately connected with its 'body' than is the case for an individual. A population and its associated territory comprise the physical foundations of a state, and yet both of these can exist without the state, or at least without any particular state. Conversely, damage to territory and population does not affect the survival of the state nearly so directly as damage to the human body effects individual survival. We can infer from these points that the state exists, or has its essence, primarily on the social rather than on the physical plane. In other words, the state is more a metaphysical entity, an idea held in common by a group of people, than it is a physical organism. To be sure, the state depends on a physical base, and past a certain point cannot exist without it. Armenians, and other exiled groups, for example, keep alive the idea of a state, but cannot give it physical expression without command of the appropriate territory. The state also generates physical expressions of itself in the familiar institutions of law and government. A purist anarchist would argue that the state could exist without these institutions, but although they are a vital part of its being and survival, they do not constitute, though they may express, its essence. Without a widespread and quite deeply-rooted idea of the state among the population, the state institutions by themselves would have great difficulty functioning and surviving, though as dictatorships like that of Somoza in Nicaragua indicate, strongly-held state institutions can prevail for long, perhaps indefinite, periods against majority disapproval.

Tracing the essence of the state to the social level gives us a major clue about how to approach the idea of national security. If the heart of the state resides in the idea of it held in the minds of the population, then that idea itself becomes a major object of national security. Since the idea of the state might take many forms, and might even be quite different among those who could reasonably be said to share a common loyalty to a particular state, this notion raises security problems of a very different nature from those normally associated with individual security. Although it would not be impossible, individuals are not usually described in terms of some essential idea. If idea implies purpose, then one tends to think along the physical lines of individual survival and reproduction, which are so closely connected to biological imperatives as scarcely to count as independently existing ideas. Grander ideas of human purpose are not in short supply ranging from religious and philosophical perfection of the spirit, to the conquest of material knowledge and the founding of Galactic empire. But these ideas are not as central to the existence of individuals as similar ones are to the existence of states. Humans may sacrifice their lives for these ideas, but they do not cease to exist without them. Because of this difference between the nature of individuals and states, we must expect national security to be vastly more varied and complex than individual security. Not only is there a huge scope for diversity of ideas about the state, but also the distinction among the idea, the institutional expression, and the physical base of the state provides a more numerous, fragmented and potentially contradictory range of security objects than does the more integrated structure of the individual.

This line of analysis suggests a simple descriptive model which we can use to guide our exploration into the nature of the state and national security. The model is given in Figure 2.1, and represents the three components of the state discussed above. It is not meant to suggest that the three components stand separately, for they are obviously interlinked in myriad ways. Rather, the model is meant to emphasise merely that these three elements are distinguishable from each other to a sufficient extent to allow them to be discussed as objects of security in their own right.[4]

Figure 2.1 *The component parts of the state*

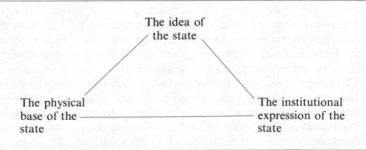

The idea of
the state

The physical
base of the
state

The institutional
expression of the
state

The model also suggests that units must meet certain criteria before they can be considered as states. Whereas individuals define themselves in strict biological terms – problems of soul, severe mental retardation, and definitions of death aside – states do not make such a self-evident category, and it is worth clarifying this matter before we examine the components of the model. What are the defining characteristics of states as a class of objects? The model points out several necessary attributes of statehood. States must have a physical base of population and territory; they must have governing institutions of some sort which control the physical base; and there must be some idea of the state which establishes its authority in the minds of its people. These features alone, however, do not add up to statehood. An agricultural commune, a factory, a family household, and numerous other social units could meet these criteria. The additional factors which make states a distinctive group of entities are size and sovereignty.

Although no strict bottom limit on size exists, there is unquestionably a strong sense of mass attached to the idea of the state which casts doubt on units with small populations. A unit with a population of ten or 100 would never qualify as a state, and even a population between 1000 and 10,000 would generally be considered inadequate. A population of 100,000 is still considered dangerously small, but begins to approach the level of acceptability. Peter Willetts argues that the United Nations has acted to ease the criteria for statehood, and in evidence there are now many quasi-state units, particularly small islands, recognised by the UN.[5] The full status of many of these as states, however, remains in doubt, and they form a kind of buffer zone between states and other social units. Size counts because states are supposed to be relatively permanent creations fulfilling the wide range of functions necessary for self-government. Without sufficient size, the unit is too fragile in the company of its larger fellows, and lacks the capability to perform all the tasks of self-rule. Thus traditional micro-states like Andorra and Liechtenstein are incapable of mounting defence and foreign relations establishments, and depend on larger neighbours to perform these functions for them. Many of the new post-colonial micro-states find themselves in the same position. Although exceptions may occur, such as the Vatican, and a variety of quasi-states may persist, the necessities of what might be called critical political mass will continue to draw a fairly high bottom line for the population size of states. Similar arguments might also be made about territorial size, but since the state is primarily a social phenomenon, population takes precedence. An adequate population will anyway tend to come with a sufficiency of territory, as demonstrated by extreme cases like the city-state of Singapore (232.4 square miles, 1970 population 2 million).[6]

Size alone still does not allow us to distinguish states from other units, because some large units of other types might still meet the criteria – large corporations for example. Sovereignty provides the crucial element dividing states from all other social units, and much of the argument about size in the preceding paragraph hinges on the need to provide sufficient capability for sovereignty to be exercised. Sovereignty, simply put, means self-rule. It requires denial of any higher political authority, and the claiming by the state of supreme decision-making authority both within its territory and over its citizens. Sovereignty can be divided, as in the case of those micro-states which claim it only over their domestic affairs, but the mark of the true state is that it claims undivided sovereignty in all temporal affairs. Sovereignty is divided among states, but not within them. The claim to sovereignty makes the state the highest form of social unit, and explains its centrality to political analysis.

That said, however, the concept of sovereignty can itself be contested, and harbours a number of practical problems. Can sovereignty exist without being exercised? In other words, is it primarily a legal idea which exists as a right? Or is it primarily a political idea, which comes into being only when exercised? If the latter, what distinguishes it from power? If sovereignty is an attribute of the state, where is it located? Does it reside with the population in some way? Is it vested in a ruler or governing institutions? Or is it somehow diffused throughout all aspects of the state? Who, in practice, exercises the authority it confers? And if that right is concentrated in an individual or an institution, what distinguishes the ruler from the state? Since the planetary supply of sovereignty has been divided up among states, is sovereignty an attribute that derives primarily from within the state? Or is it in some sense conferred externally by the recognition of other states?

These problems, though formidable, do not endanger our present line of analysis, and need not detain us long. Although conceptually difficult, sovereignty is usually easy to recognise in practice. Social units which claim it must do so openly, and failure to exercise it, or disputes over the right to do so, will usually be fairly evident. Most social units do not claim it, and signify this by subordinating themselves to one of those that does.

How, then, does this discussion leave us in relation to states as a class of objects? As Waltz points out, categories define groups of things on the basis of their similarity in some respects only.[7] Thus all apples will share a wide range of characteristics, though individual apples will differ somewhat in weight, shape and taste. But the category of fruit describes a considerably looser set of objects which may display more differences than similarities, as, say, between bananas and oranges. On this basis, states make a looser category than do individuals. Although states share several types of features, including physical (territory and population), functional (the tasks of self-government), institutional (the structure of government), and legal (their status as sovereign entities), the differences among these features are enormous.[8] If we extend Waltz's analogy, individuals form a category more like that of apples, while states form one more like that of fruit. Differences in size, power, physical geography, relative location, character of population, resources, domestic political economic and social structures, and degree of independence, are so obvious and so great as not to require illustration.

Even sovereignty, which is conventionally assumed to be a key defining characteristic of statehood, and therefore identical across all states, may not, in fact, be equally distributed. If we take Waltz's definition of sovereign as meaning that a state 'decides for itself how it will cope with its internal and external problems, including whether or not to seek assistance from others and in doing so to limit its freedom by making commitments to them',[9] then we clearly run into problems with satellite-states. One has to question seriously whether states like Poland since 1945, or Cuba before Castro, really had much option about seeking assistance from others and limiting their freedom in the process. There is a world of difference between the qualification Waltz offers, which is having the independence to make one's own decision even though one's circumstances are highly constrained, and the situation in which the constraints intrude into the heart of the decision-making process itself. Can Czechoslovakia and Poland really be said to be equally sovereign to Britain and West Germany in terms of deciding for themselves how they will cope with their internal and external problems? If they cannot, then it has to be conceded that sovereignty, like power and independence, also varies in degree among states, since all four countries enjoy recognition as states by virtually every standard criteria.[10] Even Canada, a state enjoying unquestioned sovereign status for many decades, did not gain from Britain the legal power to amend its constitution until 1982.

We must conclude, then, that states form a category rather like those formed by aircraft, galaxies and mountains. In each case, the category is united by some outstanding feature or features which distinguishes its members from the universe of all other things. But although the link among the members is both unique and strong, it does not prevent enormous diversity in many vital respects amongst them. Thus, when we compare members of the category with each other, we may well be struck much more by their differences than by their similarities. What has Concorde in common with a child's glider compared with their differences, or Everest in common with Fuji, or the Soviet Union in common with Fiji, compared with their differences? This feature of the category of states necessitates a further break in the analogy between them, and the much tighter category of individuals, where similarities and differences appear more even in proportion. Unfortunately for the analyst, it is more the differences among states than their similarities which determine the character of international relations in general, and the national security problem in particular.

Because of the importance of what is different among states in determining their relations with each other, we cannot expect the concept of national security to exhibit much unity of meaning in any general sense. The meaning of security will be nearly as diverse as the condition of the different states to which it applies, which not only adds to our difficulties in analysing the concept, but also adds a hazard to its use in any general sense at all. The problem of diversity in the meaning of security will recur again when we come to consider security in the context of relations among states at the system level. On that level, interactions among states with similar views of national security would be difficult to assess, but interactions among states whose notions of national security may share few common assumptions become nightmarishly complicated. Because national security is such a fragmented concept it cannot be compared with more stable, and rigorously definable concepts like wealth, and it certainly cannot be pegged to any simple indicator like military capability. For this reason, attempts to build theories of security along market economy lines seem unlikely to enjoy much success.[11]

Starting with the idea of the state, we shall survey the three elements of the model with a view both to filling in some of their detail, and identifying the vulnerability to threats which makes them objects of national security.

The Idea of the State

The idea of the state is the most amorphous component of our model, but in a sense also the most central. The notion of purpose is what distinguishes the idea of the state from its physical base and its institutions. The physical base simply exists, and has to be dealt with because of that fact. The institutions are created to govern, and to make the state work, but their functional logic falls a long way short of defining the totality of the state. Although institutions are, as we shall see, closely tied to aspects of the idea of the state, it is, as Kenneth Dyson points out, a 'category error' to conflate the idea of the state with its apparatus.[12] The European Community, for example, has institutions, but to the dismay of Mitrany-style functionalist theorists and others, these have failed by themselves to act as a gravitational core for the accretion of a European super-state. The missing element is a sense of purpose. No consensus exists about what the Community should be doing, how it should be doing it, or what it should, as an evolving political entity, be striving to become. With states, we should expect to find a clearer sense of both purpose and form, a distinctive idea of some sort which lies at the heart of the state's political identity. What does the state exist to do? Why is it there? What is its relation to the society which it contains? Why some particular size and form of state, when a glance at any historical atlas will reveal a variety of possible alternatives? In defining the idea of the state, reference to basic functions of providing civil order, collective goods and external defence does not take us very far. Although these functional considerations inevitably form part of the idea of the state, they indicate little about what binds the people into an entity which requires such services. Something more than a simple desire to escape the state of nature is at work in the creation and maintenance of states. Otherwise there would be no barrier to the founding of a universal state which would solve the state of nature problem without causing the troublesome intermediary of a fragmented international system of sovereign states.

A broad hint as to one direction worth exploring in search of the idea of the state is given by the term national security itself. Why *national* security? National security implies strongly that the object of security is the nation, and this raises questions about the links between nation and state. A nation is defined as a large group of people sharing the same cultural, and possibly the same racial, heritage, and normally living in one area. If the nation and the state coincide, then we can look for the purpose of the state in the protection and expression of an independently existing cultural entity: nation would define much of the relationship between state and society. This fact would give us some handles on what values might be at stake, and what priorities they might have, in the definition of national security. If the purpose of the state is to protect and express a cultural group, then life and culture must come high on the list of national security priorities. A pure modal of the nation-state would require that the nation precede the state, and in a sense give rise to it, as in the case of Japan, China, Germany and others. But it is obvious from a quick survey of the company of states that very few of them fit this model. Some nations have no state, like the Kurds, the Palestinians, the Armenians, and, before 1947, the Jews. Many nations are divided into more than one state, like the Koreans, the Germans, the Irish and the Chinese. And some states contain several nations, like India, the Soviet Union, Nigeria and the United Kingdom.

Given this evidence, either national security in a strict sense is a concept with only limited application to the state, or else the relationship between state and nation is more complex than that suggested by the primal model. The definition of nation imposes no condition of permanence, and since both culture and race are malleable qualities, there is no reason why states cannot create nations as well as be created by them. The United States provides an outstanding example of this process by which diverse territories and peoples can be forged into a self-regarding nation by the conscious action of the state. The possibility of state institutions being used to create nations, as well as just expressing them, considerably com-plicates and enriches the idea of nation. Since nations represent a pattern which covers the whole fabric of humanity, new nations cannot be created without destroying, or at least overlaying, old ones. The only exception to this rule is where new nations can be created on previously uninhabited territory, since mere emigration need not destroy the contributing nation(s). The United States benefited from this factor, though it destroyed the Indian nations in the process, but contemporary efforts at nation-building must take place in the more difficult context of *in situ* populations, there being no more large, habitable areas outside state control.

One obvious implication of this expanded view of the nation is that extensive grounds for conflict exist between natural nations and the attempts of states to create nations which coincide with their boundaries. The civil war in Nigeria, and the struggles of the Kurds, illustrate this problem, which provides an ironic level of contradiction in the meaning of national security. Clearly, from the point of view of efficient government, having state and nation coincide provides tremendous advantages in terms of unifying forces, ease of communication, definition of purpose, and such-like. The nation-state is therefore a powerful ideal, if not a widespread reality.[13]

From this discussion we can conclude that the link between state and nation is not simple, and that the nation as the idea of the state, particularly in national security terms, will not be simple either. Several models of possible nation – state links suggest themselves. First is the primal *nation-state*, of which Japan is probably the strongest example. Here the nation precedes the state, and plays a major role in giving rise to it. The state's purpose is to protect and express the nation, and the bond between the two is deep and profound. The nation provides the state with both a strong identity in the international arena, and a solid base of domestic legitimacy – solid enough to withstand revolutionary upheavals, as in the case of France at the end of the eighteenth century, or defeat and occupation by foreign powers, as in the case of France and Japan during the 1940s.

The second model has been called the *state-nation*, since the state plays an instrumental role in creating the nation, rather than the other way around.[14] The model is top-down rather than bottom-up. As suggested above, this process is easiest to perform when populations have been largely transplanted from elsewhere to fill an empty, or weakly held, territory. Thus the United States, Australia and many Latin American countries provide the best models. The state generates and propagates uniform cultural elements like language, arts, custom and law, so that over time these take root and produce a distinctive, nation-like, cultural entity which identifies with the state. Citizens begin to attach their primary social loyalties to the state-nation, referring to themselves as Americans, Chileans, Australians, and such-like, and eventually, if all works well, an entity is produced which is similar in all respects except history to a primal nation-state. The state-nation model can also be tried in places where the state incorporates a multitude of nationalities, though here it requires the subordination of the indigenous nations on their own territory, a much tougher task than the incorporation of uprooted immigrants. Many African states, faced with complex tribal divisions, seem to look to the state-nation process as their salvation, and even a multi-nation state like India sometimes appears to lean in this direction.

While a mature state-nation like the United States will differ little from a nation-state in respect of the security implications of the state – nation link, immature state-nations like Nigeria will be highly vulnerable and insecure in this regard. The idea of the state as represented by the nation will be weakly developed and poorly established, and thus vulnerable to challenge and interference from within and without. Separatists may try to opt out, as the Ibos did in Nigeria. Or one domestic group may try to capture the nation-building process for its own advantage, as the whites tried to do in Rhodesia. Or the whole fragile process may be penetrated by stronger external cultures, as symbolised by the 'Coca-colaisation' of many Third World states, and the general complaint about western cultural imperialism. So long as such states fail to solve their nationality problem, they remain vulnerable to dismemberment, intervention, instability and internal conflict in ways not normally experienced by states in harmony with their nations.[15]

The third model is the *part-nation-state*. This is where a nation is divided up among two or more states, and where the population of each state consists largely of people from that nation. Thus, the Korean, Chinese, and until 1973 the Vietnamese nations were divided into two states, while the German nation is split among three, though here some might argue that Austria, like Denmark and the Netherlands, is sufficiently distinctive to count as a nation in its own right. This model does not include nations split up among several states, but not dominant in any, like the Kurds. A variant of this model is where a nation-state exists, but a minority of its members fall outside its boundaries, living as minority groups in neighbouring states. Germany during the 1920s and 1930s, and Somalia today, illustrate this case. The mystique of the unified nation-state frequently exercises a strong hold on part-nation-states, and can easily become an obsessive and overriding security issue. Rival part-nation-states like East and West Germany, and North and South Korea, almost automatically undermine each other's legitimacy, and the imperative for reunification is widely assumed to be an immutable factor that will re-emerge whenever opportunity beckons. Germany's reunification drive during the 1930s, and Vietnam's epic struggle of nearly three decades, illustrate the force of this drive, and explain the intractable nature of what is still referred to as 'the German problem' in Europe. Part-nation-states frequently commit themselves to an intense version of the state-nation process in an attempt to build up their legitimacy by differentiating their part of the nation from the other parts. The frenzied competition between the two systems in

North and South Korea provides perhaps the best contemporary illustration of this strategy, which, given time, has some prospects of success. Part-nation-states, then, can represent a severe source of insecurity both to themselves and to others. Their case offers the maximum level of contradiction in the idea of national security as applied to states, for it is precisely the nation that makes the idea of the state insecure.

The fourth model can be called the *multination-state*, and comprises those states which contain two or more substantially complete nations within their boundaries. Two sub-types exist within this model which are sufficiently distinct almost to count as models in their own right, and we can label these the *federative state* and the *imperial state*. Federative states, at least in theory, reject the nation-state as the ideal type of state. By federative, we do not simply mean any state with a federal political structure, but rather states which contain two or more nations without trying to impose an artificial state-nation over them. Separate nations are allowed, even encouraged, to pursue their own identities, and attempts are made to structure the state in such a way that no one nationality comes to dominate the whole state structure. Canada and Jugoslavia offer clear examples of this model, and countries like Czechoslovakia, the United Kingdom, New Zealand and India can be interpreted at least partly along these lines. Obviously, the idea of a federative state cannot be rooted in nationalism, and this fact leaves a dangerous political void at the heart of the state. The federative state has to justify itself by appeal to less emotive ideas like economies of scale – the argument that the component nations are too small by themselves to generate effective nation-states under the geopolitical circumstances in which they are located. Such states have no natural unifying principle, and consequently are more vulnerable to dismemberment, separatism and political interference than are nation-states. Nationality issues pose a constant source of insecurity for the state, as illustrated by Jugoslavia, and national security can be easily threatened by purely political action, as in the case of General de Gaulle's famous 1967 'Vive le Quebec libre' speech in Canada.

Imperial states are those in which one of the nations within the state dominates the state structures to its own advantage. The hegemony of the Great Russians within the Tsarist and Soviet states provides one example, the dominance of the Punjabi's in Pakistan another. Several kinds of emphasis are possible within an imperial state. The dominant nation may seek to suppress the other nationalities by means ranging from massacre to cultural and racial absorption, with a view to transforming itself into something like a nation-state. It may seek simply to retain its dominance, using the machinery of the state to enforce its position without trying to absorb or eliminate other groups, or it may adopt the more subtle approach of cultivating a non-nationalist ideology which appears to transcend the national issue while in fact perpetuating the status quo. Imperial states contain possibilities of transformation into all the other types, and, like federative states, are vulnerable to threats aimed at their national divisions. Such states may be threatened by separatism, as in Ethiopia, by shifts in the demographic balance of the nations, as often mooted about the Soviet Union, or by dismemberment, as in the case of Pakistan. The stability of the imperial state depends on the ability of the dominant nation to retain its control. If its ability is weakened either by internal developments or external intervention, the state structure stands at risk of complete collapse, as in the case of Austria-Hungary after the First World War. Political threats are thus a key element in the national security problem of imperial states.

These models represent ideal types, and as with any such classification, not all real world cases fit smoothly into them. Numerous ambiguities occur on the boundaries of the models, and some minor 'special case' categories can be found. Switzerland, for example, contains fragments of three nations organised along federative lines, but has no distinctive or dominant national group of its own. France fits most closely into the nation-state mould, but Breton nationalists might claim with some justice that, from their minority viewpoint, the French state appears more imperial in nature. Similarly, French-Canadians might claim that Canada is more imperial than federative, just as smaller and weaker groups in Jugoslavia complain about Serbian dominance. Conversely, imperial states like the Soviet Union may try to disguise themselves as federative ones. Appearances may also be deceptive in that periods of strength and prosperity may hide domestic rifts and give the appearance of a nation-state, only to give way to separatism when prosperity or central authority diminishes. The rise of regional nationalism in declining Britain illustrates this case.

Despite these difficulties, the models give us a useful framework within which to consider the links between state and nation. They make it clear that national security with regard to the nation can be read in several different ways, and that consequently different states will experience very different kinds of insecurity and security in relation to the nationality question. Some states may derive great strength from their link to the nation, whereas for others the links between state and nation might define their weakest and most vulnerable point. The importance of the nation as a vital component in the idea of the state has to be measured externally as well as internally. Unless the idea of the state is firmly planted in the minds of the population, the state as a whole has no secure foundation. Equally, unless the idea of the state is firmly planted in the 'minds' of other states, the state has no secure environment. Because the idea of national self-rule has a high legitimacy in the international system, a firmly established link between state and nation acts as a powerful moderator on the unconstrained operation of the international anarchy, and is therefore a vital element of national security. We shall explore this point in more detail when we come to look at international security. On that level, the confluence between the nation as a legitimising idea underpinning the state, and sovereignty, as the principle idea underpinning the anarchical society of the international system as a whole, becomes centrally important to developing a concept of international security.

While the concept of nation provides us with considerable insight into the idea of the state, it falls short of exhausting the subject. Nationalism adds a fundamental and ubiquitous demographic factor to the basic functions of the state, but it still leaves plenty of room for additional notions of purpose. There is great scope for variety in the way in which the state fulfils its responsibility to the nation, and there is even scope for higher ideological purposes aimed at transcending nationalism. These additional notions, however, differ from nationalism in that they tend to be less deeply-rooted, and therefore more vulnerable to disruption. A firmly established nation reproduces itself automatically by the transfer of culture to the young, and once established is extremely difficult to remove by measures short of obliteration. The well-founded nation is, in this sense, more stable and more secure than the state. What might be called the 'higher' ideas of the state, such as its principles of political organisation, are fragile by comparison, and thus more sensitive as objects of security. For example, fascism as an idea of the state was largely purged out of Germany, Japan and Italy by relatively brief and mild periods of foreign occupation. Similar measures would scarcely have dented the sense of nation in those countries.

The idea of the state can take many forms at this higher level, and our purposes here do not require us to explore these definitively. An indication of the types and range will suffice to give us an adequate sense of their security implication. Organising ideologies are perhaps the most obvious type of higher idea of the state. These can take the form of identification with some fairly general principle, like Islam or democracy, or some more specific doctrine, like republicanism. Many varieties of political, economic, religious and social ideology can serve as an idea of the state, and will be closely connected to the state's institutional structures. In some cases, an organising ideology will be so deeply ingrained into the state that change would have transformational, or perhaps fatal, implications. Democracy and capitalism, for example, are so basic to the construction of the United States that it is hard to imagine the American state without them. In other cases, organising ideologies have only shallow roots, and large changes in official orientation occur frequently. Many Third World states display this tendency, as organising ideologies come and go with different leaderships, never having time to strike deeper roots among the population. Since these ideologies address the bases of relations between state and society they define the conditions for both harmony and conflict in domestic politics. If the ideas themselves are weak; or if they are weakly held within society; or if strongly held, but opposed, ideas compete within society; then the state stands on fragile foundations.

Different organising ideologies may represent different ends, as in the case of the Islamic state which emerged in Iran after the fall of the Shah, in comparison with the monarchist and materialist values which preceded it. But they may also represent different convictions about means, as in the liberal democratic versus the communist approaches to achieving material prosperity. They can also come in both positive and negative forms. The United States, for instance, pursues democracy and capitalism as positive values, but at the same time gives anti-communism almost equal weight as a negative organising principle. Since organising ideologies are so closely tied to state institutions, we can deal with much of their security side when we discuss the institutional component of the state.

Other concepts can also serve as, or contribute to, the idea of the state. A sense of national purpose can spring from ideas about racial preservation, as in South Africa, or from ideas relating to a larger civilisation, as in pre-1917 Russian images of the Tsarist empire as a third Rome. Even simple fear or hatred of some external group might provide a substantial part of the idea of the state. One would expect to find this in a state occupying a highly exposed position, as, for example, in the Austrian empire at the height of the Ottoman expansions.[16] Power, as suggested in the Introduction, can also be seen as a purpose of the state. In a pure Realist view, states seek power not only as a means to protect or pursue other values, but also as a means of advancing themselves in the Social-Darwinistic universe of the international system. Power is thus the end, as well as the means, of survival, each state struggling to prove its superiority in the context of a ceaseless general competition. Each state will have its own unique idea, which in reality will be a compilation of many elements. In Japan, for example, the nation, and the values associated with national culture, would constitute a large slice of the idea of the state, but democratic and capitalist ideas would also weigh significantly. In the Soviet Union, nationalism would perhaps count for less, with pride of place going to the ideological foundations of the Soviet state.

The problem is how to apply a concept like security to something as ephemeral as an idea, or a set of ideas. Where the idea is firmly established, like that of an ancient nation, the problem of security is mitigated by the inherent difficulty of instigating change. But for higher ideas, even defining criteria for security is not easy, let alone formulating policies. Most organising ideologies are themselves essentially contested concepts, and therefore impossible to define with precision, and probably in a constant process of evolution by nature. Given this amorphous character, how is one to determine that the idea has been attacked or endangered? The classic illustration here is the old conundrum about democracy and free speech. If free speech is a necessary condition of democracy, but also a licence for anti-democratic propaganda, how does one devise a security policy for democracy? The component ideas which go to make up a concept like democracy change over time, as any history of Britain over the last two centuries will reveal. Even the cultural ideas which bind the nation do not remain constant, as illustrated by the 'generation gap' phenomena, in which older generations clash with younger ones about a wide range of cultural norms and interpretations. The natural ambiguity and flexibility of these ideas mean that security cannot be applied to them unless some criteria exist for distinguishing between acceptable and unacceptable sources and forms of change, a task beyond reasonable hope of complete fulfilment given, among other things, the weakness of our understanding of many of the cause-effect relationships involved. Ideas are, by their very nature, vulnerable to interplay with other ideas, which makes it extraordinarily difficult to apply a concept like security to them.

In part because of this indeterminate character of the ideas, it is possible to see them as potentially threatened from many quarters. Organising ideologies can be penetrated, distorted, corrupted, and eventually undermined by contact with other ideas. They can be attacked through their supporting institutions, and they can be suppressed by force. Even national cultures are vulnerable in this way, as illustrated on a small scale by French sensitivity to the penetration of the national language by English words and usages. Because of this broad spectrum vulnerability, an attempt to apply the concept of security to the idea of the state can lead to exceedingly sweeping criteria being set for attaining acceptable levels of security, a fact that can give rise to a dangerous streak of absolutism in national security policy. Making the idea of the state secure might logically be seen to require either a heavily fortified isolationism aimed at keeping out corrupting influences, or an expansionist imperial policy aimed at eliminating or suppressing threats at their source. Thus, one reading of German and Japanese expansionism up to the Second World War is that neither nation could make itself secure without dominating the countries around it. The Wilsonian idea of making the world safe for democracy by eliminating other forms of government has overtones of this theme about it, as does the idea common to many new revolutionary governments that they can only make their own revolution secure by spreading similar revolutions beyond their borders.

Before examining the institutions of the state, it is worth considering who holds the idea of the state. An important undercurrent of the above discussion has been that a strong idea of some sort is a necessary component of a viable state, and the clear implication has been that the idea of the state must not only be coherent in its own right, but also widely held. Unless an idea is widely held, it cannot count as part of the idea of the state, but only as one of the ideas contained within the state, as in the distinction between a nation-state and a federative multi-nation state. From this perspective, it does not matter if ideas like nationalism and democracy stem from, and serve the interests of, particular groups or classes, so long as they command general support. Indeed, one of the advantages of an ambiguous idea like democracy is that its very looseness and flexibility allow it to attract a broad social consensus. Narrower ideas almost by definition imply greater difficulty in generating a popular base, and thus point to a larger role for institutions in underpinning the structure of the state. If the idea of the state is strong and widely held, then the state can endure periods of weak institutions, as France has done, without serious threat to its overall integrity. If the idea of the state is weakly held, or strongly contested, however, then a lapse in institutional strength might well bring the whole structure crashing down in revolution, civil war, or the disintegration of the state as a physical unit.

The Institutions of the State

The institutions of the state comprise the entire machinery of government, including its legislative, administrative and judicial bodies, and the laws, procedures and norms by which they operate. In many countries, this machinery represents a very substantial proportion of the national substance, and one that has been growing in proportion to the rest of the state since before the beginning of this century. In Britain, for example, government spending as a percentage of GNP has risen from below 10 per cent at the end of the nineteenth century, to around 50 per cent during the 1970s. Governments obviously vary enormously in extent and character, and we cannot even begin to survey their details here. Think, for example, of the contrasts between the government machinery of the Soviet Union and that of the Republic of Ireland. We can, however, say something about the nature of governments as an object of security, and point out some significant criteria for evaluating differences among them.

Perhaps the easiest way to approach this problem is to look at an extreme case. In the previous section, it was argued that ideas made up an important element of the state, providing it with coherence, purpose and definition, and also providing a social mechanism for persuading citizens to subordinate themselves to the state's authority. Strong and widely held ideas thus served to bind the state into something like an organic entity. It was also argued that organising ideologies were closely linked to the machinery of government, a point to which we shall return shortly. The question then arises: is it possible to have a state in which the idea of the state is very weak or non-existent, and in which the institutional component therefore has to take up all its functions? This question raises the image of a maximum state in which an élite commands the machinery of government, and uses it to run the state in its own interest. The idea of the state in such a case would amount to little more than the ruling élite's definition of its own interest, and the coherence of the state would be preserved by unstinting use of the state's coercive powers against its citizens. Fear would replace more positive ideas as the primary unifying element, and the government would command obedience rather than loyalty. In such a case, the government would almost literally be the state.

This model has just enough of an echo in the real world to give credence to the idea that institutions can, to a very considerable extent, replace ideas in the overall structure of the state. Cases like the rule of the Duvalier dynasty in Haiti, Somoza in Nicaragua, Amin in Uganda, and Nguema in Equatorial Guinea, come to mind, as do cases of government by a foreign occupying power, like those set up by the Germans during the Second World War, and those established by European colonial powers in places like India, Vietnam and the Middle East, where a local tradition of state structures was already well established. Although some cases approach the pure institutional model of the state quite closely, many more appear to be mixed models, in which the institutions of the state compensate for weaknesses in the idea of the state, rather than replacing it completely. The model of the imperial state from the previous section fits this category, because rule is not just by an élite, but represents a group within the state which may be a minority of the population, like the Austrians in the Austrian empire, or a weak majority like the Great Russians in the Tsarist and Soviet empires.

The weakness in the idea of the state may be along ideological rather than national lines, as in the case of almost any state captured by a dogmatic political creed. Both Nazi Germany and the Soviet Union had to devote considerable police resources to suppressing dissidents, especially in the early years of their rule. It should not be ignored also that the state itself can represent an enterprise of considerable extent in relation to the total national substance, as suggested of Britain above. Because of this fact, what might be characterised as self-interested élite rule, can encompass a rather large group. Since the state machinery disposes of relatively great resources, it can attract and co-opt support from significant numbers of people without the aid of any idea more potent than self-interest. If sufficient people can be recruited in this way, perhaps with the aid of a leader cult and a negative ideology, then the coercive and administrative arms of the state can be sustained without any general element of popular support. This is especially so if the public attitude is one of indifference, either because the public is not politically mobilised, or because the government has not made its exploitation intolerable. A negative ideology might also prove a useful means of attracting external resources, as in the case of Latin American regimes which draw aid from the United States by touting an anti-communist line.

On this basis, then, we might posit something like a sliding-scale, on which ideas and institutions can, to a considerable, but not complete, extent be substituted for each other. Substitutability would decline at either end of the scale, because even a strong idea of the state needs government machinery, and even strong institutions need, or at least prefer, to be supported by some idea. It seems fair to note that institutions can substitute more for ideas than the other way around. An extreme institutional model of the state – rule by pure coercion – has some empirical credibility, whereas a pure idea model – government without institutions – appears not to exist outside the fantasies of a few anarchists. Against this, however, has to be set the strong disposition of governments to create unifying ideas, either by cultivating an ideological orthodoxy, or by embarking on the state-nation process described in the previous section. This line of thought leads to a rather different characterisation of the relationship between institutions and ideas, where they are not so much distinct and substitutable elements, as complementary and interlinked components.

Although the nation as an idea does not suggest much about

appropriate forms of government – except in the case of multi-nation states – organising ideologies are intimately connected with governmental structures. Ideologies have, for the most part, much broader roots than the state in that they exist independently, and outside the boundaries, of any particular state. For this reason, governments can draw legitimacy from identifying with an ideology because it ties them to interests and purposes larger than those of the individuals in office. This link cannot be made without incurring quite stringent structural obligations, since the institutions of the state will have to be arranged so as to express and amplify the ideology. These implications are fairly obvious, and do not require discussion here. The familiar literatures on fascism, communism, democracy, monarchy, and feudalism, all cover the complementary and constraining interaction between ideas and institutions. The main point of interest from our perspective is that the ideas and the institutions are inseparably intertwined. The idea of democracy or communism is useless without the institutions to put it into operation, just as the institutions would be pointless without the idea to give them purpose. This interdependence means that institutions and ideas tend to stand or fall together in the context of any particular state, and this fact has obvious implications when we consider either, or both, as objects of security.

The institutions of the state are much more tangible than the idea of the state as an object of security. Because they have a physical existence they are more vulnerable to physical threats than are ideas. Institutions can be uprooted and destroyed much more easily than can ideas, and they do not suffer from, or enjoy, the same level of ambiguity which makes ideas so difficult as an object of security. They can be threatened by force, or by political action based on ideas which have different institutional implications. The Nazi government was overthrown by external military force, and replaced by institutions reflecting the ideologies of the conquering powers. Minor political reforms might take place with little use of force, as in the change from the Fourth to the Fifth Republic in France; but major transformations usually require either revolutionary violence, as in Russia in 1917, or very long periods of incremental reform, as in the transformation of Britain from monarchy to democracy. Since institutions must adapt themselves to meet changed conditions, some of the same ambiguities which apply to ideas also complicate security policy for institutions. How does one judge, for example, whether advocating the abolition of the House of Lords in Britain should be interpreted as a threat to the institutions of the state, or as a wise and timely move to adapt the institutions to the conditions of the twentieth century?

When institutions are threatened by force, the danger is that they will be overpowered, and the remedy is defence. When they are threatened by opposing ideas, the danger is that their legitimacy will be eroded, and that they will collapse for lack of support. Armed force might sustain them, as argued above, but institutions without popular support are much more precariously positioned than those with it. On this basis, state institutions vary enormously from case to case in terms of their domestic stability and, for many, the principal threat to security comes from within the state rather than from outside it. These domestic threats may range from small, relatively isolated groups of militants, as in West Germany; through powerful, centrally located groups of *coup*-makers, as in Bolivia, or substantial guerrilla movements, as in El Salvador during 1980–1; to widespread popular discontent, as in Poland during 1980–1, or full scale revolution, as in Cuba during the late 1950s. This whole problem of governing institutions that are unstable in relation to their domestic environment raises immense difficulties for the concept of national security. Because governments stand for the state at the international level, any externally mounted threat to the government clearly constitutes a national security problem. But on the domestic level, the governmental institutions constitute only part of the whole fabric of the state, existing in a condition of more or less permanent tension with other parts. Institutions can change without interrupting the continuity of the state, and this fact means that the security of the government can be differentiated from the security of the state on the domestic level in a manner not possible on the international level where state and government are inseparably bound together. This would be a manageable, if complicated, state of affairs if the domestic and international environments remained isolated from each other. Unfortunately for the analyst, domestic isolation is more the exception than the rule and, consequently, national and international politics spill into each other.

From an international perspective, governments are a perfectly legitimate target in the game of nations. Since governments largely determine the international activity and orientation of states, and since changes in government, even for purely domestic reasons, can result in significant shifts in international behaviour, it is no surprise that states interfere in each other's domestic politics. Such interventions can range from the subtle and nearly invisible, to the blatant; their style and effectiveness depending on a host of factors, not least of which is the stability of domestic politics in the target state. American concern to prevent the establishment of communist governments in the western hemisphere illustrates the kinds of motives involved in these interventions, and the lesson of the 1930s about the failure to intervene against Hitler perhaps gives them a lingering aura of legitimacy. American actions against the government of Fidel Castro in Cuba furnish many illustrations of the range of techniques available.[17] At the lower end of the spectrum come actions like propaganda against the organising ideology, provision of funds and facilities to opposition groups, and denial of recognition. In the middle range we find actions like encouragement of armed revolts, assassination attempts, and the mounting of external economic pressures in an attempt to undermine the government's domestic credibility. In the upper range, come actions like sponsored invasions and direct intervention by armed force. Where the intervening state is a great power and the target state a minor one, relatively small resources devoted by the former might have a large impact on the latter. It is not difficult to imagine circumstances in which externally provided funds could exceed the resources available from domestic sources in a small state.[18] Intervention can, of course, also take the form of assistance to a friendly government which is under challenge from domestic, foreign, or some combination of domestic and foreign, opposition. Soviet and Cuban aid to Angola in the late 1970s and British aid to Oman, illustrate this approach.

Because all of these options for intervention exist, and because motives for them are strong and opportunities tempting, the fusion between government and state which properly exists at the international level, frequently gets transferred to domestic politics. If a government is under attack by foreign intervention in the domestic political process, then it can legitimately invoke national security in its own defence. Drawing the line between indirect foreign intervention and legitimate internal political struggle, however, is not easy. The position of communists in the United States provides a good illustration of the dilemma. Should American communists be considered as agents for the Soviet Union and therefore treated as a national security problem? Or should they be treated as a legitimate manifestation of democratic politics within the domestic domain and therefore not be subjected to the repressive machinery of the state? The Soviet Union cannot help influencing and encouraging such individuals, even if it does not do so by channelling resources to them. Its very existence acts as a stimulant and inspiration to those who share its ideology, just as the existence of the United States motivates dissidents within the Soviet Union. In large, politically-stable states, the government need not feel unduly threatened by such linkages, but in states where the government institutions have only superficial roots this issue can be of much greater significance.

The problem for national security in all this is that governments can easily exploit the linkage between their own security and that of the state in order to increase their leverage over domestic politics. Governments can be assumed to have their own interests, both organisational and individual, apart from the state interest which they represent. By importing national security issues into the domestic environment, governments can increase their powers against domestic opponents, particularly as regards the use of force. The use of force is more legitimate in the international than in the domestic arena, but if national security can be invoked, then it acquires greater legitimacy in the domestic context. If domestic security can be permanently tied into national security, then the government can protect itself with the whole apparatus of a police state, as, for example, in the Soviet Union and South Korea. This is not to argue that such linkage necessarily indicates nefarious intent on the part of the government, for there obviously does exist a significant national security front in the domestic arena. Cases of political intervention by one state in the domestic affairs of another are too numerous to mention, and range from the 'comradely' Soviet occupations of Afghanistan and Czechoslovakia, to anti-communist funding supplied by the United States to right-of-centre parties in Italy. But it is to argue that a great temptation exists for governments to invoke national security in their own defence by identifying domestic political opposition with the policies of some foreign state. This temptation must be particularly strong for governments which are weakly founded in their domestic environment, and which consequently face strong, and often politically unsympathetic, opposition. One consequence of this situation is to confuse and corrupt the meaning of national security.

This problem would appear to be unsolvable especially since the decline in the legitimacy of territorial seizures has diverted effort into ideological competition among the powers. Since we have to live with it, one useful approach to reducing its unhelpful impact on the concept of national security is to formulate a distinction among types of governments to which we might try to apply security. The critical factor emerging from the preceding discussion appears to be the level of domestic stability displayed by the institutions of the state, or, to put it another way, whether the dominant threat to the government comes from outside or inside the state. A separate book would probably be required to develop this distinction into anything approaching an operational formulation, and a few observations will have to serve our purposes here.

Stable institutions are those which enjoy general support from the population. They usually rest their legitimacy on an idea of the state which is both strong and widely held, and which they are structured to reflect and uphold. The stability of the institutions expresses itself in the existence of orderly and durable mechanisms for transferring power within them, the transfer not involving use of force. Stable institutions do not require external support against domestic opposition, though they may require it against external threats. They do not necessarily enjoy complete freedom from opposition, including violent opposition, but their rule over the great majority rests on authority rather than coercion, and domestic political violence is normally on a small scale and isolated from mainstream political opinion. Democracies meet these criteria most easily, such countries as the United States, West Germany, the Netherlands and Britain providing examples. But other forms of government are by no means excluded. Stable institutions existed in Japan before 1945, in many monarchies before the French Revolution, and probably in North Vietnam prior to the merger with the South in 1975. Democracy may be currently popular as a basis for stable institutions resting on foundations of authority, but it is not logically the only format in which institutional stability can be achieved.

Unstable institutions do not enjoy general support from the population. Often this is because the idea of the state is weak, and therefore no basis for legitimising the exercise of government exists. There may be no agreed idea of nation among the population, as in Ethiopia, Pakistan and Nigeria, thereby encouraging different sections of the population to direct their cultural loyalties elsewhere than the state. Or there may be no consensus on organising ideology, thus creating opposed factions each struggling to impose a different set of institutional structures on the state, as in Spain during the 1930s, in Russia during the Revolution, and in many Third World countries, like Argentina and Chile today. Under such conditions, the institutions of the state necessarily rest more on coercion than on political authority, and force becomes a central rather than a peripheral feature of domestic political life. Such institutions live in a condition of perpetual siege, and may require external support in order to maintain themselves. In extreme cases, they may even be puppets of outside interests more than expressions of any domestic political process, as might be said of the late government of South Vietnam, and the Vietnamese-backed government in Kampuchea dating from 1979.

Unstable institutions do not normally achieve orderly mechanisms for the transfer of power, because such mechanisms require general agreement on principles of continuity which do not exist where the idea of the state is weak. Because they rely on coercion, unstable institutions are themselves vulnerable to the use of force, whether within themselves, as in the tradition of Latin American *coups*, or externally in the domestic political arena of the state as a whole, as in mass rebellions against the institutions of the state like that in Nicaragua. Where the use of force has become the regular means by which power changes hands, the institutions of the state have degenerated to the point at which the concept of security cannot be applied to them. What does security mean when threats cannot be distinguished from the normal process of government? Under these conditions, government by the military is an obvious recourse, the armed forces being by definition the organisation most capable of imposing order in the absence of a generally accepted authority. Indeed, the existence of a military government which is not justified by either the degree of armed threat from other states, or the extensive engagement of the state concerned in external imperial ventures, might almost be taken to indicate unstable institutions.

States obviously do not fall into two neat classes on the basis of this distinction, but they can be arranged along a spectrum in which the main threats to institutions are internal to the state at one end, and external to it at the other. Thus, countries like Australia, the United States, Switzerland and Norway would all cluster at the end where threats were primarily external, domestic threats being of minor concern. Countries like Bangladesh and Burma would be at the other end, where external threats were a relatively minor concern compared to domestic ones. Many countries end up in the middle ranges, like Argentina, Ethiopia, Pakistan, and the Soviet Union, where threats to institutions arise from both internal and external sources. These placings indicate nothing about the level of threat faced, so that two similarly placed countries, like New Zealand and Norway, might have to deal with quite different orders of external threat.

This kind of exercise is very difficult to operationalise on other than an impressionistic level because of the near impossibility of defining and measuring threat. One would also need to solve the problem of how to distinguish between purely domestic threats, and those fomented or encouraged by outside powers. Nevertheless, the impressionistic distinctions appear to have a strong empirical foundation, and they point to the conclusion that states cannot be treated as equal in terms of their political integrity as states. In other words, not only are states weak or strong according to the traditional criteria of relative power, but they are also weak or strong *as members of the category of states*. States like Chad, Ethiopia, Zaire and Burma are so weak as states that they can hardly be compared with states like France, Austria, Vietnam or Portugal as objects to which a concept like national security can be applied. What is it that is to be made secure when the major ideological and institutional features of the state are heavily disputed from within? We shall return to this question at the end of this chapter.

The Physical Base of the State

The physical base of the state comprises its population and territory, including all of the natural and man-made wealth contained within its borders. It is much the most concrete of the three components in our model, and consequently the easiest to discuss as an object of security. Because of its relatively concrete character, the physical base is also the area in which states share the most similarities in relation to security. In contrast to the ideas and institutions of the state, the basic quality of territory and population as objects of security does not vary much from state to state. Although population and territory vary enormously among states in terms of extent, configuration, level of development and resources, the threats to the state's physical base are common in type to all states because of the similar physical quality of the objects involved. Threats to physical objects are necessarily more direct and obvious in terms of seizure or damage than are threats to more amorphous objects like ideas and institutions.

Territory can be threatened with seizure or damage, and the threats can come from within or outside the state. Since the state covers a more or less precisely defined territory, threats against this component of the state can be determined with considerable precision. A state usually claims a specified territory as its own, and this claim may or may not be recognised by other states. In theory, there is no necessary connection between any given state and a particular territory, the argument being that state boundaries are determined only by the ability of other states to hold their ground. Powerful states like Russia and Germany could and did expand their territories into weakly-held areas like Poland. Even with nation-states, where we might expect to find a home territory defined by the settlement pattern of the national group, no permanent delimitation occurs because of the prospect of migration and conquest. The case of Germany and the *Lebensraum* question between 1870 and 1945 provides the most dramatic contemporary illustration of the fluidity of the relationship between nation-state and territory. The territory of the state tends to be clearly fixed at any given point in time, but is not constrained by indigenous determinants over the longer run of history.

That said, however, it may well be that the past flexibility of state boundaries no longer serves as a reliable guide to the future. The advent of the United Nations, combined with a situation in which nearly all available territory is already claimed by states nearly all of which recognise each other, has produced an appearance of unprecedented territorial stability. It may well be that territorial instability is characteristic of immature state systems, and that as states acquire longer histories of themselves they begin to identify permanently with quite closely-defined territories. Longstanding states like France, for example, have a clear and powerful attachment to a specified national territory which is inseparably associated with the history of the French state. Contraction of it would be unacceptable, as demonstrated by the case of Alsace-Lorraine, and no strong indigenous imperative exists to expand it beyond its present borders. This situation contrasts markedly with that of many newer states, like Somalia, Libya, Israel, Bolivia and Iraq, where strong domestic pressures for territorial expansion chafe against the norms of the UN system.

A state's territory can be threatened with seizure both by other states, as in Somali threats to both Ethiopia and Kenya, and by internal secessionist movements, as in the case of Canada and Quebec. Secessionists may wish either to establish their own state, like the Ibos in Nigeria, or to join with another state, like the Republicans in Northern Ireland. Secessionist movements offer a wealth of opportunity for foreign intervention, and rarely occur without importing some level of national security into the domestic arena. Territorial losses do not necessarily, or even usually, threaten the state with extinction. Germany, Pakistan, Mexico and Poland have all lost substantial areas without disrupting the continuity of the state over what remained. Although as a rule states will contest all challenges to their territorial integrity, some pieces of territory are clearly more valuable than others. This value may arise because of resources, like oil in the areas contested between Iran and Iraq, because of transporation access, like the Polish Corridor, for reasons arising from historical tradition or the nationality of occupants, like Alsace-Lorraine, for symbolic reasons, like Berlin, or for strategic reasons, like Gibraltar. Such territory will have much higher priority as an object of security than other areas, and some territory will have very low priority. India clearly places a much lower priority on the remote mountain areas seized by China in 1962 than on the dispute with Pakistan over Kashmir. The Russian sale of Alaska to the United States in 1867 probably illustrates the nadir of national identification with territory. States possessing territory with strategic significance beyond their own boundaries, like Turkey and the Dardanelles, may easily find that their territory becomes a source of more general threat to the state, as well as simply an object of security in its own right.

Territory can also be threatened with damage as well as with seizure. Taking territory in the broad sense of national property (not including the population), it is clear that policies like deterrence and compellence work in part through threats to territory. The United States and the Soviet Union constrain each other's behaviour not through threats of territorial annexation, but by threats to wreak huge damage on each other's physical property. The American bombing of North Vietnam was in part an attempt to coerce the North Vietnamese into changing their behaviour by damaging their territory; and Israel has used similar threats of damage against its Arab foes. Threats to territory tie in at this point to threats to the population, since the two are normally so closely associated that one cannot be damaged without damaging the other. While territory can be annexed without its population, as in the case of mass migrations of Germans westward at the close of the Second World War, threats of annexation and damage are usually aimed at both population and territory. Deterrence works not only because the laboriously acquired material wealth of the nation is under threat, but also because the population itself is held hostage to destruction. Since the state ultimately rests on its physical base, the protection of territory and population must count as fundamental national security concerns, though they may sometimes be sacrificed in considerable measure to protect the other two components of the state. The enormous losses of the Soviet Union during the Second World War illustrate this type of trade-off, and point to the bleak calculus of deterrence with its assumption of 'unacceptable damage'. Given the social nature of the state, progressive destruction of its physical base would, at some point, effectively obliterate all values associated with it. Short of that point, however, very considerable damage to the base can be sustained without endangering either the institutions or the idea of the state. Here the argument links to that in chapter 1 about disharmonies between individual security and national security. It also links to the arguments above about the idea of the state, because it can be threatened either by destroying the individuals who carry it, or by changing their minds about what its content should be.

Before concluding this section it is worth noting some anomalies that arise in relation to the physical base as an object of security. Although the state is normally taken to encompass a specified territory and population, ambiguities frequently exist. Many boundaries are either ill-defined or actively disputed, as between India and China, Japan and the Soviet Union, Argentina and Chile, and numerous others. Recent extensions in maritime boundaries have amplified this problem considerably.[19] Acknowledged disputes of this type tend to have a less inflammable character than violations of boundaries generally accepted as settled, and can acquire a semipermanent status as zones of uncertainty, like the Senkaku (Tiao Yu Tai) islands disputed among Taiwan, Japan and China.[20] A more serious anomaly arises in the case of states which define their security in terms of territory and population *not* under their control. This can occur because members of the nation are occupying territory outside the bounds of the nation-state, as in the case of the Sudeten Germans; or because the state has been deprived of some territory seen as crucial to the national interest, as in the case of Bolivia's corridor to the sea annexed by Chile in 1880. In such cases, the security dimension of the physical base takes on a quite different quality from the interest in protecting an already acquired domain outlined above.

Conclusions: Weak and Strong States

We have now surveyed the three components of our state model at some length. What, as a result, can we conclude about the state as an object of security?

Perhaps the most obvious conclusion refers back to one of the observations with which we began, namely that states are exceedingly dissimilar as objects of security. Each of the components we examined offers large numbers of options and, when added together, these results in a limitless array of combinations around which a state might be structured. Because of this diversity, the nature of security as a problem necessarily differs substantially from state to state. All states are to some degree vulnerable to military and economic threats, and many also suffer from a fundamental political insecurity. The different components of the state appear vulnerable to different kinds of threat, which makes national security a problem in many dimensions rather than just a matter of military defence. The idea of the state, its institutions, and even its territory can all be threatened as much by the manipulation of ideas as by the wielding of military power. Since the ideas underpinning the state are themselves subject to evolution, the problem is not only difficult to solve, but may even be hard to identify. The multi-layered nature of the state opens it to threats on many levels, particular vulnerabilities depending on the unique structure and circumstances of the state concerned. This diversity of states as referent objects for security underpins the argument in the Introduction about the impossibility of devising a useful general definition for national security. The concept of security can be mapped in a general sense, as we are doing here. But it can only be given specific substance in relation to concrete cases. Ideally, work at each of these levels, the general and the specific, should inform and complement work at the other.

If the diversity of national security problems is the most obvious conclusion to arise from this investigation of the state, the most important one is a refinement by which we can transform a universe of unique cases into a spectrum of distinguishable types. It becomes clear from our analysis, Waltz's arguments about states as 'like units' notwithstanding,[21] that states vary not only in respect of their status as powers, but also in respect of their weakness or strength as members of the category of states. When the idea and institutions of a state are both weak, then that state is in a very real sense less of a state than one in which the idea and institutions are strong.

Strength as a state neither depends on, nor correlates with, power. Weak powers, like Austria, the Netherlands, Norway and Singapore, are all strong states, while quite substantial powers, like Argentina, Brazil, Nigeria, Spain, Iran and Pakistan, are all rather weak as states. Even major powers, like China and the Soviet Union, have serious weaknesses as states. The Soviet Union lacks a comprehensive nationalist idea, and neither it nor China enjoys a domestic consensus on organising ideology. Both are obliged to maintain extensive internal security establishments, and neither has a reliable, long-term mechanism for the transfer of political power. Many factors explain why some states are stronger than others as states. The existence of a strong state may simply reflect a long history during which the state has had time to develop and mature. France and Britain clearly benefit in this way, whereas newer states like India and Indonesia are still in the early stages of state development, and are thus not surprisingly more fragile. Strong states may benefit from a good fit with a well-developed nation, like Japan, while weak states may have inherited, or had thrust upon them, boundaries which include a diversity of nations, like Jugoslavia, Nigeria, Ethiopia and Iraq. Weak states may find themselves trapped by historical patterns of economic development and political power which leave them underdeveloped and politically penetrated, and therefore unable to muster the economic and political resources necessary to build a stronger state. The relationship between Latin American states and the United States is often characterised in these terms, and the *dependencia* school of thought, in general, emphasises the role of external factors in the creation and maintenance of weak states.[21]

Whatever the reasons for the existence of weak states, the distinction between weak and strong states is vital to any analysis of national security. In order to facilitate discussion, we shall adopt here the following usage: weak or strong *states* will refer to the usage discussed above (i.e. the status of the unit concerned as a member of the class of states); weak or strong *powers* will refer to the traditional distinction among states in respect of their military and economic capability in relation to each other.[23] The principal distinguishing feature of weak states is their high level of concern with domestically-generated threats to the security of the government, in other words, weak states either do not have, or have failed to create, a domestic political and social consensus of sufficient strength to eliminate the large-scale use of force as a major and continuing element in the domestic political life of the nation. This definition connects back to the internal security dimension of the relationship between the state and its citizens which we explored in the previous chapter.[24] It raises again the awkward problem of defining a boundary in levels of domestic use of force, because even the strongest states require some level of domestic policing against criminals, violent dissidents and foreign agents. Establishing such a definition would require a separate study.

The kind of range with which we are concerned can be illustrated by the following cases. A normal level of civil policing, where the political content is relatively minor (which is not to say insignificant) occurs on a regular basis in countries like Canada, the Netherlands and the United States. At the opposite extreme come police states and military states where rule is extensively supported by the use of force against the population. Amin's Uganda, Pinochet's Chile and Zia's Pakistan are a few of the large number of contemporary cases. In between these extremes lie a complex variety of cases, including states with a local problem requiring abnormal use of force, like Britain and Ulster, those with well-institutionalised heavy police regimes, like the Soviet Union, and those with severe problems of external penetration, like the two Germanies and the two Koreas.

Where the state is strong, national security can be viewed primarily in terms of protecting the components of the state from outside threat and interference. The idea of the state, its institutions and its territory will all be clearly defined and stable in their own right. Approved mechanisms for adjustment and change will exist, and will command sufficient support so that they are not seriously threatened from within the state. Where the state is weak, only its physical base may be sufficiently well-defined to constitute a clear object of national security. Because its idea and its institutions are internally contested to the point of violence, they do not offer clear referents as objects of national security because, by definition, they are not properly national in scope. Because of this, it is probably more appropriate to view security in weak states in terms of the contending groups, organisations and individuals, as the prime objects of security. The concept of national security requires national objects as its points of reference, and in a state like Amin's Uganda these hardly exist aside from the national territory. To view such a state in the same terms as one would view Switzerland or Japan is not only absurd but also misleading. When there is almost no idea of the state, and the governing institutions are themselves the main threat to individuals, national security almost ceases to have content and one must look to individuals and sub-state units for the most meaningful security referents. Foreign intervention becomes much harder to assess in national security terms (unless other states are trying to seize parts of the physical base, in which case the threat is clearly on a national scale), because outside powers will be helping factions which are themselves in conflict. Thus, neither western aid to UNITA, nor Soviet and Cuban aid to the MPLA during the Angolan civil war can be described as threats to the national security of Angola, because no national political entity existed to threaten. Who should be classed enemy and who ally simply depends on one's point of view, or, in the longer term, on which side wins.

This distinction between states with serious domestic security problems and those whose primary security concerns are external, is crucial to the understanding of national security. The weaker a state is, the more ambiguous the concept of national security becomes in relation to it. To use the term in relation to a weak state, as if such a state represented the same type of object as a strong state, simply paves the road for the importation of national security into the domestic political arena, with all the attendant confusions, dangers and contradictions this implies. The security of governments becomes confused with the security of states, and factional interests are provided with a legitimacy which they do not merit. In a strong state, we might expect a considerable, though by no means total, correlation between the government's view of national security and the array of referent objects discussed in this chapter. In weaker states this correlation declines, and we need to be much more suspicious of the assumption that national security is what the government deems it to be. There will almost always be useful grounds, in either weak or strong states, for testing government assertions about national security against the range of factors discussed here.

To suggest this type of distinction between weak and strong states runs very much against the grain of orthodoxy in International Relations as a field, and it is worth examining the reasons for this attitude, which is typical also of Strategic Studies. The illusion that all states are basically the same type of object springs not only from their common possession of sovereignty, but is also much encouraged by the habit of looking at them from an external, system level, perspective. When looked at from outside, states appear to be much more definite and similar objects than when they are viewed from within. From outside, they nearly all appear as sovereign entities in which governments exercise control over territories and populations which are, for the most part, neither ruled nor claimed by other states. Most of these states either recognise, or treat with, one another as sovereign equals, and even the weakest states can usually exercise their right to vote in international bodies like the General Assembly. From this perspective, it is easy to slip into the assumption that states are similar objects, and, indeed, for many aspects of international relations such an assumption is both reasonable and analytically useful as, for example, in the study of international negotiations.

The argument here is that this external perspective distorts the view in relation to national security by covering over the domestic security dimension. National security cannot be considered apart from the internal structure of the state, and the view from within not infrequently explodes the superficial image of the state as a coherent object of security. A strong state defines itself from within and fills the gap between its neighbours with a solid political presence. A weak state may be defined more *as* the gap between its neighbours, with little of political substance underlying the façade of internationally-recognised statehood. Since the object itself is so tenuous, the concept of national security lacks many referents other than basic territoriality. Hence, behaviour within the state can be understood better in terms of individual and sub-group security than in terms of national security. National security properly refers to the relationship of the state to its environment, and becomes profoundly confused to the extent that the state is insecure within itself. In other words, the concept of national security can only be applied sensibly to the external side of the state's Hobbesian security functions. Unless the internal dimension is relatively stable as a prior condition, the image of the state as a referent object for security fades into a meaningless blur.

Notes

1 For discussions on the problem of the individual-state analogy, see Hedley Bull, *the Anarchical Society* (London, Macmillan, 1977), pp. 47–52; and Robert E. Osgood and Robert W. Tucker, *Force, Order and Justice* (Baltimore, Johns Hopkins University Press, 1967), pp. 270–84.
2 On idiosyncratic versus role variables, see James N. Rosenau, 'Pre-theories and Theories of Foreign Policy', in R. Barry Farrell (ed.), *Approaches to Comparative and International Politics*, (Evanston, Northwestern University Press, 1966), pp. 27–92.
3 Ralph Miliband, *The State in Capitalist Society* (London, Quartet Books, 1973), p. 46.

4   An exercise partly parallel in form to this model, though rather different in intent, is undertaken by R.W. Cox, 'Social Forces, State and World Orders', *Millennium*, 10:2 (1981), who notes (p. 127) that, 'there has been little attempt within the bounds of international relations theory to consider the state/society complex as the basic entity of international relations'.

5   Peter Willetts, 'The United Nations and the Transformation of the Inter-State System', in Barry Buzan and R.J. Barry Jones (eds), *Change and the Study of International Relations* (London, Frances Pinter, 1981), pp. 112–14.

6   John Paxton (ed.), *The Statesman's Yearbook 1978–1979* (London, Macmillan, 1978), p. 1051.

7   Kenneth N. Waltz, *Theory of International Politics* (Reading, Mass., Addison-Wesley, 1979), pp. 96–7.

8   For discussions of states as a class of objects, see *ibid*, pp. 95–7; and P.A. Reynolds, *An Introduction to International Relations* (London, Longman, 1980, 2nd edn), pp. 262–3.

9   Waltz, *ibid.*, p. 96.

10 For opposing views on the trend towards more equality among states, see R.W. Tucker, *The Inequality of Nations* (London, Martin Robertson, 1977); and R.P. Anand, 'On the Equality of States', in Fred A. Sonderman, W.C. Olson and D.S. McLellan, *The Theory and Practice of International Relations* (New Jersey, Prentice-Hall, 1970), pp. 23–9.

11 For examples of this approach, see Ian Bellany, 'Towards a Theory of International Security', *Political Studies*, 29:1 (1981); and Mancur Olson and R. Zeckhauser, 'An Economic Theory of Alliances', *Review of Economics and Statistics*, 48 (1966).

12 Kenneth H.F. Dyson, *The State Tradition in Western Europe* (Oxford, Martin Robertson, 1980), p. 3. Dyson goes on to explore the intellectual history of the idea of the state in great depth. His purpose is not, as mine is here, to find referents for a concept like security. Instead, he charts the development of ideas about the fundamental character of the state as a collective entity, and tries to relate these developments to the conditions of their times. I am trying to sketch a contemporary cross-section of the idea of the state, whereas Dyson shows how we arrived here. Those interested in either the dynamic of the idea of the state, or its character at various points in the past, should consult this work.

13 On nations and states, see Leonard Tivey (ed.), *The Nation-State* (Oxford, Martin Robertson, 1981); Ralph Pettman, *State and Class* (London, Croom Helm, 1979), ch. 4; Ivo D. Duchacek, *Nations and Men* (Hinsdale, Illinois, Dryden Press, 1975, 3rd edn), chs. 1–3; Hugh Seton-Watson, *Nations and States* (London, Methuen, 1977); Mostafa Rejai and C.H. Enloc, 'Nation-States and State-Nations', in Michael Smith *et al.* (eds), *Perspectives on World Politics* (London, Croom Helm Open University Press, 1981). For a useful discussion of nations as minority ethnic groups within states, see Vernon Van Dyke, 'The Individual, the State and Ethnic Comminities in Political Theory', *World Politics*, 29:3 (1977).

14 Rejai and Enlock, *ibid.*, use this term in relation to the nation-building attempts of many Third World states.

15 One view would have it that even the primal nation-states are merely longstanding products of the state-nation process, having been themselves welded together by the agency of the state during earlier historical periods. This view implies a spectrum of development ranging from those states newly embarked on the nation-building process, to those where the nation has long since become a stable and self-sustaining feature of political life. See Cornelia Navari, 'The Origins of the Nation-State', in Tivey (ed.), *op. cit.* (note 13), ch. 1; and Dyson, *op. cit.* (note 12), p. 245. A developmental view of this type would raise interesting questions about intervening variables. Could one, for example, find any uniform impact on the state-nation process arising from the difference between self-generated states and states created through the agency of an external colonising power?

16 On shared hates as a factor, see Duchacek, *op. cit.* (note 13), pp. 53ff.

17 Warren Hinckle and W.W. Turner, *The Fish is Red: The Story of the Secret War Against Castro* (New York, Harper & Row, 1981).

18 For an extended discussion of this problem in relation to Third World countries, see Barry Buzan, 'Security Strategies for Dissociation', in John G. Ruggie (ed.), *The Antinomies of Interdependence* (New York, Columbia University Press, 1983).

19 See Barry Buzan, 'A Sea of Troubles? Sources of Dispute in the New Ocean Regime', *Adelphi Papers*, no. 143 (London, IISS, 1978).

20 Barry Buzan, 'Maritime Issues in North-east Asia', *Marine Policy*, 3:3 (1979), pp. 194–8.

21 Waltz, *op. cit.* (note 7), pp. 95–7.

22 This perspective is discussed in more detail in chapter 4.

23 It does not seem possible to avoid the confusion that arises from the synonymous uses of 'states' and 'powers' in the literature. By my usage, for example, Michael Handel's book, *Weak States in the International System* (London, Croom Helm, 1981), should be titled *Weak Powers*. My usage of weak and strong *states* also differs from the meanings proposed by Youssef Cohen, B.R. Brown and A.F.K. Organski, 'The Paradoxical Nature of State-Making: The Violent Creation of Order', *American Political Science Review*, 75:4 (1981), pp. 905–7; and Stephen D. Krasner, *Defending the National Interest: Raw Materials Investments and US Foreign Policy* (Princeton, Princeton University Press, 1978), ch. 3. Cohen *et al.* define the spectrum of weak to strong states by using the measure of tax receipts as a proportion of GNP. This useful measure gives them insight into the relative strength of governing institutions as compared with the societies they are trying to rule. Krasner is also concerned with the strength of governing institutions, *vis à vis* society, but he focuses on the degree to which decision-making power is diffused as opposed to centralised. Both these approaches provide very helpful insights, though they give rather different results. Krasner is concerned to argue that the United States is a weak state because the decision-making power of its governing institutions cannot dominate its strong

society. Cohen *et al.* produce a view of the weak-strong state spectrum which correlates with the spectrum of underdeveloped-developed states. In my view, both arguments are based on Kenneth Dyson's 'category error' of conflating the idea of state with its apparatus, noted on p. 44. Both are aiming to define aspects of government. My proposal is to confine the use of the term 'states' to the more comprehensive conception outlined in this chapter which includes, but is not confined to, the governing institutions. R.W. Cox, *op. cit.* (note 4), p. 127, refers to this broader conception as 'the state/society complex', and much of its holistic sense is also expressed in the more widely-used term 'nation-state', on which see Leonard Tivey (ed.), *op. cit.* (note 13).

24 An interesting variation on this theme is provided by Cohen, *et al. ibid.*, pp. 901–10. They argue that domestic violence is a *necessary* feature of 'primitive central state power accumulation'. If they are correct, then the process of state-building necessarily involves a phase of internal conflict during which contradictions between individual and national security will be extreme.

3 National Insecurity and the Nature of Threats

Threats and Vulnerabilities

In the previous chapter we began our inquiry into level 2 by examining the state as an object of security. This was a largely static exercise, and although it uncovered some aspects of threat, we now need to look at threats in their own right. Only when we have established a reasonable idea of both the nature of threats and the vulnerabilities of the objects towards which they are directed, can we begin to make sense of national security as a policy problem. Insecurity reflects a combination of threats and vulnerabilities, and the two cannot meaningfully be separated. If Poland is thought to be historically insecure, then not only must its vulnerabilities in terms of limited population, poor resources and indefensible boundaries be taken into account, but also the threats posed to it by powerful, expansionist neighbours on either side. If Germany and Russia were empty lands, Poland's vulnerabilities would be of little consequence. And if Poland were stronger, and possessed defensible mountain borders, the threats from Germany and Russia would be less serious than they have been. Nevertheless, the distinction between threats and vulnerabilities points to a key divide in security policy, namely that units can seek to reduce their insecurity either by reducing their vulnerability or by preventing or lessening threats. These alternatives underlie, respectively, the ideas of national and international security, and they provide the link which connects security policy between levels 2 and 3.

Much of what was said in the previous chapter about the components of the state was to do with their vulnerability, and does not need to be repeated here. It is clear that vulnerability connects intimately with both weak states and weak powers. Weak powers are a well understood phenomenon, and require little elaboration. Their weakness is relative to the capabilities commanded by other states in the system, particularly the great powers of the day, and frequently stems from the fact that they are relatively small. Although wealth, skill and willpower can compensate for smallness to some extent, as illustrated in different ways by the histories of Prussia, the Netherlands, Israel and the Gulf oil-states, they cannot compensate in the long run for the lack of a broader physical base. Weak powers may be able to muster themselves to considerable effect in a single sector, but they cannot make more than a short-term impact in military terms. Even Israel can only deploy its formidable military machine for short periods before the strain on the national fabric becomes too great.[1] Weak powers can usually only prosper by specialising their economies, like many of the smaller European states have done, and this almost by definition produces a host of vulnerabilities.

Weak states, whether or not they are also weak powers, are vulnerable for the political reasons explored in the last chapter. An underdeveloped idea of the state, as in Ethiopia, and/or unstable institutions, as in Zaire, open the state to domestic disruption and foreign intervention. When a state has the misfortune to be both a small power and a weak state, like Chad, its vulnerability is almost unlimited. If, additionally, it possesses some attribute of importance to others, be it a natural resource like Zaire, a vital waterway like Turkey, or a strategic position like Poland, then external pressure on these vulnerabilities is bound to occur. By contrast, states which are strong both as states and as powers, like the United States, France and Japan, suffer far fewer vulnerabilities. Their internal political structures have sufficient mass, momentum and stability to be able to withstand anything but a large-scale intervention. The state commands ample resources in many sectors, and consequently is able to adapt to, absorb or deter many threats which would present overwhelming challenges to countries like Tanzania and Jamaica. This is not to say that such states are invulnerable, for the oil squeeze and the threat of major war stand as obvious refutations to any such contention. But it is to argue that their vulnerabilities are neither numerous nor easy to exploit and, therefore, that they are neither excessively tempting nor particularly cheap to threaten. Even with such states, however, geostrategic factors do make a considerable difference. West Germany, for example, is clearly more vulnerable to military threats than is France or Japan.

While vulnerabilities are fairly obvious, the question of threats is rather more difficult. What constitutes a threat to national security? Invasions and blockades clearly fall within the category, but there is a broad grey area between these obvious threats and the normal difficulties of international relations. Should threats to fish stocks or weak industries be considered threats to national security? Or should illegal immigration, or the promulgation of unpopular political views? Unless we can answer these questions with some clarity, we cannot establish a firm basis on which to assess national security policy. Since we are still confining this analysis to level 2, we shall defer for the time being the whole issue of what causes threats, and look first at the general types and forms of threat as they might bear on any particular state. The different character of the components which go to make up the state suggests that threats to the state can come in a variety of types. These types can be classified by sector as military, political, economic and ecological, and we shall examine each briefly.[2]

Types of Threat by Sector

Military threats occupy the traditional heart of national security concerns. Military action can, and usually does, threaten all the components of the state. It subjects the physical base to strain, damage and dismemberment. It can result in the distortion or destruction of institutions, and it can repress, subvert or obliterate the idea of the state. Military actions not only strike at the very essence of the state's basic protective functions, but also threaten damage deep down through the layers of social and individual interest which underlie, and are more permanent than, the state's superstructures. Since, as we have argued, the state is more a social entity, an idea, than it is a physical being, the use of force threatens to overthrow a self-created rule by consent, and replace it with an imposed rule by coercion. For all these reasons, and also because the use of force can wreak major undesired changes very swiftly, military threats have normally been accorded the highest priority in national security concerns. Military action can wreck the work of centuries in the political, economic and social sectors, and as such stimulates not only a powerful concern to protect achievements in these sectors, but also a sense of outrage at unfair play. Difficult accomplishments in politics, art and all human activities can be undone by the use of force. Human achievements, in other words, are threatened in terms other than those in which they were created, and the need to prevent such threats from being realised is a major underpinning of the state's military protection function. Images like the Roman destruction of Carthage, the Nazi occupation of Poland, and the devastation likely to result from a nuclear Third World War, all support the high concern attached to military threats.

That said, military threats come in many types, not all quite as drastic as the picture sketched above. At the most extreme end are threats of invasion and occupation aimed at obliterating the state.

Poland is the classic case here, most recently in 1939. Invasion and occupation may have less drastic objectives, involving merely loss of some territory as between France and Germany in 1870, or a change in idea and institutions as in the German occupation of Norway in 1940, or both, as in the Allied occupations of Germany and Japan in 1945. In such cases the state is not destroyed, and although its institutions, organising ideology and territory may be altered, its national identity, in the strict sense, may not be severely attacked. Military threats may also be in the form of punishment, the objective here usually being to force a change in government policy, rather than to seize territory or to overturn institutions. Nuclear deterrence is built on this principle, and both American and Chinese attacks on Vietnam offer examples of attempts to apply the idea on a conventional level. The range of possible effects here is great, for threats of damage can be of nuclear obliteration at one end of the spectrum, or the harassment of fishing boats at the other.

The level of threat thus varies greatly. Objectives can range from the specific, as in the American use of warships sailing into coastal waters to indicate non-recognition of expansive territorial sea claims, to the general, as in the case of 'Finlandisation' where military superiority provides the backdrop to the broad spectrum conditioning of the policies of less powerful neighbours. Military threats can also be indirect, in the sense of not being applied to the state itself, but rather being directed at external interests. Threats to allies, shipping lanes, or strategically-placed territories would all come under this heading, and the current western concern over the security of oil supplies is a good illustration. Military threats occupy a special category precisely because they involve the use of force. The use, or threat, of force implies a breach of normal peaceful relations. In that sense, it involves the crossing of an important threshold which separates the normal interplay of political, economic and social sectors from the much less restrained competition of war. The existence of this threshold goes a long way towards explaining the disproportionate emphasis given to military security at a time when threats in other sectors appear to offer greater and more immediate danger.

Military threats usually have political objectives (seizure of territory, change of government of institutions, manipulation of policy or behaviour), but some political objectives can also be pursued by political means. The idea of the state, particularly its organising ideology, and the institutions which express it, are the normal target of political threats. Since the state is an essentially political entity, it may fear political threats as much as military ones. This is particularly so where the ideas and institutions are internally contested, for in such cases the state is likely to be highly vulnerable to political penetration. Even when the state is both strong and powerful, political threats might still be a source of concern. States like France, Italy and Japan are all strong on national grounds, but are all significantly divided in terms of organising ideology. In such cases political interference might win substantial rewards in terms of changed policy and alignment. Political threats stem from the great battle of ideas, information and traditions which is the underlying justification for the international anarchy. In the twentieth century, liberal, democratic, fascist and communist political ideas contradict each other in practice just as much as monarchical and republican ideas did in the nineteenth century. Because the contradictions in the ideas are basic, states of one persuasion may well feel threatened by the ideas represented by others. Cultivating an anti-ideology, as the Americans have done with anti-communism and the Soviets with anti-imperialism, is one answer, but it carries the cost that the cultivation of negatives might begin to override the positive values which they are supposed to protect, as in the case of the McCarthy episode in the United States.

The competition among ideologies is extraordinarily complex. This fact makes it difficult to define exactly what should be considered a political threat. In one sense, the mere existence of a state espousing an opposing ideology constitutes a threat on the grounds of the 'one rotten apple in the basket' principle. To take this seriously, however, would require an interminable military crusade, the costs of which would far outweigh the objectives. More specific political in-terventions by one state in the domestic affairs of another might define the category more usefully, but even here the boundaries are hard to draw. Should propaganda of the Radio Moscow and Voice of America kind be considered a threat to national security, or as part of the general interplay of ideas and information? At the lower levels of intensity, even the interplay of ideas and communication can produce politically significant social and cultural threats. Matters of language, religion and local cultural tradition all play their part in the idea of the state, and may need to be defended or protected against seductive or overbearing cultural imports. If the local culture is weak or small, even the unintended side-effects of casual contact could prove disruptive and politically charged.[3] Unintended cultural-political threats blend upwards into more intentional political meddling, such as propaganda support for political groups of similar persuasion, and from there into the funding and creation of such groups, all the way up to the quasi-military activities of political assassination and arms aid to rebels. Such activity can be exceedingly difficult to distinguish from domestically-generated dissent, as anyone who follows Islamic politics among the Arab states can testify. Because of this difficulty, political threats will almost always involve the confusion between domestic and national security outlined in the previous chapter.

Political threats can be intentional, like those emanating in many directions from Colonel Qadhafi's Libya, those directed by the United States against radical regimes in Cuba, Chile, Guatemala and elsewhere, those posed by the Soviet Union under the Brezhnev Doctrine, and those mounted by Castro's Cuba against a variety of right-wing governments in Latin America. They can also be structural, which is to say that they result more from the nature of the situation than from the particular intentions of one actor towards another. In a broad sense, for example, one might argue that the whole *Zeitgeist* of the twentieth century has posed a political threat to monarchical rule. The Shah of Iran was but the latest in a long line of such rulers to be swept away by mass-based political movements of various persuasions. Such events cause no puzzlement, although they may cause considerable surprise. The mystery is how such anachronistic forms of government manage to survive at all when the entire political environment of the times acts to corrode their legitimacy. Trying to make such a government secure from political threats must be, in the long run, virtually impossible.

In more specific terms, structural political threats arise when the organising principles of two states contradict each other in a context where the states cannot simply ignore each other's existence. Their political systems thus play a zero-sum game with each other whether they will it or not. Relations between apartheid and black-ruled states in Southern Africa have this character, as do ideological relations between China and the Soviet Union, ideological and national relations between the two Koreas, and the global rivalry between the United States and the Soviet Union. The achievements and successes of one automatically erode the political stature of the other, and this often leads, naturally enough, to more intentional forms of political threat.

India and Pakistan offer a particularly tragic case of structural political threat. Their historical, geographic and cultural ties do not allow them to ignore each other, but their organising principles pose a permanent threat to each other; a threat amplified by the fact that both states are politically vulnerable. Pakistan is organised on the principle of Islamic unity, and so stands for the definition of the state along exclusively theological lines. India is constituted on secular, federative lines and can only exist by cultivating harmony among the various large religious groups within its borders, including more than 60 million Moslems. The principle of India thus threatens Pakistan's major *raison d'être*, and provides grounds for Pakistan to fear absorption by an omnivorous India. The principle of Pakistan likewise threatens India's basic *raison d'être*, raising the spectre of a breakdown of the Indian Union into a number of independent, single-religion, successor states. Such a breakdown would solve Pakistan's permanent inferiority to a much larger India. The tension between them is neatly institutionalised in their dispute over Kashmir. Since the population of that province mostly adheres to Islam, both states view their claims to it in the light of their national integrity. The political threats posed to each other by India and Pakistan clearly define a central element in the national security problem of each of them, and illustrate the extensive ground for confusion between internal politics and national security.[4]

Economic threats are more difficult to relate to national security than military and political ones, because the normal condition of actors in the economic domain is one of risk, competition and uncertainty. If insecurity in the economic domain is the normal condition, then it is difficult to locate the boundary at which issues acquire special status as threats to national security. Furthermore, the state is often only one among many levels of economic actor, and its responsibilities and interests are not as clear in the economic sector as they are in the political and military ones. Economic threats are more narrowly bound than military ones, in that they operate only against the economy of the target state. Secondary political and military consequences may occur from a threat implemented against the economy, as we shall see, but there is no *direct* threat to other sectors as there is with military threats. This means that economic threats tend to be neither swift nor precise in their effect, and at lower levels may easily become indistinguishable from the normal rough-and-tumble of economic practice. The national economy is in one sense part of the physical base of the state, but it is also strongly connected with the organising ideology and institutional elements. Its dynamics are extremely complicated, and its susceptibility to quite dramatic fluctuations in performance is only poorly understood, and neither reliably predictable nor effectively controllable. Because of this, the economy presents a much more ambiguous target for threats than do more concrete elements like territory and government institutions. If one cannot determine the normal condition of something, then it is hard to calculate what actions might pose threats to it. What might seem a threat in the short term, like oil embargoes or inflated prices, might turn out to be a boon in stimulating more rational energy policies and technologies over the longer run.

A huge number and variety of economic threats exist which cannot reasonably be construed as threats to national security. Export practices, import restrictions, price manipulations, default on debts, currency controls, and a host of other actions may have serious effects on the economies of other states. These range from loss of income to the destruction of whole industries, but they all fall within the merciless norms of competitive economic activity. Inability to compete or adapt is a risk of the game, and decline may result as much from internal as from external causes. A sustained and drastic economic decline, like that of Britain, is not normally seen in national security terms even when it cuts deeply into the state's military capability. For self-reliant great powers, however, economic performance is the crucial foundation on which their relative status in the system rests. Just as Britain and France feared the rapid economic expansion of Germany from the later nineteenth century until the Second World War, so the United States feared the prospect of Soviet economic success providing the Soviet Union with a power base large enough to overawe American influence. In this sense, the economic expansion of a rival power might be seen as a broad spectrum threat to the whole national security position.

Specific economic threats to national security, as suggested above, are hard to distinguish from the pitfalls of normal economic competition, but two cases do stand out. The first involves the traditional link between economic factors and military capability. In a general sense, military capability rests on economic performance, but this level is too broad to deal with in terms of economic threats. More specifically, military capability rests on the supply of key strategic materials, and where these must be obtained outside the state, threats to security of supply can be classified as a national security concern. Thus American military industries depend on supplies of manganese and nickel, neither of which is produced in the United States in significant quantities.[5] Concern over the reliability of supply underlies American interest in developing technology to obtain these minerals from the deep seabed. Similarly, the Royal Navy became dependent on supplies of various kinds of ship timber from overseas when domestic forests ceased to be able to cope with demand in the later days of sail. Threats to such supplies feed quite quickly through into military capability, and can thus almost be seen in the same light as military threats.

The second case is of more recent concern, and involves what might loosely be called economic threats to domestic stability. These occur when states pursue economic strategies based on maximisation of welfare through extensive trade. Over time, such policies result in high levels of dependence on trade in order to sustain the social structures that have grown up with increasing prosperity. Some countries become specialised as raw material producers, and depend on sales of their products, while others become industrial centres, and depend both on supplies of raw materials and on markets for their products. Australia, Gabon and Zaire are fairly extreme examples of the former type, while Japan, Singapore and Belgium exemplify the latter. Even countries with large domestic resources and markets, like the United States, can become significantly locked into the structure of trade. Where such complex patterns of interdependence exist, many states will be vulnerable to disruptions in the pattern of trade.[6] Concern over the supply of oil is only the most manifest example of such vulnerability and, because socio-political structures have come to depend on sustained growth rates, domestic political stability may be undermined by a drop in economic performance resulting from external factors.

Under such conditions, interruption to the supply of a crucial material like oil could cause economic havoc in countries the welfare of which has come to depend on oil-powered production. Especially where economic manipulations occur for political reasons, they take on an aspect which fits easily into the framework of threats to national security. The other side of this coin is the set of complaints from Third World countries which underlies their call for a New International Economic Order. They claim, with considerable force, that the economic system of complex interdependence locks them into a position of permanent economic disadvantage, so preventing them from solving the numerous problems which make them weak both as states and as powers. From their perspective, the whole system is a threat to their national security. This line of argument eventually blends into the Marxist critique that capitalism as a system is, in the long run, a threat both to everyone who participates in it, and to those who try to remain outside.

Although the case for economic threats to be counted as threats to national security is superficially plausible, it must be treated with considerable caution. The problem with it is that it raises once again the dilemmas of distinguishing between domestic politics and national security. Economic threats do resemble an attack on the state, in the sense that conscious external actions by others results in material loss, and in strain on various institutions of the state. The parallel with a military attack cannot be sustained, however, because while a military attack crosses a clear boundary between peaceful and aggressive behaviour, an economic 'attack' does not. Aggressive behaviour is normal in economic affairs, and risks of loss are part of the price that has to be paid to gain access to opportunities for gain. From this perspective, economic threats can be self-inflicted in as much as a choice is made to participate in a pattern of production and exchange in which such risks are endemic.

Military threats cannot normally be described in these terms, and do not tie directly into domestic affairs in the same way. Since the economic domain has no necessary fixed form, not only is the question of damage hard to assess, but also responsibility for creating vulnerabilities may well lie largely within the realm of domestic politics. Economic threats might thus be seen not so much as emanating from the iniquitous acts of foreigners, but as stemming from inept play on the part of those responsible for managing the nation's economic affairs. Such a view drives inquiry inexorably towards basic questions of domestic politics like 'Who governs?', and raises grounds for asking whether organising ideologies are being improperly implemented, or whether they are in some way themselves basically flawed. All of these things, including the continued testing, questioning and modification of organising ideologies, are essentially domestic political matters. As with the overlap between national security and the security of governments, there would appear to be both ample incentive and ample opportunity, for sub-national actors to appropriate national security in defence of their own vested interests.

While there is a real danger that vested interests will usurp the idea of economic security for their own ends, this hazard should not be allowed to obscure the real economic threats which are part of the national security problem. Only occasionally will specific economic threats deserve to be ranked as a national security problem. For the most part, the day-to-day inconveniences and disruptions of complex economic relations should be viewed as a normal cost of such activity. Attempts to elevate particular economic issues onto the national security agenda should be treated with suspicion as a matter of routine. On the broader level of the overall structure of economic relations, however, a much clearer case can be made for economic threats to national security. At level 3, the pattern of economic relations has major implications for the stability of the system. Not only can these larger patterns threaten the peace of states, but also they can render meaningless for weaker actors the assumptions of choice and responsibility in domestic economic policy discussed above. These system-level economic threats will be analysed in more detail in chapter 5.[7]

Threats to national security might also come in ecological forms, in the sense that environmental events, like military and economic ones, can damage the physical base of the state, perhaps to a sufficient extent to threaten its idea and institutions. Traditionally, ecological threats have been seen as natural, and therefore not part of national security concerns.[8] Earthquakes, storms, plagues, floods, droughts, and such-like might inflict war-scale damage on a state, as in Bangladesh in 1970, but these were seen as part of the struggle of man against nature, and not in terms of competition among men. With increases in the scale, diversity and pace of human activity, however, ecological threats to one state might well stem identifiably from activities within another. Trans-frontier pollution is an obvious example, and attempts at weather modification is an example which may become of greater importance in the not too distant future. There is a substantial domestic side to this problem in the self-polluting activities of states, but this can usually be distinguished from external threats. Ecological threats may appear to deserve a relatively low priority compared with the other forms of threat discussed above, but some of the more extreme scenarios (greenhouse effects and melting polar caps, diminution of oxygen supply through ocean poisoning and deforestation) have enough plausibility to command attention. They raise interesting and important questions about how national security should be viewed, both in temporal terms and in terms of priorities. They also raise questions as to whether or not the state is the most appropriate level on which to consider such threats, and we shall pick up this theme when we discuss level 3.

Other Threat Variables: Source, Intensity and Historical Change

Threats can also be differentiated along a number of other dimensions than the sector in which they come, and some of these have been suggested in the preceding discussion. Threats can vary as to source. They may come from an internal source, as in the case of secessionist movements, or, more likely, they may come from one of a variety of external sources. Other states are the most common external source, but non-state entities, like terrorist groups or transnational corporations might also play this role. Palestinian terrorist organisations, for example, have been seen as a source of threat by many states since the late 1960s, and ITT (International Telephone and Telegraph) played an active part in threatening Chile in the early 1970s. It is conceivable that international organisations might be a source of political, economic or even military threat to some states, although this might be hard to disentangle from state threats working through the organisation. The United Nations has been seen as a source of threat by Israel, South Africa and China, and many non-democratic states might see a political threat in the norms espoused by UN bodies. The IMF (International Monetary Fund) has the power to make economic threats, and the European Common Market is seen as a threat by countries like New Zealand, whose exports suffer because of it. Sources of threat may be very specific, like that which the British saw in the German navy between the turn of the century and the First World War, or like that which the strategic nuclear arsenals of the United States and the Soviet Union have posed to each other since the 1960s. Conversely, they can be very diffuse, as when the threat is seen to arise from some process, rather than from a particular object or policy. Thus, the spread of communism (or capitalism), nuclear proliferation, both weapons and civil power technology, and the arms race are all examples of broad processes which are frequently identified as threats.

Threats can also vary enormously in what might be called intensity, and several factors operate to determine this. The first is range: Is the source of threat close at hand, as Germany was to France after 1870? Is it at some middle distance, as Japan was for the United States during the 1930s, or as communism in Vietnam seemed to many Americans during the 1960s? Range applies most easily to military threats, because closeness correlates strongly with ability to under- take effective military action, though this consideration has declined in importance with the development of long-range strike weapons. It is much less relevant to political and economic threats in general, though strong arguments to the contrary might come from those located close to centres of economic and political power, like Canada in relation to the United States, and the Gulf states in relation to the politically charged religious regime which succeeded the Shah in Iran. For most states, range exists as a commonsense geographical factor. But for some, especially those great powers who view their security in global terms, range can reflect other priorities as well. Britain, in 1938, for example, saw Czechoslovakia as 'a faraway country', at the same time as it placed one frontier of its own security on the Himalayas.

The second factor is range in the temporal rather than in the spatial sense. Is the threat an immediate one, or will it take some time to develop or be implemented? Some threats are fairly easy to assess in this way, and some are not. The British, for example, could calculate the timing of the naval threat from Germany before 1914 by working out construction rates for dreadnoughts in the German shipyards. Similarly, the Soviet Union can usually obtain quite reliable infor- mation on the timing of American military deployment programmes. Perhaps the most famous example here is the mobilisation timetables which played such a large part in the security perceptions of the European great powers before 1914.[9] Other kinds of threat, however, are temporally complex. Many, like the threat of a nuclear strike, have two temporal characteristics. The first is precise, in that it is known how many minutes the threat will take to implement once a decision is taken to do so. The second is highly uncertain, in that the threat may remain in being indefinitely, and there is no way of telling at what time, if ever, it will be used. Threats by OPEC to cut off oil supplies fit this pattern, as do most threats of military attack. Many threats, especially those of a process kind, display few temporal certainties. Thus, widely-feared threats, like nuclear proliferation, the arms race, pollution, over-population, and economic stagnation, tend to be, or to be seen as being, in a constant state of becoming worse. Since there is no reliable way of assessing the risk from these threats, they generate endless argument about the level of priority and immediacy they should be accorded.

The third factor in the intensity of threats is the probability that any given threat will, in fact, occur. In trying to assess threats, probability usually has to be weighed against a fourth factor, their measure of seriousness. How serious will the consequences be if the threat is carried out? During the Vietnam war, for example, the North Vietnamese had to make calculations of this kind all the time. If they continued, or escalated, their campaign in the South, what would be the probability of an American counter-escalation, and what would be the consequent damage inflicted on the North if such counter-escalation occurred? They must have calculated that the probability of a major escalation, for example to nuclear weapons, was quite low, and therefore that the risk was worth running even though the consequences would be catastrophic if the Americans did in fact resort to nuclear weapons. Where the probabilities were higher, like increased levels of conventional bombing, the North Vietnamese calculated that the consequences were acceptable in the light of their larger objectives. Threat assessments of this type lie at the heart of security policy. Accurate assessment of either risks or probabilities, however, requires an ability to predict which is notoriously lacking in international relations. The universal preparations for a short, sharp war in 1914, British and French assessments of the risk from Hitler before 1939, and the American conduct of the war in Vietnam, illustrate both the weakness of prediction and the lack of progress towards improvement.

Most actions in the international arena, and particularly military ones, encounter hosts of complex factors which make both their direct outcome and their broad consequences highly uncertain. Even if information was not limited and distorted, as it is, and even if subjective perceptions accorded with reality, which they usually fail to do, the complexities of events would still defy accurate prediction and assessment. Objectively minor events, like Soviet restrictions on access to West Berlin, can assume major symbolic dimensions in the calculus of Soviet/American rivalry, while objectively enormous threats, like that of nuclear war in Europe, get subordinated to more politically defined security priorities. Additional to thse problems is the natural propensity of those responsible for national security to hedge their bets by thinking in worst-case terms. Worst-case analyses have the advantage not only of reflecting a prudent distrust of other actors in the system – a position easily justified by reference to history – but also of creating a strong position in the domestic struggle for allocation of resources. The American military establishment, for example, is without doubt the foremost advocate of the strength and effectiveness of the Soviet armed forces.[10] For all these reasons the intensity of threats is extraordinarily difficult to determine with any certainty, and, as we shall see, this causes serious problems for national security policy-making.

Threats also have an historical dimension which adds further to the complexities of assessment. The character of threats, in other words, does not remain constant over time, but changes in response to both new developments in the means of threats, and to evolutions in states which alter the nature of their vulnerabilities. Raymond Aron refers to this phenomenon as the 'law of change', which he defines as being that 'the military, demographic or economic value of a territory varies with the techniques of combat and production, with human relations and institutions',[11] Military technology provides the easiest, but not the only, illustration of this point. Weapons of a certain type are characteristic of any given historical period, and the particular capabilities of these weapons largely defines the nature of military security problems which states face at that time. Unless defences are continually evolved to meet new capabilities, military security deteriorates rapidly. Fortified castles and cities provided a good measure of military security before the introduction of gunpowder and cannon, but the high, relatively thin walls which served well against the pre-gunpowder techniques of siege provided ideal targets for the gunners. Similarly, Britain remained secure behind the wooden walls of its ships of the line for several centuries, but by the middle of the nineteenth century, a host of developments in steam power, metal construction and artillery began to make such vessels obsolete. By 1870, only a madman would have considered venturing out in a wooden-hulled, sail-powered ship to offer serious battle to enemy naval forces.

Changes of this type affect the whole system, because the first to introduce a new military technology holds a decisive advantage over all those who fail to adapt to it. Thus, the introduction of Dreadnought battleships by Britain in 1906 greatly reduced the military utility of all existing battleships. Jet fighters made propeller-driven varieties obsolete, and nuclear weapons required the rethinking of most elements of conventional military wisdom ranging from air defence, through battlefield tactics, to amphibious landings. Taken together, such developments change the entire condition of threat and vulnerability. The relatively leisurely pace and modest scale of military activity in eighteenth-century Europe escalated remarkably during the Napoleonic wars under the influence of mass conscription. Forces and tactics designed for the earlier age proved hopelessly inadequate, and the threat of complete occupation became much more immediate and widespread than it had been before.

By the late nineteenth century, industrial technique had added its force to the cause of military mobilisation, and this meant that huge forces could be transported quickly and supplied abundantly. The German victory over France in 1870 is generally taken as a landmark in the speeding up of warfare through the use of both mechanised transport and pre-organised mobilisation schemes. It signalled an erosion in warning times against attack, a process which has continued to the present day. The advent of long-range bombers during the 1930s opened the prospect of almost immediate attack, a trend brought to global reality during the 1960s by the deployment of nuclear-armed intercontinental missiles. One implication of this trend has been the squeezing of time both for diplomacy and defensive preparation. Defences not in permanent readiness have little value, and whole concepts of defence and vulnerability have been transformed. Britain ceased to be a sanctuary from continental wars during the 1930s, and by the 1960s even the United States was no longer protected from strategic bombardment. The calculation of military threats would be hard enough without such change, but the continuous and rapid transformation of military instruments requires constant reassessment, often on the basis of skimpy and uncertain evidence. As demonstrated by the Polish cavalry charges in 1939, and the outflanking of the Maginot line in 1940, the consequences of miscalculation can be catastrophic.[12]

The character of political and economic threats also changes over time in response to developments in the internal structures of the units making up the system. In many parts of the world, for example, threats to territory have declined because the historical trend of nationalism has increased the identity between land and people, thereby reducing the political acceptability of annexations. This situation contrasts markedly with that prevailing in the nineteenth, eighteenth and earlier centuries, when boundaries were much more fluid, and the main significance of territorial transfers derived from their impact on the balance of power. Note, for example, Israel's difficulty in establishing the legitimacy of its territorial conquests.

Similarly, the shift away from forms of government based on hereditary principles, towards forms based on representation and/or ideology, has changed the prevailing character of political threats. Intrigues over the lineages of succession no longer occupy centre stage as they once did in the murky borderlands between domestic and international politics. Instead, mutual meddling takes place in the broader context of political factions, party politics, elections, insurgency and manipulation of public opinion. The threat has broadened from fear of foreign interference in the affairs of the ruling family to fears of external corruption of mass politics.

Economic threats have changed not only as states have become less self-reliant in terms of being able to maintain their norms of domestic welfare, but also as the nature and source of trade materials have changed according to the economic requirements of the day. Things like oil, mineral ores, computers and automobiles have replaced things like silk, tea, opium and ship timbers as main items of trade, though many things like food, money, weapons and textiles have retained a continuing importance. These changes, plus the continuing evolution in the economic roles and capabilities of states, produce a dynamic pattern of interests and vulnerabilities which requires continuous updates and revisions in the assessment of economic threats. The Soviet Union can, to some extent, be threatened by embargoes on food and high technology exports, the United States can be threatened by restrictions on oil exports, Britain, as was demonstrated in the 1956 Suez crisis, had become vulnerable to financial pressure, and many countries, particularly in the Third World, are vulnerable to price manipulations, fluctuations in demand for their export products and squeezes on credit.

While the range of possible economic threats is large, however, the nature of the economic system makes them difficult to implement. Alternative suppliers and markets can often be found to circumvent threats, and, because of this, the threatener may find he is inflicting more damage on himself than on his target. Monopolies are hard to create and maintain in most sectors, and without them, threats can be difficult to apply.

Conclusions: The Ambiguity of Threats

We can conclude from this discussion that national insecurity is a highly complicated phenomenon. Each state exists, in a sense, at the hub of a whole universe of threats. These threats define its insecurity, and set the agenda for national security as a policy problem. They do not, unfortunately, constitute a clear set of calculable and comparable risks like those faced by players of chess or bridge. Threats to the state come in diverse forms which cannot easily be weighed off against each other, and which are frequently in a state of constant evolution. They vary enormously in range and intensity, pose risks which cannot be assessed accurately, and depend on probabilities which cannot be calculated. Because threats are so ambiguous, and because knowledge of them is limited, national security policy-making is necessarily a highly imperfect art. It requires constant monitoring and assessment of threats, and the development of criteria for allocating policy priorities, and for deciding when threats become of sufficient intensity to warrant action. Since threats can be found everywhere, and since national security resources are limited, some cut-off point has to be set below which threats are considered inconsequential or worthy only of monitoring.

The possible range of choice is still huge because, depending on one's resources, and on one's willingness to allocate them to national security, one can choose between a relatively passive policy of waiting until threats loom large, or a relatively active policy of meeting them while they are still small, or merely potential. Since threats increase in number the harder one looks for them, and since there is a well-known tendency to adopt a worst-case view, an active policy has no theoretical limit. It raises the dangers of exhaustion, paranoia, creation of an aggressive appearance to others, and unnecessary concern about low-level threats which, left to themselves, might well never develop into larger problems. An excessively passive policy, on the other hand, raises the danger that threats will become too large to deal with except at great cost, although it has the significant advantage of allowing serious threats to separate themselves out from minor ones. United States' policy offers a partial illustration of these two extremes, excessively passive during the 1920s and 1930s, until bombs were dropping on Pearl Harbor and a massive war effort was necessary to turn the tide, and excessively active after 1947, finding an American security interest in almost every corner of the globe.[13]

Since threats can only be assessed in relation to a particular state as a target, security policy requires not only to understand the threats themselves, but also the vulnerabilities of the state as an object of security. As we have seen, this is no straightforward matter. Cause-effect relations between threats and vulnerabilities are poorly understood at best, even for relatively calculable forms like military attack. No one knows how a Soviet attack on western Europe would unfold, just as no one knew that the First World War would end up stalemated in the trenches, or that the Second World War would not be started by aerial gas attacks against cities. For economic and political threats, the problem of distinguishing threats from normal, or at least acceptable, activity is much more difficult to begin with. Trying to assess such threats in relation to vulnerabilities raises the host of problems discussed above of disentangling domestic interests of various kinds from interests that can legitimately be considered to constitute national security issues. If the national security policy process has itself been captured by an interest group, then confusion mounts alarmingly. To add to these problems of uncertainty about threats and vulnerabilities, there are the further unknowns arising from the interaction between threats and counter-measures. How does one stave off threats without creating new problems when military defence leads to arms races and threats of holocaust, and both autarky and interdependence seem to lead to international friction?

We shall take up these problems in more detail when we come to look at national security as a policy problem. In this chapter we have examined threats simply as a set of conditions faced by any particular state. While this perspective was useful for illuminating one side of the national security policy problem, it largely ignored the deeper causes and dynamics of threat which lie beyond the state in the international system as a whole. Any sound security policy must, as suggested at the beginning of this chapter, address threats in both these ways: dealing with them as they come, like reducing vulnerability by preparing defences against invasion, on the one hand; and dealing with their causes, like seeking peaceful settlement of the dispute, on the other. For this reason, we must move on to explore security at the international system level – level 3 – before we can attempt to understand national security as a policy problem.

Notes

1   For a useful discussion of the military problems of weak powers, see Michael Handel, *Weak States in the International system* (London, Cass, 1981), pp. 77–94.
2   There does not seem to be a strong literature on threats, probably because of the intractable problem of distinguishing between the subjective and the objective aspects of the phenomenon. Charles F. Doran, K.Q. Hill and K. Mladenka, 'Threat, Status Disequilibrium and National Power', *British Journal of International Studies*, 5:1 (1979); and Kenneth Boulding, 'Toward a Theory of Peace', in Roger Fisher (ed.), *International Conflict and Behavioural Science* (New York, Basic

Books, 1964), ch. 4. Both attempt to make some general remarks on the subject.

3 On this theme, see K.J. Holsti *et al., Why Nations Realign* (London, Allen & Unwin, 1982).

4 See G.S. Bhargava, 'India's Security in the 1980s', *Adelphi Papers*, no. 125 (London, IISS, 1976).

5 For an argument against excessive emphasis on the security of strategic resources in the American case, see Charles L. Schultze, 'The Economic Content of National Security Policy'; *Foreign Affairs*, 51: 3 (1973), esp. pp. 522–9. For an argument against the simple correlation of economic growth with military power, see James R. Schlesinger, 'Economic Growth and national Security', in Fred A. Sonderman, W.C. Olson and T.S. McLellan (eds), *The Theory and Practice of International Relations* (New Jersey, Prentice-Hall, 1970), pp. 155–64.

6 See Robert O. Keohane and J.S. Nye, *Power and Interdependence*, (Boston, Little Brown, 1977), esp. chs. 1 and 2; Edward L. Morse, 'Interdependence in World Affairs', in James N. Rosenau, K.W. Thompson and G. Boyd (eds), *World Politics* (New York, Free Press, 1976), ch. 28; and 'Crisis Diplomacy, Interdependence, and the Politics of International Economic Relations', in Raymond Tanter and Richard Ullman (eds), *Theory and Policy in International Relations* (Princeton, Princeton University Press, 1972); Wolfram F. Hanrieder, 'Dissolving International Politics: Reflections on the Nation-State', *American Political Science Review*, 72 :4 (1978); Kenneth N. Waltz, 'The Myth of Interdependence', in Charles P. Kindleberger, *The International Corporation* (Cambridge, Mass., MIT Press, 1970).

7 For a useful review of this area, see Klaus Knorr and Frank N. Trager (eds), *Economic Issues and National Security*, (no place of publication, Regents Press of Kansas, 1977).

8 It is interesting to note, however, that the National Security Council in the United States takes an interest in earthquakes, and even commissioned a study of earthquake risks in California. *Science News*, 119 :16 (18 April 1981), p. 254.

9 On which, see Maurice Pearton, *The Knowledgeable State* (London, Burnett, 1982), pp. 69–76, 117–39.

10 See, for example, *Soviet Military Power*, US Department of Defense, 1981.

11 Frank N. Trager and Philip S. Kronenberg (eds), *National Security and American Society: Theory, Process and Policy* (Lawrence, Kansas, University Press of Kansas, 1973), p. 59.

12 There is a rich literature on the evolution of military technique and technology. See, for example, Robert E. Osgood and Robert W. Tucker, *Force, Order and Justice* (Baltimore, Johns Hopkins University Press, 1967), chs. 2–3; Michael Howard, *War in European History* (Oxford, Oxford University Press, 1976); Michael Howard, *Studies in War and Peace* (London, Temple Smith, 1970), chs. 6 and 11; Tom Wintringham and J.N. Blashford-Snell, *Weapons and Tactics* (Harmondsworth, Penguin, 1973); Bernard and Fawn M. Brodie, *From Crossbow to H-Bomb* (Bloomington, Indiana University Press, 1973). A useful, if not

wholly convincing critique of the view that technology itself provides the
major impetus for change in military affairs can be found in Bernard
Brodie, 'Technological Change, Strategic Doctrine and Political Outcomes', in Klaus Knorr (ed.), *Historical Dimensions of National Security
Problems* (Lawrence, Kansas, University Press of Kansas, 1976).
Pearton, *op. cit.* (note 9), is particularly focused on the problem posed for
national security policy by the continuous evolution of military
technology.

13 Stanley Hoffmann makes the interesting argument that the range of
security policy expands not only with the growth of power, but also as a
result of expanded perceptions of vulnerability and threat. He sees the
range of Soviet security policy expanding for the former reason, and that
of the United States for the latter. See 'Security in an Age of Turbulence:
Means of Response', in 'Third World Conflict and International
Security', Part II, *Adelphi Papers 167* (London, IISS, 1981), pp. 4–5.

4 The State and the International Political System

In the last three chapters we have concentrated primarily on the attributes of the pieces in the great game of international relations. In this chapter and the next, we shall focus mostly on the nature of the board. States occupy a number of systems or environments, which provide both the context and the forum for their behaviour towards each other, and which heavily condition the whole national security problem. These systems not only generate many of the threats which define the national security problem, but they also constitute a major target of national security policy. In as much as these systems are the source of insecurity, states have an interest in trying to shape them into more congenial and security-enhancing forms. This interest provides a major link between levels 2 and 3 in international relations. In this chapter and the next, we shall take a broad look at the two major systems which make up the security environment of the state: the international political system, and the international economy.[1] The purpose of the exercise is to lay a foundation from which we can move on to examine the dynamics of security in more detail, concentrating on processes like the security dilemma which lie at the heart of the security problem.

The Nature of the International Anarchy

The international political system is the most important part of the environment of states for the obvious reason that states are essentially political constructs. Indeed, the political connection between states and system is so intimate that one is at risk of introducing serious distortion even by speaking of states *and* the international system as if they were distinct entities. Although they are distinguishable for some analytical purposes, the essential feature of states and the international system is that they represent opposite ends of a continuous political phenomenon. The international political system is an anarchy, which is to say that its principal defining characteristic is the absence of overarching government. The principal defining feature of states is their sovereignty, or their refusal to acknowledge any political authority higher than themselves. Thus the essential character of states defines the nature of the international political system, and the essential character of the political system reflects the nature of states. If units are sovereign, their system of association must be anarchy, and if the system is anarchic, its members must reject overarching government. This link is much more than a mere analytical nicety or glib tautology. It means that levels 2 and 3 are inextricably associated with each other, and that problems which appear to arise from the anarchic nature of the system cannot be treated purely as systemic, or level 3 matters. If the international anarchy is to be criticised as a system, then one cannot avoid extending the critique to the character of the states which comprise the system.[2]

Since the international anarchy defines the structure of relations among states, and since states are generally conceded to be the prime source of threat to each other, we need to examine the nature of the anarchy in some detail in order to understand its role in the problem of national security. Anarchy is a politically emotive concept. Its basic definition as the absence of government implies that it is a negative condition, along the lines of poverty and illness, which is characterised by a deficiency of some positively valued or normal attribute, in these cases, order, wealth and health. The use of anarchy as a synonym for chaos and disorder reinforces its negative image. This prevalent view of anarchy produces a misleading conception of how the international system works. In relation to the international system, anarchy should be viewed in the strict sense of simply absence of government. This absence describes a structural condition, and contains no necessary inference of chaos or disorder. The association between anarchy and chaos probably arises from the Hobbesian image of mankind in the state of nature.[3] Under such conditions, and because of the acute vulnerability of individuals, anarchy seems quite likely to result in chaos. But as argued in chapter 2, the analogy between individuals and states is false in so many respects that it cannot be used to support a parallel set of assumptions about states. An anarchy among states may or may not result in chaos, but it certainly does not necessarily, or even probably, do so. Because states are much larger, more durable, more easily defended, more self-contained, fewer in number and less mobile than individuals, an anarchic system among them has a much better chance of avoiding chaos than does a similar system among individuals.

The idea of an international anarchy does not automatically ascribe a single characteristic (chaos) to the system of states. Rather, it defines a basic structure of relations among them, within which many varieties and styles of system might emerge or be built. The fact that a single structural form can be expressed in a variety of ways is central to our analysis of security at level 3, because it is in the nature of the possible variations that the factors crucial to security are found. Simple illustrations of variations on the theme of anarchy are provided by possible variations in the number and power of members in the system. An anarchic system could be composed of two or 200 members. Power could be distributed evenly, or divided between a few strong and many weak members. Such variations make a substantial difference to the character of the system, and they suggest the need to distinguish between *character* and *structure*. While a system may have a single structure, like anarchy, knowledge of that structure does not allow us to infer much about its character. To explore character, we need to know more details about the particular form in which any given system expresses its structure.

Any attempt to pursue this line of inquiry runs immediately into the level of analysis problem discussed above. How do we draw a meaningful line between discussions about states and discussions about the system when the factors we need to consider apply inseparably to both? If, for example, we try to talk about the distribution of power as an aspect of system structure, we have inevitably begun to define the units at level 2: a bipolar system must have in it two super-powers. This dilemma takes us back to the connection between level 2 and level 3 argued above. Although separable for some analytical purposes, the two levels represent the linked ends of a single political phenomenon. Even in the narrow terms of structure, there is a strong tie between sovereignty and anarchy. At the broader level of character, it becomes impossible to discuss the system without delving into the nature of its component parts. The major distinction drawn by John Ruggie between the medieval and modern anarchic systems, for example, rests on differences between the component parts in the two systems, as does the definition of systems change used by Robert Gilpin.[4] Any characterisation of the system must address the interplay between the component parts and the structure, because vital factors like rules, norms, the distribution of power and the frequency of conflict make no sense if they are strictly confined to either level 2 or level 3. A system-wide norm like sovereign equality says something important about both level 2 and level 3. It cannot sensibly be restricted to either level.

The character of the system is determined in an important sense by patterns among the characters of its component parts. It is in this connective space between levels 2 and 3 that we find the material for understanding the security problem at the system level. The structure of the system defines only the general form of the security problem with none of its details. The character of the system defines the level of detail necessary to enable us to discuss the security problem in empirical terms. Although the distinction between state and system is both important and useful, there seems to be no point in enforcing it for all modes of analysis, when to do so imposes artificial barriers on the unity of the subject.

If we accept that the anarchic structure defines the basic framework of the security problem, what can we say about security and the character of the system? One useful approach is to hypothesise a spectrum of anarchies which we can label *immature* at one end, and *mature* at the other.[5]

An extreme case of immature anarchy would be where each state recognised no other legitimate sovereign unit except itself, and where relations among the units took the form of a continuous struggle for dominance. Such a system would approximate chaos. The struggle for dominance would generate endless warfare, and would not be moderated by any sense among the units of the rights of others. Insecurity would be endemic, and relations among states would be like the automatic and unthinking struggle of natural enemies like ants and termites. The ethic of such a system would be survival of the fittest, and nothing other than the distribution of power and the level of capability available would prevent the unification of the system under the strongest actor. An anarchy of this sort would be 'immature' because, in Bull's terms, it had not developed any form of international society to moderate the effects of political fragmentation. Its members would share no norms, rules or conventions among themselves, and their relationships would be dominated by fear, distrust, disdain, hatred, envy and indifference. Order, if it existed at all, would reflect only deference to superior power. In the long run, an immature anarchy would be unstable, both because of the risk of general exhaustion and collapse, and because of the risk of one actor transcending the balance of power and unifying the system under its control.

At the other end of the spectrum, an extremely mature anarchy would have developed as a society to the point where the benefits of fragmentation could be enjoyed without the costs of continuous struggle and instability. The mechanism behind this utopian anarchy would be the development of criteria by which states could recognise and accept each other's legitimacy, and at the same time increase their own. In a very mature anarchy, all states would have to be strong as states, along the lines of the criteria explored in chapter 2, in other words, the idea of the state, its territory and its institutions would have to be well-developed and stable, regardless of its relative power as a state in the system. On this basis, a strong international society could be built on the foundations of mutual recognition and acceptance. Mutual recognition of sovereign equality and territorial boundaries alone would make a substantial modification to the hazards of immature anarchy.

If all states had developed internally as nation-states or state-nations, then a Wilsonian-type norm of mutual respect for nations as self-determining cultural-political entities could be added to international society. This would have an enormous moderating impact on fragmentation, in that it would associate the pattern of states with much deeper and more durable patterns of social and territorial organisation. The state as a purely institutional entity has no natural boundaries, and a system composed of such units is likely to be conflict-prone and power-oriented. But if the notion of the state is broadened to include specified national and territorial criteria, then the state becomes at least potentially a much more fixed and defined object, with fewer grounds for posing threats to its neighbours. John Herz has labelled this idea 'self-limiting nationalism'. He argues for it not only as the view of many of the original proponents of nationalism, but also as the basic ideology of a stable anarchy, in contrast to the 'exclusivist, xenophobic, expansionist, oppressive' nationalism which has caused the world so much suffering and insecurity.[6]

Other norms, like non-interference in internal affairs, respect for different organising ideologies, avoidance of force in the settlement of disputes, and adherence to a variety of international institutions for dealing with problems of a multi-national scale, would complete the social machinery of the mature anarchy. Such a system would still place a high value on political variety and fragmentation, and it would still be as much an anarchy in the structural sense as the immature variant sketched above. But it would none the less be a highly ordered and stable system in which states would enjoy a great deal of security deriving both from their own inner strength and maturity, and from the strength of the institutionalised norms regulating relations among them.

Between these two rather unlikely extremes lie a whole range of possible international anarchies, including our own. The present anarchy lies somewhere in the middle of the spectrum, for if it is obviously a long way from the calm and stable realms of maturity, it is just as obviously well removed from unbridled chaos. Some elements of maturity are quite strongly developed in our system, such as mutual recognition of sovereign equality and its associated baggage of international law. Some are firmly established as principles, like the right of national self-determination and the sanctity of territorial boundaries, but only partially respected in practice. And others are accepted as ideals, like not using force to settle disputes and not intervening in the domestic political affairs of others, but are applied only in a limited number of cases and have only a minor restraining effect on state behaviour. The United Nations Charter stands as a model for a more mature anarchy than the one we have, and defines the progress which the system has made away from chaos. But the record of disputes, conflicts and insecurity which the modern era has produced marks the difficulty of the problem, and the distance we still have to go.

These models illustrate further the need to combine levels 2 and 3 in analysing the character of the system. To comment about a mature anarchy is to say things of significance about both the component units and the pattern of relations among them. A mature anarchy must be composed of mature states, because only states well ordered and stable within themselves could generate and support strong common norms for the system as a whole. But once such norms exist, they become a characteristic of the system, enriching, but not transforming, the basic structure of anarchy.

For our purposes, this spectrum of models serves both as a source of ideal types and as a crude scale by which to gauge the intensity of that part of the national security problem which is posed by the anarchic structure. In this chapter and the next we shall elaborate on the idea of mature and immature anarchies in the context of the further aspects of system structure and character which we have still to consider.[7]

These models imply the idea of progress from immature to mature anarchy, and so raise the whole issue of determinism.[8] Can the evolution of international political systems be compared with that of biological organisms or species? If it can, then there will be a strong, though not necessarily uniform or inevitable, tendency for the maturity of systems to increase with the passage of time. If it cannot, then movements towards greater maturity can only come about by the direction of collective effort to achieving specific structural objectives. The idea of a temporal imperative behind an evolution towards maturity has considerable appeal, and does not exclude trying to force the pace by more directed measures.

Even within the recent span of our own system one can detect substantial developments towards a more mature anarchy. The idea of national self-determination – the nation as the foundation of the state – for example, was firmly rooted in the system by the middle of the nineteenth century, as exemplified by the legitimacy attaching to the processes of national unification in Germany and Italy. While nationalist developments had a destabilising side in the power-oriented and expansionist notions of Social-Darwinism (the survival of the fittest nation), by the time of the Versailles Treaties in 1919, national self-determination was close to being a system-wide principle. Despite continiing difficulties with it, such as in the partition of Germany, Korea, China, India and Vietnam after the Second World War, it underlay the post-1945 decolonisation movement, with its gigantic transfer of political authority from imperial powers to local states.[9] Even an overtly imperial power like the Soviet Union recognises the nationality principle both in its domestic constitutional structure and in its relations with its satellites.

Similar signs of evolving maturity can be read into the development of international organisations like the League and the United Nations, and the attempts through them to fix territorial boundaries and to establish norms and principles aimed at restraining the use of force. In addition, the historical development of states themselves seems to add weight to the maturity of the system over time. Long-established states have had time both to develop their own ideas and institutions, as well as to reach accommodation with their neighbours on boundaries. The western European states, and the United States and Canada, come to mind as examples of relatively mature states among which force has ceased to play a significant role in relations. Younger states, like many of those in the Third World, appear weak as states because of their newness, and there is enough similarity between their situation and the earlier history of the more mature states to support some hopes of evolution.[10]

At least two major lines of criticism, unfortunately, disturb this pleasing image of historical drift towards greater maturity and security in the international anarchy. The first of these rests on an extension of the biological analogy in which a phase of maturity is followed by decline and death. This could apply either to states or to the system as a whole, and results in Toynbeean-style historical cycles which interrupt any continuous progress towards harmony. There is, of course, no way of proving that a cyclic pattern will be valid for the future even if it has been for the past, especially given the rapid and fundamental changes in human capabilities and institutions that characterise the modern era. But the image of a system that proceeds by a series of peaks and troughs is made compelling by the retreat of political order in Europe following the collapse of the Roman empire, and by the possibilities for collapse inherent in the capabilities and vulnerabilities of contemporary human social organisation.

This last point ties into the second line of criticism, which is that, if increase in maturity is a function of time, then that increase does not take place against a static background of threat, but rather is paralleled by increases in both the scale of threat and the scope of vulnerability. From this perspective, increasing system maturity cannot be seen as a process of steady gain on a problem of fixed dimension. Rather, it must be viewed as part of a larger process in which the forces of order compete endlessly against the ever-mounting capability for chaos. Thus, progress towards a more mature form of anarchy is not a cause for congratulation or complacency in its own right, but only if it seems to be outpacing the simultaneous increase in threats. The growth of threats and vulnerabilities stems basically from the increase in human numbers and capabilities, which up to the present has shown the long, steady build up, and then the rapid growth of a geometrical curve.

Three examples serve to illustrate this trend against which increasing systemic maturity has to compete. This first, and most obvious, is the escalating risk from the process of war. Human life may have been nasty, brutish and short in the primitive and immature past of the international anarchy, but at least humans posed no general threat to their own existence as a species. Steady increases in the cost and destructive power of weapons, combined with increasing capacity to mobilise human and material resources for warfare, have culminated during the present day in a half-mature international system in which some of the states are capable of wreaking massive damage on large portions of the planet. It is an understandably common view that the military arts in their own right now pose the largest imaginable threat to human society, and that progress in the evolution of the international anarchy has been totally inadequate to contain this threat.

The second and third examples concern food and civil nuclear power, and illustrate the way in which vulnerability has increased because the survival of large numbers of people has become increasingly dependent on the maintenance of high levels of social order. Some countries like Japan and Britain no longer produce enough food for their populations, and even within many countries, especially those highly industrialised and urbanised, the great majority of the people are very remote from food production. This condition reflects the pursuit of efficient economies of specialisation, but it produces a society much more vulnerable to serious total disruption than the traditional peasant economy in which most of the people were involved in, and close to, the process of food production. Unless complex distribution and production systems are maintained, people starve, and virtually the entire machinery of society collapses.[11] Since these systems are vulnerable to attack, societies dependent on them are vulnerable in a more profound sense than were those of their more primitive forebears. Similarly, the prospective construction of a large civil nuclear power sector in many states creates the long-term problem of disposal and management of radioactive wastes. At present, such wastes require active management, and if that continues to be the case, the safe storage of these materials would require a considerable measure of social stability over long periods.[12] War or social breakdown would expose the risk inherent in mortgaging the future to present needs.

There are, then, no grounds for feeling sanguine about either the past progress or the future prospects of the international anarchy. Threats and vulnerabilities multiply and evolve at the same time as the system advances towards maturity, making security a highly dynamic problem of uncertain dimensions. At this stage, it is worth looking more closely at the structure of the present anarchy, and at analytical approaches to it, in order to assess more closely its impact on national security.

The Limitations of System Structure Analysis

Perhaps the most common approach to analysing the international anarchy has been attempts to identify patterns in the structure of fragmentation, and to impute from these conclusions about the security characteristics of the system as a whole. The favoured format in this exercise has been to focus on patterns in the distribution of power in the system, and to derive from these conclusions about the probability and intensity of war. Morton Kaplan, for example, identifies six types of system, not all of them anarchies, as follows: balance of power, loose bipolar, tight bipolar, unit veto, universal and hierarchic.[13] The balance of power model drives from the European state system up to 1914, the loose and tight bipolar models reflect, respectively, the later and earlier stages of the Cold War, and the others constitute theoretical possibilities for which there are no contemporary examples. K.J. Holsti offers four models: hierarchical, diffuse, diffuse bloc and polar.[14] And Richard Rosecrance proposes a more complex scheme based on four variables: stratification, polarity, distribution of power and homogeneity.[15]

Although these efforts have a taxonomic and analytical interest in their own right, and generate interesting theoretical debates like that resulting from Kaplan's attempt to formulate rules for the balance of power system, they produce no clear conclusions about the security implications of different structures. Holsti, for example, argues that none of the models he examines produces more security for the independent political units within it than any of the others.[16] While the models produce different styles of international relations, the security risks they pose to their members are merely different, and not demonstrably higher or lower. Some interesting hypotheses do emerge. Rosecrance, for example, argues that bipolar systems will have less frequent but more intense international violence, while more diffuse systems will have more frequent but less intense violence. He also argues that more homogeneous systems (that is, those in which differences in organising ideologies are relatively small) will be less prone to international conflict than those in which ideological divisions are large.[17] On key issues, however, there is no agreement. In relation to the central contemporary issue of the impact of bipolar power structures, like those we have lived with since the end of the Second World War, opinions contradict completely. Rosecrance argues that a tight bipolar system is 'the most intractable' in terms of controlling international conflict,[18] and his view is backed up by the earlier position of John Herz that the bipolar structure produces the most unmitigated form of the security dilemma.[19] Karl Deutsch and David Singer argue that multipolar systems are preferable in security terms to bipolar ones; while Michael Haas disagrees, finding merit and cost in both forms.[20] Against these views, Waltz argues at length that a bipolar power structure is best in terms of international security because it is simpler, more stable, and less accident-prone than more diffuse systems.[21]

The balance of power deserves special mention here because of the important place it has traditionally occupied in the analysis of international relations. In one sense, it is simply another of the power structure models just discussed, and is subject to the same criticisms. As Bull notes, however, 'the term "balance of power" is notorious for the numerous meanings that may be attached to it'.[22] It refers not only to a particular type of power structure, but also to a general principle of state behaviour in an anarchic system. Both Bull and Hoffmann make the case against the utility of the model in relation to the contemporary international system.[23] Bipolarity, nuclear weapons, economic interdependence, and doubts about the validity of power theories of political behaviour, all militate against it. Even when conditions allow its application, it favours, as Bull argues, the interests of great powers, and can hardly be recommended as a general security policy for all states.[24] Hoffmann argues bluntly that 'the balance of power is not a relevant mechanism in the new arenas of world politics'.[25]

As a system model, the balance of power offers no more enlightenment on the national security problem than do other power structure models. Indeed, with its emphasis on military rivalry and great power interests, its acknowledgement of the interdependence and uncertainty of security relations, and its open-minded view about the role of war in the system, the balance of power model might better be seen as defining the problem of insecurity. Where the balance of power comes into its own, as Bull argues, is on the system level.[26] On level 3, the balance of power describes a principle which is fundamental to the preservation of the international anarchy, and which is inseparable from it. An anarchic structure can only be maintained by a balance of power. Thus, the balance of power and the international anarchy are opposite sides of the same coin. If we accept Vattel's classic definition of the balance of power as 'a state of affairs such that no one power is in a position where it is preponderant and can lay down the law to others',[27] then it becomes simply another way of describing the basic structure of anarchy. Thus, the balance of power will, by definition, last as long as the international anarchy. This is an important conclusion if we take the whole anarchic system to be an object of security, because the balance of power is essential to the preservation of such a system. It is, however, at a very high level of generality, and contributes little more to solving the national security problem than defining its basic condition. At this level of analysis, the balance of power as anarchy incorporates all the system structure models except those concerned with mono-polar or unified political orders.

At this high level of generality, then, we do not find much clear guidance about the impact of system structure on the problem of national security. The system structure approaches generate useful organising ideas for thinking about alternative system structures, or patterns of fragmentation, and they also raise questions about why, when, how, and with what consequences, the system structure changes from one form to another. Much energy has been spent arguing about the criteria for, and significance of, changes in the structure (as pattern of distribution power) of the international system,[28] though in the absence of agreement about the significance of the patterns themselves this debate is largely confined to abstract realms. Different structures can themselves be seen as objects of security if one argues, as Waltz does about bipolar systems, that they tend to produce fewer security problems than do alternative structures. In a roughly similar way, it can also be argued that system change in itself is likely to generate security problems because old systems represent vested interests that will not give way without a fight. The single transformation in system structure identified by

Waltz, for example, occurred through the agency of the Second World War. From this perspective, maintenance of the existing distribution of power can be seen as a type of status quo security interest, and the search for system stability becomes a theme of security analysis.

The problem with this whole attempt to define and compare system structures is that it is one-dimensional and ahistorical. That is to say, it attempts to generate knowledge about the conditions for security by looking at the single factor of the distribution of power, and assumes that whatever explanatory power is contained within that factor holds true across different historical periods. Thus, a five-member balance of power system should behave in a similar fashion regardless of whether it occurred under the conditions of the eighteenth or of the late twentieth century. This is clearly a case of expecting a lot of answers from rather little data. Although many different system types can be proposed, depending on how grossly the criteria for distinguishing between types are defined, cross-historical comparisons will necessarily rest on a dangerously narrow base. The conditions for security depend on a host of variables other than distribution of power, and the variance in these between historical periods will weigh heavily against any uniformities arising from similarities in system structure.[29]

The kinds of historical variables which also determine the national security problem include the following:

- the character of the prevailing military technology, particularly its destructive capacity and the range over which force can be projected;
- the availability of effectively empty territory in the system, which is to say territory which is either uninhabited, or lightly inhabited, or inhabited but not organised to a political level recognised by the major powers in the system;[30]
- the character of the states making up the system, which includes Rosecrance's 'homogeneity' variable in relation to ideologies, and also the matter of whether or not significant powers in the system are revisionist, and what form their revisionism takes, which we shall look at in chapter 7;
- the strength and pattern of war-weariness in the system, which is to say, whether or not the system, or some of its members, are close to a debilitating experience of war, like the European system after the Thirty Years War and after the First World War, and like the United States, to a lesser extent, after its experience in Vietnam;[31]
- the legitimacy of war as an instrument of state policy within the system, which, for example, has declined greatly during the present century;[32] and

 – the levels of enmity between states in the system, which, as in the case of Germany and France, can vary greatly with the shift of complex historical conditions.

For all these reasons, and more, there exist severe limits on what can be deduced about security from the rather gross variable of system structure. It simply defies credibility to assume similarities between similar system structures when one has nuclear weapons and the other not, or when one is war-weary, and the other not. Europe was a balance of power systems before the First World War as well as after it, but what a difference to the security environment the intervening few years made!

An Alternative Approach: Security Complexes

If we shift our attention from the higher levels of generality about the power structure of the system to more specific security features of particular systems, we lose some of our ability to make comparisons, but gain in the level of richness with which we can assess any particular system. This middle level of analysis is an important, but seriously neglected, area of international relations analysis. Much effort is devoted to analysis of security at the state level, both in terms of national security policy, and in terms of situation analyses of trouble spots. Similarly, a weight of analysis is oriented towards the grand abstraction of systems analysis. In between, however, we find only the hazy derived notions of regional balances of power, and sub-systems. Yet it is precisely in this middle area that the concept of security finds one of its most useful applications. Because security encompasses both subjective and objective factors, it directs inquiry more towards the nature of relations among states than towards the more rigid attempts to compare attributes which are characteristic of power analysis.

The point is that the security implications of the anarchic structure do not spread uniformly throughout the system. Complex patterns of alignment and enmity develop from historical conditions in all types of anarchic systems, more so in those which are highly fragmented. Despite the subjective, perceptual element of security relations, these patterns are often fairly durable features of the international system, and it is they, rather than the grosser system structure overall, which define the security environment of most states. I propose to use the term *security complex* to label the relevant structures at this level of analysis. A security complex is defined as a group of states whose primary security concerns link together sufficiently closely that their national securities cannot realistically be considered apart from one another. Security complexes tend to be durable, but they are neither permanent nor internally rigid.[33] The international system as a whole contains a large number of security complexes, some of which intersect or overlap, and some of which fit inside each other. Because of these complicated patterns, the boundary of any particular complex may be difficult to define with precision, and the use of the concept requires sensitivity to the situation of those states which occupy positions in more than one complex. The links which tie together a security complex together may be of many types – geographical, political, strategic, historical, economic or cultural – and states outside the complex may play a major role within it, without the complex itself being central to their security concerns.

An extended example should help to illustrate both the idea and the advantages and difficulties of using it as an analytical tool. In Chapter 3 we looked briefly at India and Pakistan in the context of the structural political threats each posed to the other, and the locking of this relationship by the longstanding, unresolved dispute over Kashmir. South Asia as a whole provides a relatively clear example of an important, middle-level security complex. The heart of this complex is the rivalry between India and Pakistan, two large states whose insecurities are so deeply intertwined that their national securities, particularly in terms of political and military security, cannot be separated. A number of much less powerful states are bound into the complex for geographical reasons, including Bangladesh, Butan, Nepal and Sri Lanka. Burma provides a neutral buffer between south Asia and the quite distinct complex of security concerns in south-east Asia. China, although an important actor in the south Asian context, is not part of the security complex because south Asia is relatively peripheral to its primary security concerns. The status of Afghanistan is rather ambiguous, more so since the Soviet occupation, but it is at best a peripheral actor in the complex. Iran, like China, is, or at least was under the Shah, an actor of importance in the complex, but has the main centre of its own security concerns outside it. Iran serves as a link state between the south Asian complex, and the exceedingly intricate and entangled complex, or set of complexes, which covers the Gulf and the Middle East.[34]

What binds the south Asian security complex together is the dominant role of local issues and relations in defining the national security priorities of the states within it. None of the south Asian states is strong as a state, though India is conspicuously better placed in this regard than is Pakistan, and consequently most of them face substantial security threats arising within their own boundaries. Because of religious, national and historical patterns which run across state boundaries, these domestic problems cannot be separated from relations among the states. Bengalis live in both India and Bangladesh, Punjabis are in both India and Pakistan, Pathans stretch across both Pakistan and Afghanistan, and the Islamic religion weaves a pattern through all of them. Pakistan has already experienced one dismemberment in 1971, which not only underlines internal fragility, but also demonstrates the way in which domestic and international politics within the complex interleave with each other. The argument about structural political threats made in chapter 3 adds another dimension to the interconnectedness of domestic insecurities between India and Pakistan.

On top of these domestic problems, but frequently linked to them, lies a layer of local, inter-state disputes which defines the principal binding insecurities of the complex as a whole. Although many boundary lines and disputes within and around the complex have been settled – for example, as between India on the one hand, and Sri Lanka, Bangladesh, Indonesia and Burma on the other – several problems remain. The most important of these is between India and Pakistan over Kashmir. As argued above, this dispute ties into the domestic instabilities of both states, and symbolises the structural political threat which they pose to each other. It has embittered relations between the two since partition in 1947, and provided a major motive for two of the three wars fought between them (1947–8 and 1965). It has also symbolised a more general power rivalry between the two, in which India has tended to assume the status of senior regional power, while Pakistan has struggled to keep itself from being overawed by the naturally greater weight of its neighbour. Arms racing has been a persistent feature of relations between the two since the mid-1950s, and although the partition of Pakistan in 1971 appeared at first to make its uphill struggle too difficult to be worth continuing, by the mid-1970s military rivalry was moving towards the great equaliser of nuclear weapons. Other rather less serious disputes exist between India and Bangladesh over water rights and refugee movements, and between Pakistan and Afghanistan over the peoples and areas of the north-west frontier.

These local rivalries and hostilities, especially between India and Pakistan, not only define the south Asian security complex, but also set the mould for its relations with the larger complexes which surround it. Two major external patterns cut through the south Asian complex, one generated by the Sino-Soviet dispute, and the other arising from the rivalry between the United States and the Soviet Union. The Sino-Soviet dispute can be viewed as a distinct, neighbouring and larger security complex in its own right, which influences security alignments worldwide. It can also be seen as part of a three-cornered global security complex in which China has become a member of the highest level complex which previously centred on the East-West struggle between the United States and the Soviet Union. Whether these patterns are viewed separately or together however, they interact with the local pattern in south Asia in such a way as to intensify it. They illustrate the way in which higher level complexes (that is, those composed of major powers which define their security in regional or global terms) penetrate and influence the pattern of relations generated within a local complex.

One hard issue does connect south Asia with these larger complexes: the Sino-India border dispute. Although relations between India and China were thought to be good during the 1950s, towards the end of the decade disputes over large, ill-defined, mountain boundary areas, and tensions over the consolidation of Chinese rule in Tibet, caused them to deteriorate. A short, sharp war in 1962 fixed an enduring pattern of insecurity for India. Not only was territory lost, and the Indian army humiliated, but also China came to be seen in India as a looming threat along its northern borders. Other than this issue, however, American, Chinese and Soviet influence on the south Asian complex has virtually all been in the context of their rivalries with each other.

To recount the full detail of this complicated history is beyond the scope of the present study, but its main features can be outlined without too much over-simplification. The initial impact was made by the Cold War. India, largely for its own reasons, chose to become a leading exponent of non-alignment during the 1950s, cultivating self-reliance, and in the process rather alienating itself from the United States, Pakistan, by contrast, saw American containment policies against the Soviet Union as an opportunity to increase its military strength against India, and so joined in the network of anti-Soviet alliances. The flow of cheap, or free, American arms to Pakistan between 1954 and 1965 had much more impact within Pakistan, and on relations between Pakistan and India, than it did on the Soviet Union. It did not help, and may well have hindered, Pakistan's domestic security, and it exacerbated tensions and hostility between India and Pakistan.[35] It also opened the door to Soviet wooing of India, which began in the mid-1950s, by pressuring India to find a supply of modern weapons with which to offset those being supplied to Pakistan. The generous terms offered by the Soviet Union clinched a major arms deal with India in 1962, starting India's long drift away from non-alignment, and incidentally benefiting from its coincidence with the emotionally charged insecurity in India arising from the border war with China.[36]

During the 1960s, American impact on south Asia declined. The 1965 war between India and Pakistan resulted in the cessation of large American arms flows to Pakistan, and the United States was anyway preoccupied with its mounting disaster in Vietnam. The seed planted by the United States during the 1950s continued to flourish, however, and contributed significantly to the pattern of Sino-Soviet penetration which followed. During the 1960s, the rivalry between the Soviet Union and China became both open and deep, and both states used south Asia as a forum for their dispute. The pattern here was already indicated. China and India were alienated by the 1962 war, while India and the Soviet Union were already well-embarked on the road to friendship. Pakistan, by its alignment policy, had established an anti-Soviet record. All that remained was for events to harden these trends.

The 1962 Sino-Indian war, and India's defeat caused the United States, Britain and the Soviet Union to rush military aid to Delhi, the odd combination of East and West reflecting western slowness to register the significance of the Sino-Soviet split. It also transformed attitudes towards military defence in India, resulting in a rapid doubling of manpower and expenditure, and the adoption of serious long-term plans for upgrading domestic defence production and procurement policies.[37] These developments caused alarm in Pakistan, not only because of the immediate shock of seeing its American ally ship arms to the enemy, but also because the burgeoning transformation of the Indian military threatened to push Pakistan into permanent inferiority on the sub-continent. A classic security dilemma was clearly in the making here, with outside powers amplifying local patterns of insecurity. On the one hand, India grew increasingly concerned at the prospect of a two-front attack by China and Pakistan. To meet this contingency, it greatly increased its arms strength, moving closer to the Soviet Union as a supplier of arms and arms industries in the process. On the other hand, Pakistan saw the growing weight of Indian arms almost wholly in relation to itself, worrying not only about its military security in general, but also about the rapidly declining prospects for resolving the Kashmir dispute in its favour.

China and Pakistan began moving closer together in what must count as one of the most unlikely political associations imaginable. Pakistan saw the need for a more reliable ally against India than the United States had proved to be, and the Chinese had demonstrated both the capability and the will to act against India in 1962. The

Chinese, for their part, could hardly miss the containment implications of a Soviet-Indian axis. From Peking's perspective, a tie with
Pakistan not only provided a politically significant territorial passage
to the Indian Ocean, but also offered prospects of deflecting India
from Soviet purposes by keeping it preoccupied with its subcon-
tinental disputes. The 1965 war between India and Pakistan quickiy
deteriorated into a military stalemate, but its political impact was to
consolidate the intrusion of the Sino-Soviet complex into the south
Asian one. Because of the war, the United States and Britain imposed
an arms embargo on both sides, thereby opening the door for Soviet
and Chinese influence. India and Pakistan were at a pitch of mutual
fear and suspicion, and sorely in need of weapons to make up their
war losses. The Soviet Union lost no time in assisting India's
rearmament, and China did what it could to resupply Pakistan. By
the later 1960s, as a result, the two security complexes, though still
distinct, were locked together by alignments, respectively, between
the two weaker and the two stronger powers in each complex. Since
the Sino-Soviet complex centred on much larger powers, however,
its impact on south Asian affairs was relatively large, whereas the
south Asian links were relatively peripheral in overall Sino-Soviet
affairs.

The 1971 war between India and Pakistan arose from the process
of Bangladeshi secession, and added further layers of external
intrusion to those already built up in south Asia. By the early 1970s,
the United States was again having some impact on south Asia. Its
relations with Pakistan were partly rebuilt, and Pakistan played a go-
between role in the establishment of relations between the United
States and China. This development relieved Pakistan of the burden
of having its two principal backers treating each other as enemies. In
response, India and the Soviet Union firmed their friendship into an
alliance, the Soviet Union having long since become India's primary
supplier of arms and licensed production facilities. Pakistan was not
saved from dismemberment, because the causes of its disintegration
were largely internal, but it was supported by its allies against the
prospect of military defeat in the western part of the country. The
balance of external powers prevented any one of them intervening
directly in the war, but their overall presence served to constrain the
range of possible outcomes.

Patterns of alignment have remained much the same since 1971,
though three developments are worthy of note. First is the growth of
nuclear rivalry between India and Pakistan as discussed above. Since
the nuclear programme in neither country is aided or supported by
allies, this development has the effect of re-internalising a major
element of rivalry within the south Asian security complex. Second is

Pakistan's assiduous playing of its Islamic card in its continuing search for external support to offset the greater relative weight of India. Starting with a security agreement with Iran in 1972, which built on ties created earlier by both states' participation in western alliances, Pakistan has steadily built up a whole range of defence, economic and political ties with the Gulf states. These links increase the connections between south Asia and the Byzantine pattern of disputes, alignments and external interests which make up the Middle Eastern security complex. While such ties raise Indian concern about Pakistan's access to the huge arms supplies of fellow Islamic oil states, they do not seem likely to cause basic changes in the south Asian complex. Third is the Soviet occupation of Afghanistan. This brings Soviet troops to bear along the many hundreds of miles of border between Pakistan and Afghanistan, and puts Pakistan in the awkward position of being unwilling sanctuary for Pathan resistance. Since the Soviet Union is India's ally, the situation raises threats to Pakistan. These threats could simply intensify the present pattern, with Pakistan forging stronger links with China and the United States. Or they could transform it, by putting such pressure on Pakistan as to make it change sides, or in some other way alter the basic pattern of relations which has defined the south Asian complex since 1947.[38]

The south Asian case, then, provides a clear example of what security complexes consist of as structural features of an international anarchy. They act as nodes in the system, not only defining intense and relatively durable local patterns, but also serving to guide and shape the impact of larger external powers on these local patterns. The local and external patterns tend to reinforce each other, but the impact on the local pattern is greater because of the disproportion in size and resources. Arms supplies played an obvious role in hardening and intensifying the local disputes, and the linking together of local and external patterns of hostility amplified insecurities all round. These effects were only partially offset by pressures for reconciliation or restraint imposed on the local complex by the outside powers, as in the case of Soviet mediation after the 1965 war, and the general constraints created around the 1971 conflict.

Security complexes are a typical product of an anarchic international structure, and they come much closer to reflecting the operating environment of national security policy-makers than do higher level abstractions about the distribution of power in the system. Almost every country will be able to relate its security perspectives to one or more complexes, and the concept provides a useful tool for organising patterns of relations, and for arranging them into lateral (south Asia and the Middle East) and hierarchical (south Asia and Sino-Soviet) categories.

More importantly, security complexes offer an approach to security which requires attention to both the macro-level of great power impact on the system, and the micro-level of local state relations. In forcing attention to both levels, security complexes emphasise the mutuality of impact between them, with external influences tending to amplify local problems, and local problems shaping and constraining external entanglements and influences. The idea of security complexes relates clearly to the traditional idea of the balance of power, since it is not difficult to interpret the linkage among states in a balance of power system, like that in eighteenth-century Europe, as the pattern which defines a security complex. Precisely because of its emphasis on power, however, the balance of power approach tends strongly to encourage a narrowly-based, top-down, view of international relations, and consequently to give relatively little weight to patterns among the minor states. Although great power can sometimes override local structures, the American experience in Vietnam indicates many of the pitfalls of taking an excessively top-down view. As Hoffman argues, 'it is a mistake to treat issues in which third parties are embroiled as if these countries were pawns in a global balancing game, instead of dealing with the issues' intrinsic merits and the nations' interests'.[39] As a tool for analysis, security complexes encompass traditional power priorities by allowing for linked hierarchies of complexes. At the same time, they stress the importance of patterns of relations and sources of insecurity at all levels through which power relations are mediated.

Security complexes go rather against the grain of the Anglo-American analytical tradition in international relations. Both because of their relative geographical isolation, and because of their status as 'top dog' states in the power leagues, Britain and the United States have tended to view the world almost exclusively in terms of the highest level security complex among the reigning great powers. These special factors insulated both countries from any constant, intense experience of their own local complex, and encouraged a rather detached view of international relations. Their experience does not, for the most part, bear comparison with that of countries like Russia, Germany, Greece and Iran, whose entire histories have been sharply conditioned by inescapable pressures from intense local security complexes. Add to this the natural propensity towards ethnocentrism in security thinking explored by Booth,[40] and the predictable result is a rather self-centred, top-down, major power-oriented, view of national security.

This perspective has its uses, and must obviously be part of any comprehensive analysis. It may even be the most efficient perspective in a system within which the differentials in power and status between the top and the bottom of the hierarchy of actors is very large. In such a system, like that of the nineteenth century, the great powers could almost treat the world as their stage, not bothering to pay much regard to local actors and patterns of relations. Their political and military power was so great in relation to the non-industrial, often sub-state entities which they encountered, that they could override or distort local patterns without even thinking about it, as was done in Africa, and earlier in the Americas. Their only concern needed to be their immediate neighbours, if any, and the other major powers.

Unfortunately, or, depending on one's point of view, fortunately, such conditions no longer exist. Decolonisation has filled the world with states, and in the process has created much higher levels of political and military mobilisation outside the great powers than existed before. Many of these new states may be weak both as states and as powers, but they nevertheless constitute an order of magnitude improvement over what existed before, particularly as regards consciousness of the rights and potentials of political self-organisation. The spread of modern weapons to the Third World also carries military significance for relations between major and minor powers, as illustrated by the cost to Britain of regaining the Falklands from Argentina during 1982.[41] As such, they represent a major, and apparently continuing, trend towards a relative diffusion of power.

The significance of this analysis for the present argument is that the diffusion of power in the contemporary system raises the importance of the actors at the bottom of the power hierarchy for the functioning of the system as a whole. If, because of their relative weakness, they still serve as the objects of great power rivalry, at least they now have some durable features of their own, and create patterns within and among themselves which to some extent condition the behaviour of the great powers. As Kolodziej and Harkavy put it, there is a trend towards the 'decentralization of the international security system'.[42] It is these features and patterns which the idea of security complexes aims to capture and bring into the field of analysis. If security complexes, and the links among them, are accepted as basic structures within the international anarchy, then they automatically provide a major counterweight to the pressures for ethnocentrism in national security analysis. The single state, self-help view of national security derives from assumptions of a relatively immature anarchy, and tends to focus attention on what the state itself can do to improve its security. National security in this approach tends to get treated as a divisible good, that is to say, one largely produced by the efforts of the actor concerned.

An approach based on security complexes focuses attention on sets of states whose security problems are closely interconnected. Security is viewed as only partly divisible, a substantial portion of it residing in essentially indivisible relational patterns among states. Ethnocentrism is avoided, because one not only has to view one's own state in the context of the complexes of which it is a member, but also has to apply the same logic to other states, be they friend or foe. Although such a procedure by no means avoids all sources of bias, it does at least ensure that all states are viewed in a relational context larger than themselves. An extreme ethnocentric perspective centred on Pakistan, for example, might tend to see India as the problem and a more powerful Pakistan with more allies as the answer. The same problem viewed through the security complex lens, as illustrated above, produces a quite different analysis, which centres on the whole relationship between India and Pakistan as the problem, and emphasises the way in which increased strength and the pursuit of external alliances amplifies the problem rather than solving it.

Security complexes can be used as either a static or a dynamic mode of analysis. As a static framework, the idea generates a perspective and a set of questions which can be applied to any situational analysis. As a dynamic framework, security complexes offer a class of durable entities whose patterns and processes of evolution are of as much theoretical, and perhaps more practical, interest as those of the power structures of the system as a whole. They have the advantage of being historically based, thereby avoiding the critique of ahistoricism to which higher level system theories are subject, and enjoying a closer relation to the empiricial realities of policy-makers. What causes a security complex to arise? What sort of evolutionary paths do they follow? And since they are not permanent fixtures, what options exist for their evolution?

On this last question, for example, at least three kinds of answers emerge from existing literature. One is the subordination model, in which a security complex is fundamentally transformed as a result of being overlaid by a more powerful complex. A.W. De Porte makes an extended argument along these lines in relation to Europe during the twentieth century.[43] A second is an internal solution in which the basic rivalries defining the complex are obliterated by the victory of one party. Europe approached this solution under Hitler and Napoleon, and it would occur in south Asia if India reabsorbed all or part of Pakistan. An opposite to this might happen if conflict broke down the major units within the complex, as would occur if India and Pakistan disintegrated into more numerous, smaller states. This would produce an entirely new pattern of relations. A third answer could be the phenomenon already known in the literature as a 'security community'.[44] Security communities exist among independent states which do not expect or fear the use of force in relations between them, such as Canada and the United States. As with security complexes, security communities imply physical propinquity among the members – one would not talk of such a community between Paraguay and Upper Volta – although among great powers, because of their ability to project power, the assumption of nearness need not apply. Security communities might be seen in one sense as resolved or matured security complexes in which basic conflicts and fears have been worked out, resulting in an oasis of relatively mature anarchy within the more fractious field of the international anarchy as a whole.

One last observation about security complexes is that they provide a useful referent on which policy can be focussed, or which can be used to evaluate policy proposals. Some of the sillier, though serious, debates and proposals now in the policy realm might be more difficult to sustain if the notion of security complexes was more firmly established in people's minds. For example, the perennial debate about whether the Israel-Palestinian conflict or the threat from the Soviet Union is the key issue in the Middle East looks completely different if viewed through the lens of a Middle Eastern security complex. The Israeli-Palestinian issue then emerges clearly as a defining dispute, one of several, within the complex, along the same lines as the India-Pakistan conflict within south Asia. The Soviet threat occurs as part of a higher level complex, and cannot be analysed without bringing in the rest of the higher complex, including the United States, as it impacts on affairs within the Middle East. The two complexes have quite separate dynamics, just as the south Asian and Sino-Soviet ones did, and the point is not to confuse them, but to sort out how they interact with each other. On this basis, security complexes can be treated as objects for policy in the sense that problems can only be resolved within the context of the relevant complex as a whole. Following on from this, it would become more difficult to float and defend misguided ideas like the Indian Ocean as a Zone of Peace (IOZP). Since the Indian Ocean in no sense forms a security complex, the idea suffers from a remarkably bad fit with the salient structures of the international system. It cuts across at least five security complexes, and could never hope to contain all the divergent interests within and across its notional boundaries.[45]

The Character of States as a Factor in System Structure

Within the overall structure of the international anarchy, we have so far examined two kinds of substructures: those based on macro-patterns in the distribution of power, and those based on distinct relational patterns which we called security complexes. The object of this exercise has been to suggest in what ways, if any, the structure of the international political system bears on the problem of national security. Before we leave this question, it is necessary to look at one more aspect of the international political system, and that is the character of the units which compose it. Although Waltz has argued that proper systemic theories should not concern themselves with the character of the units which compose the system,[46] this distinction between systemic and reductionist theories breaks down because, as argued at the beginning of this chapter, the basic character of the units (sovereignty) and of the system (anarchy) are so closely linked. Under such conditions, one cannot discuss some characteristics of the system without reference to the character of the units, as was demonstrated in the discussion of system maturity. If, as argued earlier, mature anarchies provide a more secure environment for states than do immature ones, and if system maturity depends to a considerable extent on the character of the units, then we have a legitimate area of inquiry under this heading.

The most striking feature of states as a class, as argued at length in chapter 2, is their diversity. While this diversity provides the essential motive and justification for the anarchic international structure, it also generates the impediments which make the transition from immature to mature anarchy so slow. A completely homogeneous state system would have no reason to retain an anarchic structure, and homogeneity to that extent is not necessary for a mature anarchy to exist. While thus allowing a considerable measure of political, social and economic diversity to continue, (that is, rejecting the Wilsonian image of a world in which all states have similar political ideologies and institutions), it is worth looking again at the distribution of power, and at the problem of weak states, as factors which influence the character of the security environment provided by the international political system.

One of the key distinctions drawn in chapter 2 was that between states which were weak or strong as *states*, rather than weak or strong as *powers*. This distinction reflects on the structure of the international political system in as much as the whole idea of anarchy is precisely about the nature and pattern of political fragmentation. Where states are strong, the pattern of fragmentation is clear and relatively firm. Where they are weak, the pattern is less clear and decidedly less firm. Firmness in the pattern of fragmentation is a basic condition for the development of a mature anarchy. The present system displays a highly mixed structure in this regard. Some regions like Europe, east Asia and North America contain mostly strong states. Others, most notably Africa, contain a high proportion of weak states. Complicated variations in patterns of historical evolution explain this situation, and its effect is to produce a distorted, unevenly developed anarchy which is much more mature in some parts than in others. Since we have only arrived very recently at a stage in which the state system has become universal, this situation is hardly surprising. In many ways, it can be seen as a linear extension from the era in which states only occupied part of the planetary territory, the rest being occupied by sub-state units, either of local origin, like tribes, or attached to states, like colonies.

Although these areas are now covered by states, and are thus inside the international system rather than subordinate to it, most of these new states are weak as states. Consequently, they still provide an arena for great power competition in a way that would not be nearly so marked if they were strong as states, regardless of their status as powers. The universalisation of the state system has extended the moderately mature norms of the older, stronger part of the system to cover the new members, but many of these new members are so weak as states that they cannot adequately fulfil their role in such a relatively advanced system. While system norms now make it much more difficult to occupy and annex territories than it used to be, the poorly developed and weak ideas and institutions in many of the new states provide irresistable targets for foreign intervention, and an opportunity to continue old patterns of competition in new forms.

Since territory is no longer the prime target, military threats have declined in utility as between the great powers and the new states, although not so much among the new states themselves, where many territorial issues remain to be resolved. But political threats have become much more salient. Weak states are highly vulnerable to political threats, because such threats are not, like military invasions, aimed at the country as a whole, but at the main factional disputes within it. Thus, state A does not threaten state B in a simple, direct fashion. Instead, it participates in domestic disputes between factions b1 and b2, backing whichever one seems most likely to pursue policies favourable to A. There are countless possible variations in the style of political intervention, ranging from support for existing factions in a relatively stable electoral system to encouragement of, and military assistance to, armed struggle within the target state. But the common theme is the exploitation of weak states by foreign powers competing with each other to determine patterns of international alignment. Because the state structures of weak states provide such targets of opportunity, governmental security and national security become hopelessly confused, and the development of national political life gets trapped by broader, ideological disputes among the powers.

Thus, although the universalisation of the state system has greatly moderated disputes over territory, this has simply changed the form of great power competition and intervention, rather than leading to a more harmonious and mature form of anarchy. So long as weak states constitute a significant proportion of the international community, this arrested development seems likely to remain the case. A mature anarchy can only exist when the great majority of its members are themselves also mature. On this level, the character of the units, and that of the system, cannot be separated. A mature anarchy requires members that are firm in their own definition, and can project their own inner coherence and stability out into the community of states. Only on that basis can a solid foundation be created for the promulgation and observance of mature anarchic norms based on the mutual respect of units. Zbigniew Brzezinski came close to recognising explicitly this link between national security and the flawed anarchic structure represented by weak states when he ranked 'regional conflict, the fragmentation of wobbly social and political structures in societies incapable of absorbing the political awakening of so many more people' as the second greatest threat to the United States (after Soviet power).[47]

One logical conclusion from this line of argument is support for the underlying drift of much, often incoherently-expressed rhetoric stemming from the North-South debate and the corridors of the United Nations. The UN expresses the current form and dilemma of the international anarchy very clearly, for its whole purpose is not to replace the anarchy with some transcendent form of world government, but to make it work better. The redistributional pleas and demands which constitute its major output, though frequently distorted by vested interests, can be seen as one way of saying that the anarchy will continue to be unbalanced, unstable and conflict-prone, until its weaker members have become more firmly established as states. Only when they can project a basic solidity into the system, rather than a basic fragility as now, will the system as a whole be able to advance in maturity. The incentive for the better-established states in all this is that a more mature system would provide more security, though perhaps less opportunity, all round.

The most obvious line of objection to the above argument is the traditional one, that it is the distribution of power which dominates the anarchy and which conditions relations within it. On this basis, great powers will dominate, and interfere with, small powers simply on the grounds of power differentials between them, and regardless of more esoteric considerations like degrees of strength or weakness as states. To some extent this is true, as attested by the fate of weak powers like the eastern European states. I would argue, however, that the two factors are worth distinguishing, and that as the system continues to develop, political strength will tend to gain in importance relative to gross power. The arguments about the greater vulnerability of weak states, and about their impact on the system overall, stand on their own merits. While even great powers might hesitate to tackle medium powers like Brazil, Turkey or Iran on military grounds, the fact that those countries are relatively weak as states makes them much more vulnerable to political meddling.[48]

The straight power factor is also diminished in force by the decline in relative power differentials as more and more actors move away from the very bottom of the scale. Given a sufficient degree of political mobilisation, even small states can now put up a costly resistance. In addition, the development of mature anarchic norms, like sovereign equality, non-interference, inviolability of boundaries, and such-like, make it more difficult, because less legitimate, to throw one's power about than it used to be. Weak states still provide considerable opportunity for such behaviour because of the difficulty of applying system norms to units which are so poorly defined and internally infirm in their own right. Stronger units would make norms more valid and thereby provide less opportunity for the exercise of power.

None of this is to deny that the overall balance and distribution of power in the system plays a crucial role in the security environment. All of the norms and niceties discussed above would be swept away, along with much else, in a war between the super-powers, and the military stalemate between them is clearly a factor of immense significance. However, the failure of those engaged in systemic power distribution analysis to come up with firm conclusions about security indicates the hazards of trying to use the power factor in isolation. If the current stability owes more to nuclear weapons than to the distribution of power, then we are dealing with an independent factor with a potential historical continuity much greater and more salient than bipolarity.

The issue of power raises the question of whether or not a more mature anarchy is better served by a more even distribution of power than by the huge inequalities between the United States and Burundi which we have at present. On the face of it, it would seem that more equal units might well provide a more manageable anarchy, because each would have difficulty mobilising sufficient resources to threaten others seriously, assuming all other factors, such as strength as states, to be also roughly equal. This question is worth raising, even though it cannot be resolved, for the light it casts not only on the matter of desirable anarchic structures, but also on the norms of, and process of evolution towards, a more mature anarchy. We might speculate, for example, about the relationship between system structure and security as it affects the norms and standards around which states themselves are organised.

There appears to be an historical trend towards ever larger political aggregates which might be significant for assessments of the current anarchic structure. City-states initially commanded sufficient relative power to build great empires, and presumably the 'invention' of cities had a catalytic effect in promoting their spread. More recently, nation-states have provided the model, with the unifications of Italy and Germany in the last century providing clear examples of the transformation from earlier forms. Most of the current system is based on the nation-state idea, although inefficiently for the reasons argued in chapter 2. This is despite the fact that on its European home-ground, the nation-state is widely seen as inadequate in scale to fulfil many economic and security functions. It is interesting to ponder whether, in addition to their many other troubles, most of the new states may have adopted, or had thrust upon them, a form which is being replaced in the more advanced, or more historically coherent, parts of the system by super-states. In this perspective, the United States and the Soviet Union provide catalytic models for a further stage of political aggregation, because only states organised on a continental scale can provide adequate military and economic security under contemporary historical conditions.[49] Countries like China, India, and perhaps Brazil, start with an advantage of scale, while the integration difficulties of western Europe illustrate the problems of breaking away from familiar, but inadequate, older forms.

A trend towards a system composed of relatively large units (super-states) in relatively small numbers, might well facilitate the development of a more mature anarchy. Such units would better be able to provide the internal strength and stability which is necessary for a harmonious anarchy, and would aggregate international interests more efficiently than is possible under the current degree of fragmentation. As the case of China illustrates, even a relatively underdeveloped super-state can allocate enough resources to security to create an effective stand-off between itself and more advanced superpowers. Aggregation into super-states might thus help to compensate for the differences in economic and industrial strength which appear likely to persist in the international system. Furthermore, a world of super-states might more easily achieve a multi-sided balance of terror. The military paralysis engendered by a balance of terror transforms the logic of the balance of power. With such paralysis, the balance not only preserves the anarchic structure, but also does much more to preserve the particular pattern of states than is the case under the more fluid regime of a simple balance of power. A system-wide balance of terror serves national as well as systemic security. These advantages at level 3, however, might have costs at level 1. Aggregation into super-states is likely to affect individual security adversely in two ways: first, by undermining the nation-state synthesis which provides a useful framework for mediating between individuals and the state; and secondly, by increasing the political distance, and therefore the potential for alienation, between individual citizens and their government. In a system of super-states, a few remaining nation-states on the old model would occupy a status not unlike that of the remaining principalities (Andorra, Monaco, Liechtenstein, and others) in the present system.

Although this projected future is highly speculative, it does serve to illustrate a middle-range ideal model for the international anarchy, which can be offered as an alternative to utopian projections of world government. It also gives some idea of the possible historical forces involved, and suggests some security implications of the link between the character of units and the nature of the system.

Conclusions: Anarchy and Security

The character of the international political system has a major bearing on the problem of national security. As we have seen, the international anarchy does not constitute a single form with relatively fixed features, but rather a single condition around which many large variations in character can be arranged. Some forms of anarchy heighten the problem of national security, whereas others mitigate it, and the 'natural' trends affecting the matter are contradictory, with improvements in the system structure racing against an expanding universe of threats and vulnerabilities. The systemic perspective not only gives a clearer view of the sources of threat to national security, but also enables us to take a broader and more contextual view of national security itself. It helps us to identify a number of features, like levels of maturity, security complexes, and patterns in the distribution of power, which offer potentially important targets for national policy in as much as they represent opportunities to manipulate the system into forms more conducive to the enjoyment of national security. The systemic view emphasises the indivisible side of security because it highlights relational patterns and general structures. But it also ties this aspect into the divisible side of security by revealing the link between the character of states and the character of the system as a whole. As well, it provides us with a sound basis for looking at system dynamics relevant to security, and with a sense of the whole domain within which national security policies need to be formulated. State and system are clearly so closely interconnected that security policies based only on the former must be both irrational and inefficient.

Before we turn to examine the international economic system, it is worth commenting briefly on the alternatives to an anarchic international political system. The discussion above has been confined to anarchies partly because those are what we have, and partly because they seem to this writer to be what we are likely to have for the foreseeable future. Short of some gigantic catastrophe like nuclear war, we are unable to go back to pre-anarchic systems when the level of contact among units was too low to justify the notion of an international political system. The principal alternatives to the innumerable varieties of anarchy are thus unitary systems, either world empires or world federations of some sort. Despite a persistent liberal enthusiasm for world government, neither current conditions nor apparent trends favour either such development. Both power and the degree of fragmentation have become more diffuse, and there are no signs of either sufficient power, or sufficient political consensus on an organising ideology, on which to base a unitary political system. The anarchy we now find ourselves living with is much more an imposition of history on the present generation than it is a matter of conscious, preferred choice. No grand design over the centuries has produced it. Its maker has been a myriad of apparently unconnected decisions, actions and capabilities. Nevertheless, as Bull argues, the anarchy may not be as bad as it sometimes seems:

The system of a plurality of sovereign states gives rise to classic dangers, but these have to be reckoned against the dangers inherent in the attempt to contain disparate communities within the framework of a single government. It may be argued that world order at the present time is best served by living with the former dangers rather than by attempting to face the latter.[50]

Although we did not choose to make the anarchy we have, once conscious of it, we can choose to mould it into more – or less – mature forms. The character of anarchy can take very different forms, from providing an ideal arena for raw power struggles at one extreme, to sustaining diversity with security at the other. From this perspective, international anarchy need not be seen as an obstacle standing in the way of world government and universal peace. Instead, it can be seen as a field of opportunity offering attractions different from, but no less morally appealing than, those which sustain support for world government. Improved anarchies, though by no means within easy reach, are not so far off as world government. They may be seen in one sense as necessary developments on the way to a planetary federation. But keeping the profound differences between states and individuals in mind, they may also be seen as an ideal form of international association, and thus as desirable objectives in their own right.

Notes

1 Other systems also exist as part of the security environment of states, but limitations of space forbid a detailed exploration of them here. Two obvious ones are the human geographic system, hinted at in the discussion of nations in chapter 2, and the physical geographic system of the planet itself. The possible security implications of ecological factors, for example, was touched upon in chapter 3. Since the physical environment can no longer be treated as a constant, as has tended to be the case in the past, examination of these areas would open up an increasingly rich dimension of the national security problem.

2 On the links between state and system, see Richard K. Ashley, *The Political Economy of War and Peace* (London, Frances Pinter, 1980), ch. 1, esp. pp. 48–9. For a very useful discussion of sovereignty and anarchy, see John G. Ruggie, 'Continuity and Transformation in the World Polity: Toward a Neo-Realist Synthesis', *World Politics* (forthcoming January 1983). Ruggie explores the medieval system as a form of international anarchy. If accepted, his view precludes the use of the neat formulation that sovereignty defines anarchy, and anarchy defines sovereignty. While the first part of the proposition would still hold, the second would not. Anarchy *might* define a system of discrete sovereign unites, but might also express itself in much messier forms, like the medieval system, in which the actors had not aggregated sovereignty into exclusive units. This argument does not disturb my conclusion that sovereignty and anarchy need to be treated as aspects of a single phenomenon. The anarchic structure could not be replaced unless states as currently constituted ceased to exist. The equation is a little less clear in the other direction: states could transform themselves without undoing the anarchic system structure (for example, by reversion to some neo-medieval form of layered, partial sovereignties), but the nature of their transformation could also replace the anarchy (for example, by subordination of states into a world federation). See also Oran R. Young, 'Anarchy and Social Choice: Reflections on the International Polity', *World Politics*, 30:2 (1978).

3 Thomas Hobbes, *Leviathan* (Harmondsworth, Penguin, 1968), ch. 13.

4 Ruggie, *op. cit.* (note 2); and Robert Gilpin, *War and Change in World Politics* (Cambridge, Cambridge University Press, 1981), pp. 39–42.

5 A distinction along these lines is hinted at by Hedley Bull, *The Anarchical Society* (London, Macmillan, 1977), p. 68; and Stanley Hoffman, *Primacy or World Order* (New York, McGraw-Hill, 1978), p.

108, both of whom develop dualistic notions of the systems' character. Bull distinguishes between the unifying features of 'international society' and the fragmented structure of the international anarchy; and Hoffman between 'troubled peace' and 'state of war' models of the system.

6   John H. Herz, 'The Territorial State Revisited', in J.N. Rosenau (ed.), *International Politics and Foreign Policy* (New York, Free Press, 1969), pp. 82, 89.

7   An extended systematic presentation of the mature-immature anarchy idea would, in my view, be a feasible and worthwhile project. It would require the identification of the different variables which one would want to measure in order to place them on the spectrum. It would also have to deal in some way with the possibility of uneven development where either one part of the system is more mature than the rest, or where system-wide development is more advanced along one variable than along others. One advantage of this approach would be to correct what is, in my view, the false polarisation between international anarchy and international society. Anarchy would be properly confined to structure, while society would be seen to consist of a number of variables determining the character of the system. Unfortunately, this task is beyond the scope of the present volume. For an interesting attempt to discuss some of the conditions necessary for a mature anarchy, see Stanley Hoffmann, 'Regulating the New International System', in Martin Kilson (ed.), *New States in the Modern World* (Cambridge, Mass., Harvard University Press, 1975), pp. 188–97.

8   The idea of progress is not strongly developed in international relations, not least because of reluctance to take risks with normative or deterministic positions. On the national policy level, ideas of progress are commonly either very short-term, or non-existent, excepting those states governed by forward-looking ideologies. Progress is, anyway, much easier to define for revisionist than for status quo powers. For the international system as a whole, hazy ideas about a more peaceful world provide almost the only yardstick for a sense of progress.

9   Decolonisation, it must be stressed, was a highly distorted and imperfect implementation of national self-determination. *States* were made independent, but these often reflected arbitrary colonial boundaries rather than nations, leaving the new states with a formidable task of nation-building along state-nation lines.

10   This parallel cannot be pushed too far. Contemporary Third World states face much more serious problems of external intervention by more highly developed states than did the European countries in their state-building phase. On the modern state, see Joseph R. Strayer, *On the Medieval Origins of the Modern State* (Princeton, NJ, Princeton University Press, 1970); Heinz Lubasz, *the Development of the Modern State* (London, Macmillan, 1964); Leonard Tivey (ed.), *the Nation-State: The Formation of Modern Politics* (Oxford, Martin Robertson, 1981); and Kenneth Dyson, *The State Tradition in Western Europe* (Oxford, Martin Robertson, 1980).

11   This vulnerability at the system level replaces, of course, the feudal system in which *local* collapse was the main threat.

12   On the problem of nuclear waste management, see Walter C. Patterson, *Nuclear Power* (Harmondsworth, Penguin, 1976), pp. 103–14; and Raymond L. Murray, *Nuclear Energy* (Oxford, Pergamon Press, 1980), pp. 225–8.

13   Morton A. Kaplan, *System and Process in International Politics* (New York, Wiley, 1964). See also the critique in Kenneth Waltz, *Theory of International Politics* (Reading, Mass., Addison-Wesley, 1979), pp. 50–9.

14   K.J. Holsti, *International Politics: A Framework for Analysis* (New Jersey, Prentice-Hall, 1967), p. 91.

15   Richard Rosecrance, *International Relations: Peace or War?* (New York, McGraw-Hill, 1973), pp. 107–23.

16   Holsti, *op. cit.* (note 14), pp. 93–4.

17   Rosecrance, *op. cit.* (note 15), pp. 118, 122.

18   *Ibid.*, p. 124.

19   John H. Herz, *International Politics in the Atomic Age* (New York, Columbia University Press, 1959), p. 241.

20   Karl W. Deutsch and J. David Singer, 'Multipolar Power Systems and International Stability', *World Politics*, 16 (1964); Michael Haas, 'International Subsystems: Stability and Polarity', *American Political Science Review*, 64:1 (1970).

21   Waltz, *op. cit.* (note 13), ch. 8.

22   Bull, *op. cit.* (note 5), p. 109.

23   Ibid., ch. 5; and Hoffmann, *op. cit.* (note 5), pp. 168–77.

24   *Ibid.*, pp. 107–8.

25   Hoffmann, *op. cit.* (note 5), p. 176.

26   Bull, *op. cit.* (note 5), pp. 106–7.

27   Quoted *ibid.*, p. 101.

28   Waltz, *op. cit.* (note 13), is based on this problem.

29   On the problem of historical comparisons, see Klaus Knorr, 'On the Utility of History', in K. Knorr (ed.), *Historical Dimensions of National Security Problems* (Lawrence, Kansas, University Press of Kansas, 1976), pp. 1–4; Young, *op. cit.* (note 2), p. 245; and Rosecrance, *op. cit.* (note 15), pp. 200–7.

30   Rosecrance, *op. cit.* (note 15), ch. 6, deals with this under the useful concept of environmental supply.

31   For an elaboration of this argument, see Robert E. Osgood and Robert . Tucker, *Force, Order and Justice* (Baltimore, Johns Hopkins University Press, 1967), pp. 88–120.

32   *Ibid.*, p. 195.

33   The idea of security complexes is, I think, new, though shadows of it can be found in earlier writings about local balances of power and sub-systems. Security complexes differ from power balances, as the names indicate, on the basis of the organising principles involved. Security is the broader idea, and security complexes include, but are not limited to, balances of power. Sub-system is an extremely broad notion, and

security complexes could be seen as a type of sub-system. Attempts to apply the idea of sub-systems have tended to take a regional approach, and have concentrated either on questions of war and stability (for example, Haas, *op. cit.* (note 20)), or on questions of integration (for example, Bruce M. Russett, *International Regions and the International System* (Chicago, Rand McNally, 1967)), or on simply increasing the attention paid to local factors in the general analysis of international relations (for example, Michael Brecher, 'International Relations and Asian Studies: The Subordinate State System of Southern Asia', *World Politics*, 15:2(1963)). Security complexes take a specific functional idea, security, as their defining principle, and thereby avoid the broad regionalism which has sapped interest in the utility of sub-systems approaches. Michael Haas seemed to be moving towards the idea with his notion of 'international military-strategic subsystems', (*op. cit.* (note 20), pp. 100–1), but I am not aware that this notion was ever developed along similar lines.

34 The Middle Eastern complex is probably the most tangled and difficult case in the present system. It contains at least two dozen countries, and stretches from Iran and Somalia in the east, to Morocco and Algeria in the west. It contains no single core conflict or dominant power like south Asia. Instead, it is composed of four, or possibly five, sub-complexes (the Gulf, the Arab-Israeli, the Horn, north-west Africa, and possibly one centred on Libya). These sub-complexes all have independent, locally-generated security dynamics, but they are all tied together into a super-complex because of the links created by Arab and Islamic politics. Nearly all of the states within the super-complex involve themselves in the security affairs of other members, and this process often produces bizarre patterns of alignment. Syria, for example, is an opponent of Iraq (most of the time) in the context of the Gulf sub-complex, but an ally in the Arab-Israeli one. For a discussion of the Middle East super-complex in the context of regional security policy, see Barry Buzan, 'Regional Security as a Policy Objective', in Alvin Z. Rubinstein (ed.), *The Great Game: Rivalry in the Persian Gulf and South Asia.* (New York, Praeger, forthcoming, 1983).

35 J. Ansari and Mary Kaldor, 'The Bangladesh Crisis of 1971', in Mary Kaldor and A. Eide, *The World Military Order* (London, Macmillan, 1979), ch. 5.

36 Onkar Marwah, 'India's Military Power and Policy', in O. Marwah and J.D. Pollack (eds), *Military Power and Policy in Asian States: China, India, Japan* (Boulder, Col., Westview Press, 1980), pp. 111–13; SIPRI, *The Arms Trade with the Third World* (Stockholm, Almqvist & Wiksell, 1971), pp. 472–86.

37 Marwah and SIPR, *ibid.*, Emile Benoit, *Defence and Economic Growth in Developing Countries* (Lexington, 1973), ch. 4.

38 On the south Asia security complex generally, see, in addition to the sources cited in notes 35–7, S.D. Muni, 'South Asia', in Mohammed Ayoob (ed.), *Conflict and Intervention in the Third World* (London, Croom Helm, 1980), ch. 3; G.S. Bhargava, 'India's Security in the

1980s', Adelphi Paper, no. 125 (London, IISS, 1976); R.J. Jackson, 'The Great Powers and the Indian Sub-Continent', *International Affairs*, 49 : 1 (1973); B.S. Gupta, 'Waiting for India : India's Role as a Regional Power', *Journal of International Affairs*, 29 : 2 (1975).

39 Hoffmann, *op. cit.* (note 5), p. 175.

40 Ken Booth, *Strategy and Ethnocentrism* (London, Croom Helm, 1979).

41 On the diffusion of military power to the Third World, see Edward A. Kolodziej and Robert Harkavy, 'Developing States and the International Security System', *Journal of International Affairs*, 34 : 1 (1980).

42 *Ibid.*, p. 59.

43 A.W. De Porte, *Europe Between the Superpowers: The Enduring Balance*, (New Haven, Yale University Press, 1979).

44 Holsti, *op. cit.* (note 14), ch. 16; and Karl Deutsch *et al., Political Community and the North Atlantic Area* (Princeton, Princeton University Press, 1957).

45 Barry Buzan, 'Naval Power, the Law of the Sea, and the Indian Ocean as a Zone of Peace', *Marine Policy*, 5 : 3 (1981).

46 Waltz, *op. cit.* (note 13), ch. 4.

47 Quoted in Larry W. Bowman and Ian Clark (eds), *the Indian Ocean in Global Politics* (Boulder, Co., Westview Press, 1981), p. 99.

48 It is important here not to confuse weak states, in my usage, with the narrower idea of states with weak governing institutions. A weak state might well have institutions that were strong in the sense of being authoritarian. Such institutions would be necessary for the country to be considered a medium power. Thus, countries like Pakistan and Iraq are both medium powers and weak states with authoritarian institutions.

49 This line of argument extends from earlier attempts like that of John Herz, 'The Rise and Demise of the Territorial State', *World Politics*, 9 (1957), to argue that the territorial state *per se* was being made obsolete because of the collapse of its defence functions in the face of nuclear threats. Developments since then suggest that deterrence is an adequate security policy to sustain the legitimacy of the state, and that super-states have the advantage of being large enough both to provide some sense of security and defensibility (whether false or not). Super-states additionally dispose of sufficient resources to arm themselves fully with the most modern military technology required for effective deterrence, an option not open to smaller powers. Robert Jervis, 'Cooperation Under the Security Dilemma', *World Politics*, 30 : 2 (1978), p. 172, argues for the stabilising effect of large, powerful actors. Waltz, *op. cit.* (note 13), ch. 8, and 'The Myth of Interdependence', in Charles P. Kindleberger, *the International Corporation* (Cambridge, Mass., MIT Press, 1970), pp. 213–22, can also be interpreted in this light, although their main burdens are to argue, respectively, the merits of bipolarity, and the limits of interdependence in relation to super-states.

50 Bull, *op. cit.* (note 5), p. 287.

5 The State and the International Economic System

The international economic system is an entire subject in its own right, and we can do no more here than touch on those elements of it which are crucial to an understanding of national security. Major disputes exist about the basic structure and process of the international economy, and hence we are denied the support of even such a modest orthodoxy as that which attends the international political system. The focus of what follows will not be on the international economy as an independent phenomenon, but on its relationship with the international political system and the relevance of the links between them for the problem of security.

The Nature of the International Political Economy

The international political system is characterised much more by its pattern of fragmentation than by what binds it together. The international economic system, by contrast, presents a more balanced structure in which substantial elements of division are matched by powerful forces of integration. Although economic activity generates many fragmentations – for example, into classes, corporations and national economies – the international economy as a whole is also powerfully tied together by patterns of trade, production, capital and technology. Cheaper, more efficient production in one part of the system, for example, cars in Japan, affects the ability of others to pursue similar activity elsewhere, as illustrated by the problems of Chrysler and British Leyland. Technological innovations, once made, create powerful pressures for emulation elsewhere, both by their impact on production costs, and by their effect on consumer preferences. If trade is pursued as a means of increasing efficiency and welfare, then complicated patterns of dependency arise

128

in which economic activity in one place depends on a host of external conditions, and market pressures permeate the whole system.

If autarky is pursued, then pressures arise to secure necessary suppliers through direct political control, and competition for resources and markets ensues. Even attempts to drop out have their limits. The overall dynamic of the system is so strong that severe political measures are necessary to sustain isolation from it. These measures have profound domestic impacts, as in the Soviet Union, and require constant defence against the material temptations surrounding the borders. The high status – and black market price – of blue jeans in the Soviet Union, and the role of hard currency in the Polish economy, provide trivial, but indicative illustrations of this problem. Even if isolation can be sustained effectively, the deeper pressure of global economic forces undermines it. China, for example, discovered that it could not generate the technology and industrial capacity seen as necessary to supply its military defence needs so long as it pursued economic autarky. Isolation led to a relative weakening of its economic power base, and thus to an erosion of the conditions for a highly independent policy. The heroic achievement of Chinese-built F-9 fighters counted for little when such planes would be expected to engage the aircraft of China's enemies which would be two or three generations more modern.

The problem in characterising the international economy is that from one view it appears to be a system in its own right, and from another, to be so heavily entangled with the international political system as to be indistinguishable from it in many crucial respects. From one extreme as an independent phenomenon, the international economy appears to have a structure and dynamic of its own. Capital, in combination with human needs and wants, provides the basic dynamic, and the division of labour, with its attendant pattern of class and regional differentiations, provides the fundamental structure. The system has an identifiable historical momentum, its energies being fed by factors such as population growth, technological innovation, increasing capacity for political organisation, class struggle, and the development of explicit economic theories. Over historical time, economic dynamics have generated a powerful trend towards increasing wealth and ever larger conglomerations of activity which have in some senses paralleled, and in other senses outstripped, the simultaneous aggregation process in the political sphere. Their end result to date has been the progressive expansion of locally-rooted economies, and an increase in the level of exchange among them. This, in turn, has led to an emergent global economy in which many patterns of production, consumption, class and wealth operate on, and can only be understood in the context of, a planetary scale. This world scale contrasts with, and creates an important environment for the more persistent fragmentation of the international political system. In this view, the international economy has grown up through, and transcended, the state system so that, as Robin Murray argues, international capital is becoming increasingly independent of state interests.[1]

If the international economy is viewed from the opposite extreme, in the light of a dominant international political system, a very different picture emerges. Although much of the dynamics and structure outlined above remain the same, the pattern of political fragmentation is imposed much more strongly. National economies stand out as the critical level for analysis, and the international economy becomes less a thing in itself, and more a complex pattern of interaction among national economies. Emphasis is placed on the growing economic role and power of governments, on national definitions of economic priorities, on states as economic units, and on the numerous links between state power and economic activity. From this perspective, the class structure appears to be more important within states than above them, and economic activity becomes interesting not so much because of its own dynamics, but because it forces states to interact with each other, and thus provides a major behavioural force within the international political system.

Arguments over whether the political or the economic system should be given primacy need not detain us here. Both systems clearly possess main structures and dynamics which are strong enough to be identified independently. Just as clearly, however, the two systems are so closely intertwined that neither can be understood in the absence of the other. The international economy is just as thoroughly penetrated by state structures and the dynamics of power and security, as the state system is cut through by patterns of production, consumption and class, and by the dynamics of wealth. Because of this, both systems can only dance partly to their own tune, the rest of their movement being prompted or constrained by ties to the partner system. Each state contains a slice of the global economy and class structure, which becomes to some extent differentiated from the global economic patterns precisely because it is contained within a particular state structure. These state structures are more than simply convenient units for intra-élite rivalry because, as we have seen, they spring from deep roots of their own which certainly constrain, and may surpass, the influence of economic and class divisions as a basis for action.

Many writers, and indeed whole literatures, have dwelt in various ways upon the interaction between the international economic and political systems. Literature on political economy before the middle of the nineteenth century tended naturally to treat the two together because they were seen as one subject, the disciplinary gulf between politics and economics having not yet opened. The literature on imperialism is premised on the juncture of the two systems, as are the much more recent literatures on interdependence, and on con-temporary international political economy.[2] Current writers like Wallerstein, Galtung and Ashley have attempted to build general theories of international relations which are rooted firmly in both systems, and the interaction between them; while writers like Pettman have attacked the academic malaise of artificial, disciplinary distinctions which inhibit the study of crucial links between state and class.[3] Tivey pursues the matter on level 2, looking at the political economy of national-building.[4]

Galtung offers a particularly clear attempt to integrate the structures and the dynamics of the two systems. Much of the analysis in this chapter reflects the basic scheme set down in his model. Galtung argues that while class structures divide states domestically, they also correlate significantly with the overall pattern of relations among states. Thus the 'centre' versus 'periphery' (élites versus masses) class divide within states is reproduced globally in the 'centre' versus 'periphery' relations between the industrialised states and the Third World countries. Elites within the periphery states share many interests with élites at the centre. But while both sets of élites are at odds with their domestic peripheries, those in the Third World are more so than those at the centre, because they have fewer resources to distribute (because they are the periphery in the system overall). There is no harmony of interests between the periphery of the centre and the periphery of the periphery, because the relative advantage of the former depends on the maintenance of the system which exploits the latter. Although there are risks of over-simplification in a sweeping analysis of this type, it does have the considerable merit of clarifying how class interests permeate state behaviour, as in the case of North-South issues, and how state divides contribute to intra-class conflicts, as in the protectionist empire-building of the interwar years.

This dualistic approach to the international system(s) introduces three important factors into the analysis of national security: First, it enables us to refine the analysis of weak states by adding to it economic and class divides. Secondly, it gives us a set of economic entities to assess as objects of security. And thirdly, it opens up a new dimension of system structure which we can explore for security implications. Just as, in the last chapter, different configurations in the international anarchy were seen to have security implications, so also do different configurations in the international political economy.

Weak States and the International Political Economy

Domestic class structure, particularly the extent and intensity of disaffection between élites and masses, offers itself as an obvious factor in assessing the strength or weakness of a state. This factor can be added to the strength of the national idea to produce a crude matrix by way of illustrating how one might begin to refine the classification of states.

Figure 5.1 *Ethnic and class factors in the classification of states*

		Strength of division along national lines	
		High	*Low*
	High	India, Nigeria, S. Africa	Egypt, S. Korea, Italy
Strength of division along class lines			
	Low	Canada, Jugoslavia, Soviet Union, Belgium	USA, Japan, W. Germany Denmark

These classifications have little correlation with the strength or weakness of states as powers, but they suggest the kind of political threats to which specified states will be particularly sensitive. States which are highly divided along both lines will be vulnerable to both nationalist and leftist political attack, whereas those divided along one dimension, but relatively harmonious along the other, may, like South Korea and Canada, be able to employ the strong side to mask or mute the weak one. In some places, like South Africa and Brazil, there may be substantial correlations between ethnic and class divisions. A more far-reaching argument on the problem of weak states is opened up implicitly in the theories of Wallerstein and Galtung, and explicitly in the work of the *dependencia* school.[5] Their argument is that the relative strengths and weaknesses of state structures occur as a result of position within the capitalist world

economy, with states at the centre necessarily having strong structures, and those at the periphery necessarily having weak ones. Since
a centre-periphery structure is seen as necessary to the maintenance
of the capitalist system, we are confronted with a major intrusion of
economic dynamics into the structure of the international political
system. Even if Wallerstein, Galtung and the *dependencia* writers
have overstated their case, they have uncovered a point of great
importance to the analysis of immature and mature anarchies.

When the economic and political systems are considered simultaneously, weak states appear not only as a result of different levels of
development in a state system which is still young in historical terms,
but also as the product of a powerful economic dynamic. If weak
states were only a product of a different pace of development, then
time plus, perhaps, some external assistance would be sufficient to
ensure that they caught up. An assumption along these lines underlay
the discussion in the previous chapter about the prospects for
evolution towards a more mature form of international anarchy, and
the consequent improvement in the national security environment at
level 3. If, however, weak states also reflect an economic dynamic,
then they begin to look like a much more permanent feature of the
system, which will be maintained rather than eroded over time.
Economic and class interests operating from the centre, or linked to
it, would act to maintain the structure of weak states in the periphery
in order to sustain the relative advantage on which their dominance
rests. These are very large-scale arguments which we cannot hope to
resolve here. They raise many points of controversy, and even if they
are substantially correct may themselves eventually fall victim either
to the Marxist argument that a successful bourgeoisie works in the
long run to engineer its own downfall, or to the tendency of the
capitalist centre to shift location over time.[6]

For our present purposes, these arguments serve to highlight
several systemic aspects of the national security problem. They point
out a major security interest of the centre states which is located
outside their boundaries, and which therefore requires them to adopt
a security perspective expanded well beyond the national domain.
Part of their security is seen to rest on a pattern of economic relations
in the system, and this pattern links directly to the security problems
of weak states in the periphery. The internal security preoccupations
of periphery states can be seen to arise not only from their newness,
and their particular problems of state-building, but also from the
nature of their economic and class ties to the centre. This situation
could almost be characterised as a competition between a basic
political dynamic, which is to create strong states everywhere along
the lines of the phenomenally successful European leaders, and a

basic economic dynamic which is to sustain and expand the global economy in the interests of those élites who occupy its centre. As Calleo and Rowland put it: 'The elaborate economic interdependence of free-trade imperialism is obviously not without its political implications. It often promotes... political units lacking political or economic viability except as tributaries of the imperial power.'[7]

In pure form, the political dynamic would logically lead to a world of strong states. The pure economic dynamic, by contrast, would lead to a world divided between strong states at the centre and weak ones at the periphery, with a gradation of semi-periphery states in between. The centre would not be fixed on a particular set of states but would shift over time, as the economic forces at play migrated in search of optimum profit in response to shifting social, technological and political conditions. From this perspective, the economic factors act as a brake on the political dynamic, especially at the periphery, because the emergence of strong states there would tend to increase the disruptive penetration of national divisions into the international economy. The dropping out from the international economy of large, relatively strong states like the Soviet Union, China, and to a lesser extent, India, illustrates the economic problem posed by such political developments.[8]

These arguments identify a significant tension between economic interests and the development of a more mature international anarchy. In other words, the structure of the international economy defines some important elements of the national security problem. Not only must centre states define their security in reference to a pattern of dominance, but weak peripheral states find that their domestic security problems are part of a wider systemic phenomenon. Their insecurity is defined, in large part, by the structure of the international political economy.

Economic Entities as Objects of Security

A second issue raised by the dualistic approach to the international system(s) is the status of elements of the international economy as objects of security in their own right. The most obvious candidates here would be classes, but it is exceedingly difficult to apply a concept like security to an object like a class. As we have seen, states are decidedly ambiguous as objects of security. Classes are an even more amorphous group of entities, so much so that it is hard even to identify their physical boundaries. Classes have no behavioural unity in the physical and political senses that enable states and individuals to be identified as actors. They have interests and attitudes which can be identified, but they seldom have sufficient organisational coherence to produce policies, and cannot be seen as entities capable of providing for their own security in any collective sense. Although a class might have coherent interests, intra-class conflicts of interest are commonplace, and competition within a class may not exclude the use of force. The barons of industry are not less combative amongst themselves than were the nobility of fourteenth-century England, even if the dominant forms of struggle have altered somewhat. In addition, there is the problem of Marx's historically determinist argument about classes mentioned above. If a class like the bourgeoisie is destined to bring about its own destruction through the mechanism of its own success, how can we apply a notion like security to it in anything but the most superficial sense?

Similar sorts of problem arise in trying to apply security to other economic entities like corporations. Although one might speak of corporate security in a limited sense, the range of concerns it covers is much narrower than for national security. Corporations are, as a rule, creatures of functional convenience. They carry no sense of permanence about them as states do, and the ever-shifting environment of economic activity does not encourage great longevity in its collective players. Corporations can fail, be dismantled or be absorbed, with much less consequence than states, and such practice is a normal part of economic activity. It creates no general disturbance to the economic system, though it may, of course, have a considerable local impact.[9]

For these reasons, the concept of security is more useful when applied to political structures than to economic ones. Because of the overlap between economic and political systems, particularly in the form of the state as an economic unit, we can assume that the security interests of classes and corporations are largely vested in the states with which they are associated. This assumption tends in the direction of a now rather old-fashioned Marxist view that states are instruments of the dominant class, and therefore naturally oriented towards securing the interests of that class. As we have seen, however, the state has roots and dynamics of its own, additional to those of its ruling class. Acceptance of 'the relative autonomy of the state' is now common even amongst Marxist thinkers, and national security must therefore be seen as combining the interests of state and class without necessarily being wholly dominated by either.[10]

As we have seen, class economic interests may extend well beyond the boundaries of the state. This provides an awkward problem for national security, because it cannot be separated from state interests due to the extent to which state and class interests are intertwined. In the case of centre states, national security becomes bound up with the ability to maintain a controlling position which reaps sufficient advantage to underwrite domestic political stability. In peripheral states, the clash between state and class interests may be really stark. Ruling élites there may serve their own and centre élite interests only at the cost of a weak and strife-torn structure. Class and state security interests cannot be disentangled, and therefore neither operates unmediated by the effect of its ties to the other.

National security as a concept has to combine the two interests, and a model like Galtung's provides us with useful hints as to how to read sense into their interplay. In weak states, where the concept of national security begins to border on meaninglessness, we can look to national class structures and their external linkages to find the actors who lie at the heart of security behaviour. In centre states, where class antagonisms are usually much more muted, domestic security is a minor problem. Maintenance of that domestic harmony may well depend on continued control over external economic factors, however, and so class interests will determine a national security perspective with a substantial external orientation. In these ways, patterns deriving mostly from the international economy insinuate themselves into, and become inseparable from, the whole problem of national security. The structure and functioning of the international economy as a whole becomes a central factor in the security concerns of many of the states bound up in it, and so, like the structure of the international political system, constitutes a level 3 factor which is indispensable to understanding the apparently level 2 problem of national security.

Mercantilist versus Liberal Economic Systems

This discussion leads us to the third, and most important issue arising from the dualistic approach to the international system(s). Since we have treated the two systems as essentially separate entities, though heavily bound to each other, it becomes possible to look at the system as a whole in terms of the degree of harmony or compatibility between the economic and the political systems taken separately. That is to say, the character of the international system will vary according to whether the structures and dynamics of its economic and political sides fit together reasonably well, or are chained together at cross-purposes. Many combinations are theoretically possible, but it will be simplest to pursue this point by reference to the broad contemporary debate about the merits of mercantilist versus liberal approaches to structuring the international economy.[11] Put crudely, mercantilists seek to make the international economy fit with the pattern of fragmentation in the political system. They emphasise the integrity of the national economy, and advocate protection as a means of preserving it. By contrast, liberals seek to create a more unified, larger-scale, more interdependent global economy which transcends the fragmentation of the international anarchy by encouraging trade in a worldwide market. These alternatives can result in quite different styles of international system, in which not only the character of economic security changes, but also the character of the national security problem as a whole.

Our purpose in this exercise is to survey the arguments on both sides, and to see how they fit with the analysis of security which we have developed so far. This approach unfortunately cannot avoid the highly charged debate which surrounds the two positions. Liberalism and mercantilism represent strong normative as well as empirical schools, and their contending interpretations and prescriptions are often argued as if they represent the opposed sides in a zero-sum game. Our task would be difficult enough if these debates were only about economics, but both liberalism and mercantilism contain major assumptions and arguments about security as part of their overall doctrine. This aspect is why the debate between them is of such interest to our current inquiry. These doctrines contain almost the only coherent theories of security we have, and yet there exists very little connection between the political-economy literature in which they reside, and the Strategic Studies literature which is the principal outlet for thinking about security. In what follows we shall try to avoid the economic issues at stake as much as possible, and concentrate on how the security implications of the two doctrines mesh with the political structures of the international system. Because both doctrines are a mix of normative and empirical analysis, our argument will of necessity contain a mix – some might say a tangle – of historical and theoretical threads.

Mercantilism

Mercantilism was the reigning economic doctrine during the early centuries of the European state system, up to the triumph of Adam Smith's *Wealth of Nations*. The dominant impression it has left in the historical record is as a system of state power in which the international economy was treated as a zero-sum game. States sought economic advantage in order to increase their power, and purely economic objectives were subordinated to that end. Self-reliance was cultivated for its military utility, and the classical mercantalist system was one in which war over economic issues was acceptable practice.[12] The doctrine tolerated a conflictual international environment as the price to be paid for national security.[13]

The taint of war attached to mercantilism by its classical theory and practice was much reinforced by the advent of neo-mercantilism in the twentieth century. Both communist and fascist states espoused protectionist policies aimed at enhancing their military power. Although the swing towards mercantilism had begun in the late nineteenth century, the prime historical lesson drawn from it came from the disastrous experience of the 1930s. That decade, with its plunge into protectionism, extreme ideologies, imperialism and war, provided a case against mercantilism which, rightly or wrongly, became a principal historiographic prop of the post-1945 commitment to liberal economics. The 1930s case was widely taken as substantiating the view of mercantilism as a war-prone system, consequently justifying the turn to liberalism both as a preventive, and as a better system in its own right.[14] Since the Second World War, the negative image of mercantilism has also been sustained, at least in the West, by its association with the Soviet Union. The Soviet Union is widely perceived to fit the model of state economic control and self-reliance aimed at the accumulation of military power for aggressive purposes.

The problem with mercantilism is that, while it reduced vulnerability by encouraging the basic security of self-reliance, it accomplished this only at the cost of increased economic, political and military threats all round. Except for continental states, autarky along national lines imposes a major restraint on the imperatives towards greater economies of scale which have been a driving feature of economic development. This means that for most states greater self-reliance and firmer self-control on the national level must, under contemporary conditions of industrial economy, be bought at the risk of lower levels of economic growth. More dangerously, it means that states must contain within themselves the forces which push for economic growth if they are to avoid being impelled into economically-motivated conflict. To count on such containment may be hopelessly idealistic when the distribution of power among units is very uneven, and when the gains of one tend to equal the losses of another. In such a system states can hope to improve both their own level of domestic welfare, and their power relative to other actors, by embarking on policies of expansion. Expansion not only satisfies the economic dynamic, but also unleashes a Social-Darwinist tendency which is latent in the international political system. This tendency is free to operate unless checked by those factors we have associated with mature anarchic structures.

On this analysis, a mercantilist system would tend to produce a crude balance of power system in which the powerful states would build mercantilist blocs or empires among the weak, somewhat along the lines of the European powers up to 1914. If the imperative to growth remained unsatisfied when the system was reduced to a few large empires, then conflict among these would continue more fiercely, presumably until a universal empire, or a collapse into chaos, resulted. The danger of mercantilism is that it satisfies some level 2 criteria for security but, in so doing, creates a system structure that is unstable and conflict-prone for all its members. National security concerns in such a system would be centred either on the fear that national independence would fall victim to the economically-motivated expansion of more powerful states, or on the fear that one's relative power status and, therefore, in this dog-eat-dog system, one's security, would be eroded by the successful expansion of other powers. The security problems of mercantilism arise from the apparent inability of states to contain within themselves the factors necessary for sustained economic growth. Rather than resulting in the subordination of the economic system to the structure of the political system, the mercantilist approach risks resulting in the corruption of the state system by the forces of economic competition and expansion. As Calleo and Rowland put it: 'The great danger of mercantilism is its tendency to engage the power and prestige of states in economic competition for world markets.'[15]

Although both the classical and the neo-mercantilist experiences tend to support the view that mercantilism produces an unstable, war-prone system, there are many grounds on which that analysis can be attacked. The key question is not about what mercantilism did in the past, but about what effect it would have if applied under present conditions. The record of the seventeenth and eighteenth centuries can be largely discounted on the basis of the massive changes in economic and military conditions which have taken place since.

The 1930s experience is of much more recent vintage, and for that reason it occupies a prominent position in the case made against mercantilism on security grounds. One can argue, for example, that other factors unique to the 1930s explain its dismal record. These might include the character of the economic collapse, the violent nature of fascist ideology, the unbalanced conditions created by the First World War, the marginal roles being played by the Soviet

Union and the United States, and the peculiarly exposed economic positions of Germany, Japan and Italy. In as much as such period elements explain events, then the 1930s case is weakened as a general model for the effects of mercantilism. One can also argue that conditions found in the present era, but not available in the 1930s, contribute to invalidating any attempt to draw historical lessons. Thus nuclear weapons have adversely transformed the prospects for military imperialism.[16] Technology, population increase, and higher levels of wealth have greatly expanded the size of domestic markets.[17] The memory of the 1930s serves as a deterrent against a repeat performance.[18] And the system is now dominated by many more large actors which are inherently better suited to mercantilism than was the case in the 1930s (the United States, the Soviet Union, the European Community, China, India).

These arguments open up a broad field of debate which we do not have the space to explore here. They point to the existence of two views of mercantilism which Giplin has labelled 'malevolent' and 'benign'.[19] In the malign view, a mercantilist system is bound to reproduce its previous historical offering of competition and war. The economic dynamic, it is assumed, cannot be locked up within states without driving them into expansion, militarism and conflict. In the benign view, it is assumed that substantial protectionist behaviour can be adopted without triggering the slide into war. The crucial difference between these views, and the factor which might justify both of them, is what John Ruggie calls 'the social purpose' of the states involved. If the social purpose behind protectionism is the accumulation of state power, then the malign view is likely to be correct, because other states will be able to identify the motive and the danger. But if the intention is to serve domestic, political, economic and social objectives such as employment, monetary control, industrial adjustment and maintenance of key industries, then the outcome is much more likely to resemble the benign view, since other states will not see themselves threatened by a general power struggle. Malign mercantilism results from the pursuit of the warfare state, and benign mercantilism from pursuit of the welfare state.[20]

The benign view of mercantilism is of particular interest because it offers a form in which the political and economic systems can be brought into apparent harmony. It implies a degree of protectionism less rigorous than that of either the classical or the neo-mercantilist experience, but yet sufficient to go against the free-trade imperative of liberalism. It might be seen as the international counterpart of the mixed economy principle at the domestic level. In the context of security at level 3, benign mercantilism fits neatly into the model of a mature, super-state-based anarchy developed in the previous chapter. Super-states would provide both the internal economic scale, and the multipolar military stand-off, necessary to contain the dynamic of expansion. Furthermore, a benign mercantilist system would have a better chance of containing peacefully states with different organising ideologies. Liberal systems force a polarisation between capitalist and centrally-planned states, and malign mercantilism encourages a general alienation of each from all. Benign mercantilism perhaps offers a middle way in which divergent actors can relate to each other on more equal terms over the whole system.

Some present trends seem to favour an evolution in this direction, but many serious obstacles remain. Among these are the probability that many states now stuck in the periphery of a global centre would simply end up in the periphery of a bloc leader. If this happened, the problem of inequality and dependency would continue, but the centre-periphery structure would be transformed from a global system into a series of regional sub-systems. One might hope that a sense of regionalism would be sufficiently strong under these conditions to moderate exploitation of the periphery by the centre. In addition, considerable uncertainties still attach to even the most successful of the regional integration movements. The European Community and the Association of South-East Asian Nations (ASEAN) do not yet look like becoming super-states within the foreseeable future.

A credible, benign view of mercantilism is important because it serves not only to correct exaggerated conclusions about mercantilism generally, but also to sustain an alternative to the liberal model. If mercantilism is assumed to be malevolent, then a liberal system is the only acceptable alternative on offer. If mercantilism can be benign, however, then one is not stuck with a choice between a liberal system, and a reversion to less mature forms of anarchy.[21] Since, as we are about to argue, liberal economic systems are also deeply flawed in security terms, the availability of a third alternative becomes a matter of considerable significance.

Liberalism

In contrast to a mercantilist economic system, a liberal one exacerbates the disharmony between the economic and political structures by encouraging the development of a global-scale international economy. Although liberals have traditionally argued that free trade generates a harmony of interests, this doctrine, if it is true at all, only applies within the economic sphere. There is no convincing evidence that shared economic interests can override other sources of political dispute, especially not when the conditions necessary for their pursuit stand in serious contradiction with accepted political structures. There are many compelling arguments in favour of a liberal economic system, not the least being that it counteracts the mercantilist tendency towards zero-sum competition and war, and that it maximises the creation of wealth, which is instrumental to the realisation of so many other political values. For all its merits, however, a liberal economic system merely redefines, rather than abolishes, the national security problem. Because the international economy becomes more independent as a system in its own right, the international system as a whole becomes much more complicated. Economic actors assume important trans-national roles, and the fragmented political structure gets overlaid by the much celebrated bonds of interdependence. Patterns of production, consumption and finance spread beyond state boundaries to the point where levels of welfare, and even fulfilment of basic human needs, in any one country become dependent on activities and events in many others. In short, the liberal system gambles that high levels of economic interdependence will enhance security by reducing the motives for, and the utility of, resorts to military force. This gamble, however, is taken at the risk of increased vulnerability both to disruptive actions by others (intended or not), and to vagaries in the performance of the system as a whole.

Although the system can encourage a positive view of growth by others (if the Chinese had more money they could buy more goods produced in other places, therefore, growth in China would benefit external producers), in contrast to the more zero-sum perspectives of a mercantilist system (if the Chinese had more money, they would be more powerful and, therefore, constitute more of a threat), it does not eliminate economic threats. Higher interest rates in the United States, which may be imposed there for pressing domestic reasons, have a major impact on currency values and thus on trading positions in the rest of the system. Civil war in Iran jacks up the price of oil everywhere, and the development of more modern motorcycles in Japan destroys a long-established, but no longer innovative, industry in Britain. Asymmetries in the patterns of interdependence give some states a source of threat to wield over others, and periodic recessions, depressions and inflations run through the whole system, apparently beyond the control of any one actor.

The increased vulnerability to the performance of the world economy as a whole which results from interdependence is one of the major features which distinguishes the national security problem under a liberal system from that under a mercantilist one, where economic threats are more in the line of denial, or seizure, of vital resources. Several problems stem from it, and most of these relate to the tension created in the system by the liberal requirement to separate economic and political structures. The most obvious problem of interdependence is the significant loss of control by the state over its economic sector. If the system is working well, this loss may be more than compensated by increased levels of welfare. If the system is not working well, however, or if the state in question occupies a peripheral position within it, then the problem of interdependence may well outweigh its advantages. It is a common theme in writings on interdependence that loss of control by states over their economies raises economic issues to the status of national security problems because of the link between economic welfare and national political stability.[22]

The state must cope not only with the consequences of adverse activity elsewhere, be it fair market competition (Japanese motorcycles) or exploitation of monopolistic control (OPEC oil pricing), but also with malfunctions in the global economy as a whole. If domestic political and social structures have become conditioned or addicted to levels of welfare and expectation based on times when the system is working smoothly, then interruption of the pattern can have severe domestic impacts over which the state has only limited control. Governments can find most of their energies consumed by the problem of coping with external events in the context of an international environment that is complex and unpredictable. As Stanley Hoffmann puts it, 'each state is adrift on a sea of guesses', and each is engaged in a game of 'mutual and constant interference' in the affairs of others.[23] Disruptive inputs from the international economy can easily undermine the position of a particular government, raising the spectre of confusion between governmental and national security discussed in chapter 2. All of this occurs because of the separation between state and economic structures, and the consequent economic vulnerability of the state, which is fundamental to the liberal international economy.

The obvious answer to this problem is improved management of the global economy to even out the performance and minimise vulnerabilities, while not losing the advantage of superior productivity and welfare. We shall examine this option below, but first it is worth noting a more insidious effect of interdependence, which arises from Hoffmann's comment about 'mutual and constant interference'. While we can, as above, look at economic interdependence as a problem for states, it can also be seen more seriously as a major intrusion into, at times amounting to an assault upon, the anarchic state system itself.[24] The key issue here is the extent to which a liberal international economy imposes such critical constraints on the anarchic state system as to erode its basic character. In order to function effectively, the liberal system requires considerable uniformity of behaviour from its state members. They must allow relative freedom of economic movement, and must refrain from policies which produce gain for them at the expense of others. These restrictions on state behaviour are necessary if joint economic gain is to be pursued effectively.

Since the system is addictive, in the sense that states must restructure themselves extensively in order to participate in it, once such restructuring has occurred states increase their vulnerability to adverse behaviour by others, or to breakdowns in the system. If a country loses its self-sufficiency in basic foods in order to concentrate on more profitable export crops, then its welfare depends on the maintenance of complex trade-flows in a very fundamental way. No rapid conversion back to self-sufficiency will be possible. Because of this increased vulnerability, states naturally become more sensitive to domestic developments elsewhere which could cause disruptions in the system. Each state has a valid concern that domestic developments elsewhere do not take such a turn that damaging shock waves are sent out through the complex networks of interdependence. The converse of each state being dependent on others is that others are dependent on it, and this situation creates an intense and permanent pressure on the domestic politics of states which is wholly at odds with the underlying principles of the international political system. It means that developments in domestic politics are constrained within the rather tight confines of what will not cause damage to the functioning of the international economy. Political options which do not fit the requirements of the liberal economy become targets for external interests which would be jeopardised by their success. The pre-emptive 'destabilisation' of Allende's government in Chile to block a feared move towards a more revolutionary left regime provides a paradigm for this process.

A liberal international economy, then, cannot be separated conveniently from the state system. Its operating requirements feed back strongly into states with two effects: first, to restrict forms of government to those which are compatible with the functioning of a relatively open economy (this does not imply homogeneity, it may tend towards congenial democracies in some places and times, and repressive dictatorships in others); and second, to necessitate, and to some extent to legitimise, interventions designed to maintain or to restore such compatible governments. Both of these effects would be cause for concern about the political impact of a liberal international economy even if such an economy produced a tolerably even spread of benefits. But as argued above, there are grounds for suspicion that the liberal economy tends to produce and maintain a differentiated distribution of benefits in which a powerful centre exploits a weak periphery. Although the membership of the centre may change, the larger divide between centre and periphery is durable.

Under these conditions, the impact of the liberal economy on the international political system is much more serious, because it acts to retard the development of a more mature anarchy. Intervention in the periphery occurs to maintain governments which serve the needs of the centre, and of the international economy, even though such governments may not serve the local interest of building viable states. The resultant tension between the state-centred political dynamic and the system-centred economic one is plainly visible throughout the Third World, as a moment's reflection on cases like Brazil, Iran, Cuba and Vietnam will reveal. Many of the difficulties attending the concept of national security which we have explored in previous chapters clearly relate to this tension, not only in the context of weak states, but also as regards the impossibility of understanding a level 2 notion without extensive reference to factors on level 3. A liberal international economy both blurs the boundaries of states as entities, and gives a whole special meaning to the economic dimension of security.

Some of these problems, though not all, can be solved or mitigated by ensuring that the liberal economy works efficiently, and so provides not only the wealth with which other values can be realised, or at least pursued, but also the security of interdependence. To do this, as suggested above, requires some form of management which smooths out the performance of the system, provides the basic collective goods (such as an acceptable medium of exchange) necessary for its efficient functioning, and reduces the vulnerability risks to those participating (at the same time, of course, also reducing their opportunity to exploit asymmetric interdependence for private gain at the expense of other participants). Management on such a scale comes close to implying government, which is the one thing that the international political system in its anarchic form cannot provide.

Here again we encounter the basic tension between a liberal economy and a fragmented political system. In the absence of a higher political authority, the only feasible, effective management system is one centred on a hegemonic leader: an exceptionally powerful state capable of underwriting the international economy.[25] This role was first performed by Great Britain, and has been occupied by the United States since the Second World War. In as much as the liberal economy creates pressure for world government, as many functionalists and others of similar mind have hoped it would, then it goes directly against the statist dynamic of the international political system. Since that dynamic, as we have seen, has durable roots of its own, no resolution is at all likely, and world government enthusiasts seem doomed to a very long period of frustrated expectations. Such international institutions as have been developed so far tend much more to reinforce, than to replace the structure of the anarchic state system.[26] Although these collective organisations do not constitute an embryonic world government, their existence provides a major contribution to the maturity of the contemporary system. In as much as they resulted from the strong internationalist current which is part of liberal economic thought, they represent one of the major positive contributions of liberalism to international security.

Because these institutions play a coordinating, rather than an authoritative or commanding, role in the system, a liberal economy comes to depend for its effectiveness on hegemonic management. As a result, a whole new set of problems arises, many of them with security implications. A hegemonic leader, because of its own internal dynamics of class and state, is most unlikely to be able to separate its own domestic interests from its managerial role in the system. The managerial job is not without its costs and burdens, as well as its advantages, and it seems doubtful that any state would take it on unless its interests were already so engaged in the wider system that a broader responsibility appeared to be the best way to preserve and enhance them. The reluctance of the United States to take on the job in the interwar years is perhaps instructive in this regard, and certainly illustrates the powerful impact of domestic political factors on a state's external role. If we assume that a cost of hegemonic leadership is the adulteration of an (ideally) objective managerial role by a substantial strain of self-interest on the part of the hegemon, then several consequences of a liberal economy in the context of a political anarchy become clear.[27] Most obviously, the hegemon will tend to skew the management of the international economy in such a way as to serve its own interests. This has to be done with moderation, and with regard to other powers within the system, in order to retain general acquiescence to the hegemon's role. Such a distortion, however, points directly to the problem of centre and periphery, which we have already identified as a major embarrassment of the liberal economic system. More powerful states closer to the hegemon will gain from the management, and pay only moderately for the skew, while weak states at the periphery will be left carrying most of the strain.

An even more serious problem in the long run is the stability of a system which depends on a hegemonic power for its central management. Put bluntly, the problem is that hegemonic leaders do not last, and the process by which the role is transferred from one state to another inflicts periodic and dangerous transformations on the system as a whole. Here, the dynamic of the state system intrudes disruptively into that of the international economy. It can be argued that the role of hegemon is itself responsible for wearing out its incumbent, or merely that the distribution of power in the state system is always in motion, driven by a complex mass of factors that generate the rise and decline of states. Whichever is the case, a point comes where the presiding hegemon can no longer fulfil the managerial function. This happened to Britain during the interwar years, and by the 1970s there were signs that it was beginning to happen to the United States.

This transformational crisis could take many forms, ranging from a struggle among leading powers to capture the succession, to the decline of the system around its weakening hegemon resulting in some sort of relapse into a more mercantilist system. Collective leadership of some kind is, of course, a theoretical option, but is more difficult to establish and maintain (because requiring a much higher degree of co-operation and coordination) than a hegemonic order, and much more likely to relapse into a mercantilist system.[28] If there is a lesson from the 1930s experience, it seems to be not that mercantilist systems are necessarily dangerous and war-prone in their own right, but that the process of collapse from a liberal system into a protectionist one is where the danger lies.[29] Enthusiasts for the liberal system tend to ignore, or underrate the seriousness of the transition problem. Robert Gilpin, for example, unblushingly remarks that: 'Unfortunately, the world had to suffer two world conflicts before an American-centred liberal world economy was substituted for a British-centred one.'[30] Because national economies are geared up for the scale of a liberal system, the collapse of that system leads to concentrations of massive surplus capacity. Since domestic welfare has come to depend on utilisation of this capacity, the drive to capture resources and markets must be particularly strong in the period of retreat from a liberal system. The Japanese and German efforts during the 1930s illustrate this process.

If this analysis is correct, a major security implication of a liberal economic system is its tendency to periodic, and highly dangerous, collapse, associated with the decay of the hegemonic power. Since the liberal economic option is tied to hegemonic management, it is virtually doomed to suffer severe crises of leadership. The logic of this process becomes clearer if one assumes that liberal systems are created by hegemonic powers rather than, as it were, arising independently and generating a demand for leadership. If liberal systems are a direct product of hegemonic powers, then the fate of the system is more obviously tied to the fate of its leader. There is no reason, in theory, why a hegemonic leader could not use its advantaged position in the system to retain its capacity to dominate, but there are firm grounds for suspecting that this does not tend naturally to be the case. Put simply, the argument is that economic success tends to create political conditions which undermine, rather than sustain, ability to retain a dominant position. In a liberal system, economic success depends not only on size and wealth, but also on an ability to continue innovating at a rate sufficient to retain dominance in vital new areas of production. If economic success generates political demands which impair ability to adapt freely (in other words, if society decides to use its wealth to pursue other values, and to reduce its subordination to an unrestrained economic dynamic), then economic initiative will shift elsewhere, leading to a relative decline of the previously successful state.[31] Britain is a favourite contemporary example of a once successful economic power which has declined drastically in relative performance because domestic political constraints have severely damaged its ability to compete in an open international economy. The United States is feared by some to have the 'British disease', and Japan is the favoured example of a society somehow in tune with the needs of contemporary economic innovation and performance.

All of this adds up to a chronic cyclic leadership problem in the liberal international economy. As the hegemonic power ossifies because of its own success, it becomes increasingly less able to carry the burdens of system management. Domestic pressures force it into increasingly self-interested actions (protectionism, currency manipulations), which lead to increasing strain on the system and the erosion of confidence in it. At some point, a protectionist momentum takes over, and the system drops into a transition crisis. The crisis centring on the decline of Britain was much alleviated, though hardly made peaceful, by the existence of the United States as an obvious successor. From the middle of the Second World War, American policy could build on the widespread fear of economic collapse to restore a liberal system centred on itself. In doing so, the Americans explicitly cultivated a liberal system as a preventative of both the dangerous return to mercantilist conflict, and the spread of communism. Quite what would transpire in the absence of an obvious successor is a problem very germane to the current situation, and a major conundrum for enthusiasts of the liberal economic system.[32] The problem of recurrent leadership crises is a profound one, arising as it does from the fundamental antagonism between a global economic system and an anarchic political one. It means that, whatever its merits, while it is functioning well under a fresh hegemon the liberal system has a basic, and as yet unsolved, contradiction with the international political structure which makes it unstable over the long run.

To suggest this not only raises doubts about the overall desirability of the liberal system, but also focuses attention onto the peculiar security position of the hegemonic power itself. If the hegemonic power defines its security in terms of maintaining its role as hegemon, then it has to worry not only about external challenges to its leadership, but also about the dynamics of its own domestic development, which in the long run might pose much the greater threat to that objective than external challengers. For the hegemonic state, national security thus gets imported into the domestic sphere with peculiar force, but in a way that is very difficult to handle politically. National security so defined will depend on an ability to retain leadership in dynamic as well as in static terms. In other words, the hegemon can only retain its leadership by continuing to be the most successful economic innovator. But if occupation of the top position tends to erode conditions for superior adaptation, then the political structures resulting from success become themselves a core threat to national security. To propose, however, that one's own political structure, especially when it is that of a strong state, is itself a basic threat to national security, borders on logical absurdity, and would be a hard line to sell in a polity proud of, and confirmed by, its own success.[33]

Conclusions: Economic Systems and Security

Mercantilist and liberal economic systems create quite different international environments for national security. Although we have made only a superficial survey of the two economic alternatives, a number of key distinctions emerge. The mercantilist system carries the burden of its association with zero-sum competition and war, but because of its potentially better fit with the state system it can avoid many of the problems which come with a liberal international economy, particularly the insecurities of interdependence and the hazards of hegemonic leadership. Liberal systems, despite serious dangers, encourage an internationalist, system-oriented perspective, and undercut the link between prosperity and control of territory which drives the mercantilist system towards war. Variations in the economic system can raise threats to states either by affecting the overall propensity of the system for violent conflict, or by corroding the conditions which enable the state to function as a sovereign political entity. Economic systems also penetrate down through level 2 into level 1. The warfare versus welfare versions of mercantilism have obvious implications for individual security, as does the question of one's placing in the centre or in the periphery of the economic system. Liberal economics is strongly associated with individualist political philosophy, while mercantilism tends more to be associated with collectivist approaches. This connection takes us right back to the dilemma of minimal and maximal states discussed in chapter 1, with its essential contradiction between individual and national security.

Since neither liberalism nor mercantilism can generate a risk-free, peaceful international system, the security choice between them is not appealing. We may, however, find ourselves on the horns of a false dilemma created by the apparent mutual exclusivity of the two doctrines. As was warned above, liberalism and mercantilism contain normative as well as empirical elements. For this reason, they tend to be presented as opposed extremes, whereas in reality they exist on a spectrum where much blended middle ground exists.[34] From a security perspective, this middle ground is vital, for it offers the possibility of trying to capture the security advantages of both doctrines, while dampening their security costs. The discussion of benign mercantilism above was pushing towards this connecting zone, and there is no reason why such a system could not be labelled 'protected liberalism'. Putting a name to it, and treating it as an option in its own right, is important. Without a firm identity, the middle ground falls by default to the either/or choices which are implicit in the struggle between the proponents of liberalism and mercantilism.[35] If the choice really is either/or, then, as we have seen, the international economic system has nothing to offer us in the security realm except a choice of disasters.

We can conclude from this chapter and the last that national security cannot be dissociated from the character of the international system, in either its political or its economic dimensions. National security policy therefore must, if it is to be rational, belie its name and contain a strong international dimension.

Notes

1 Robin Murray, 'The Internationalization of Capital and the Nation State', *New Left Review*, 67 (1971), pp. 104–9.
2 On imperialism see, for example, J.A. Hobson, *Imperialism: a Study*

(London, Nisbet, 1902); V.I. Lenin, *Imperialism: the Highest Stage of Capitalism* (Moscow, Foreign Languages Publishing House, n.d.); David K. Fieldhouse (ed.), *the Theory of Capital Imperialism* (London, Longmans, 1967); David K. Fieldhouse, *Economics and Empire* (London, Weidenfeld & Nicolson, 1973); E.M. Winslow, *The Pattern of Imperialism* (New York, Columbia University Press, 1948). On interdependence see, for example, Robert O. Keohane and J.S. Nye, *Power and Interdependence* (Boston, Little Brown, 1977); R. Rosecrance and A. Stein, 'Interdependence: Myth or Reality?', *World Politics*, 26 : 1 (1974); Richard Rosecrance *et al.*, 'Wither Interdependence?', *International Organization*, 31 :3 (1977); David Baldwin, 'Interdependence and Power', *International Organization*, 34:4 (1980); J.N. Rosenau, *The Study of Global Interdependence* (London, Frances Pinter, 1980). On contemporary international political economy, see, for example, Charles P. Kindleberger, *Power and Money* (London, Macmillan, 1970); Klaus Knorr, *Power and Wealth* (London, Macmillan, 1973); David H. Blake and Robert S. Walters, *The Politics of Global Economic Relations* (New Jersey, Prentice-Hall, 1976); David P. Calleo and Benjamin Rowland, *America and the World Political Economy* (Bloomington Indiana, Indiana University Press, 1973); Joan E. Spero, *The Politics of International Economic Relations* (London, Allen & Unwin, 1977).

3   Immanuel Wallerstein, 'The Rise and Future Demise of the World Capitalist System', *Comparative Studies in Society and History*, 16 :4 (1974). For a critique, see Aristide R. Zolberg, 'Origins of the Modern World System: A Missing Link', *World Politics*, 33 :2 (1981); Johan Galtung, 'A Structural Theory of Imperialism', *Journal of Peace Research*, 8:2 (1971); Richard K. Ashley, *The Political Economy of War and Peace* (London, Frances Pinter, 1980). This is based on the earlier work by Nazli Choucri and Robert C. North, *Nations in Conflict: National Growth and International Violence* (San Francisco, W.H. Freeman, 1975); Ralph Pettman, *State and Class: A Sociology of International Affairs* (London, Croom Helm, 1979).

4   Leonard Tivey, 'States, Nations and Economies', in L. Tivey (ed.), *The Nation-State* (Oxford, Martin Robertson, 1981), ch. 3.

5   Wallerstein, *op. cit.* (note 3), pp. 390–412; and Galtung, *op. cit.* (note 3), pp. 85–91. From the *dependencia* school, see André Gunder Frank, *On Capitalist Underdevelopment* (Bombay, Oxford University Press, 1975); André Gunder Frank, *Dependent Accumulation and Underdevelopment* (London, Macmillan, 1978); Pettman, *op. cit.* (note 3), pp. 157–61; *International Organization*, 32 :1 (1978), special issue on 'Dependence and Dependency in the Global System'; Tony Smith, 'The Underdevelopment of Development Literature', *World Politics*, 21 :2 (1979); André Gunder Frank, 'The Development of Underdevelopment', *Monthly Review*, 18 :4 (1966). For a critique of these literatures, see R. Brenner, 'The Origins of Capitalist Development', *New Left Review*, 104 (July-August 1977).

6   Johan Galtung, 'A Structural Theory of Imperialism – Ten Years

Later', *Millennium*, 9:3 (1980–1), pp. 186–7, argues that the centre of capitalism is now in the process of shifting towards east Asia.

7   Calleo and Rowland, *op. cit.* (note 2), p. 11; see also ch. 9.

8   Such dropping out is clearly easier for large states than for small ones, whether they are strong or weak. Larger states tend to be more self-contained economically, as indicated by lower proportions of GNP traded externally, and therefore have an autarkic option much more easily to hand than do smaller states.

9   For one view of corporate security strategies, see John K. Galbraith, *the New Industrial State* (Boston, Houghton Mifflin, 1967). See also Robert Skidelsky, 'Prophet of the Liberal State', *Times Literary Supplement* (7 August 1981); and Calleo and Rowland, *op. cit.* (note 2), ch. 7.

10 Fred Block, 'Marxist Theories of the State in World System Analysis', in Barbara H. Kaplan (ed.), *Social Change in the Capitalist World Economy* (Beverly Hills, Sage, 1978), pp. 27–8. Few Marxists, I suspect, would accept the separate political dynamic which I have argued here as the source of the relative autonomy of the state. According to Block (pp. 33–6) their shift of view away from direct class control is more in response to the structural complexities of the pluralist politics which underlie state behaviour. This line of argument ties into the pre-occupation of liberal thinkers during the eighteenth and nineteenth centuries with the existence of a militaristic aristocracy which controlled the state and was seen to be responsible for the malaise of war. Much liberal argument was devoted to removing this class, not least by encouraging free trade so as to undermine its economic base. Notions that the character of the ruling class was responsible for war continued in the socialist tradition, but have now largely been replaced by more diffuse structural explanations for war. For an excellent review of these ideas and their development, see Michael Howard, *War and the Liberal Conscience* (Oxford, Oxford University Press, 1981 (1978)).

11 For a general outline of the mercantilist versus liberal arguments, see Robert Gilpin, 'Three Models of the Future', in his *U.S. Power and the Multinational Corporation* (London, Macmillan, 1976/New York, Basic Books, 1975), ch. 9; also in *International Organization*, 29:1 (1975). I am not using these terms to describe the two strictly-defined and highly-polarised alternatives of economic theory, but to indicate the broadly opposed tendencies of free trade versus protectionism. To avoid unnecessary complications I use the term mercantilist to include both the classical and the neo-mercantilist perspectives.

12 On mercantilism, see Philip W. Buck, *The Politics of Mercantilism* (New York, Octagon Books, 1974 (1942)); Eli F. Heckscher, *Mercantilism* (London, Allen & Unwin, 1955 (1935)); Jacob Viner, 'Power versus Plenty as Objectives of Foreign Policy in the Seventeenth and Eighteenth Centuries', *World Politics*, 1 (1948).

13 Buck, *op. cit.*, pp. 113–21.

14 Versions of this view can be found, *inter alia*, in Robert Gilpin, 'Economic Interdependence and National Security in Historical Perspective', in Klaus Knorr and Frank N. Trager (eds), *Economic Issues and*

National Security (no place. Regents Press of Kansas, 1977), p. 55; L.B. Krause and J.S. Nye, 'Reflections on the Economics and Politics of International Economic Organizations', in C.F. Bergsten and L.B. Krause (eds), *World Politics and International Economics* (Washington, DC, Brookings Institution, 1975), pp. 324–5; Fred Hirsch and Michael Doyle, 'Politicization in the World Economy: Necessary Conditions for an International Economic Order', in Fred Hirsch *et al., Alternatives to Monetary Disorder* (New York, McGraw Hill, 1977), pp. 14–20. For an opposing interpretation, see David P. Calleo, 'The Historiography of the Interwar Period; Reconsiderations', in Benjamin Rowland (ed.), *Balance of Power or Hegemony: the Interwar Monetary System* (New York, New York University Press, 1976).

15   Calleo and Rowland, *op. cit.* (note 2), p. 140.

16   This point is made by Harold von B. Cleveland, in David P. Calleo *et al., Money and the Coming World Order* (New York, New York University Press, 1976), pp. 6–7.

17   This argument relates to Hobson's point about curing imperialism by expanding internal markets. See Fieldhouse, *Theories, op. cit.* (note 2), p. 72.

18   Cleveland, *op. cit.* (note 16), p. 7.

19   Gilpin, *op. cit.* (note 11), pp. 234–5.

20   John G. Ruggie uses the idea of 'social purpose' to discuss differences between liberal regimes, but it applies also to mercantilist ones. See 'International Regimes, Transactions and Change; embedded liberalism in the postwar economic order', *International Organization*, 36 :2 (1982). I am indebted to him for several of the insights in this paragraph, and for the use of the terms 'welfare' and 'warfare' states in this context.

21   David P. Calleo, 'The Decline and Rebuilding of an International Economic System', in Calleo *et al., op. cit.* (note 16), argues for a benign mercantilist system as an alternative to the current declining liberal order. Douglas Evans, *the Politics of Trade: the Evolution of the Superbloc* (London, Macmillan, 1974), argues that a mercantilist bloc system is emerging, though he does not share Calleo's benign view of it. Hirsch and Doyle, *op. cit.* (note 14), also seem to be arguing for some kind of benign mercantilism with their suggestion for 'controlled disintegration' as an approach to the decay of the post-1945 liberal system. Charles P. Kindleberger, 'Systems of International Economic Organization', in Calleo *et al., op. cit.* (note 16), pp. 28–30, gives a critique of the mercantilist bloc position.

22   See, for example, the chapters by Klaus Knorr, C.A. Murdock and Robert Gilpin in Knorr and Trager (eds)., *op. cit.* (note 14), pp. 1–98; and Edward L. Morse, 'Interdependence in World Affairs', in J.N. Rosenau, K.W. Thompson and G. Boyd (eds), *World Politics* (New York, Free Press, 1976), ch. 28.

23   Stanley Hoffmann, *Primacy or World Order* (New York, McGraw-Hill, 1978), pp. 132, 135.

24   This theme was explored, from a different angle, in Raymond Vernon, *Sovereignty at Bay* (Harmondsworth, Penguin, 1973 (1971)).

25   Charles P. Kindleberger, *the World in Depression, 1929–1939* (Berkeley, University of California Press, 1974), is the principal advocate of the necessity for hegemonic leadership in a liberal system. A more abstract, theoretical case for the commanding advantage of hegemonic leadership can be derived from the theory of collective goods, for which the *locus classicus* is Mancur Olson, *The Logic of Collective Action* (Cambridge, Mass., Harvard University Press, 1965). For other arguments supporting this view, see Stephen D. Krasner, 'State Power and the Structure of International Trade', *World Politics*, 28:3 (1976); Robert Gilpin, *op. cit.* (note 11); and Robert O. Keohane, 'The Theory of Hegemonic Stability and Changes in International Economic Regimes 1967–1977', in Ole Holsti *et al.* (eds), *Change in the International system* (Boulder, Col., Westview Press, 1980). Two other possibilities exist for managing a liberal world economy. The first is collective management leadership of some sort. Writers who otherwise disagree seem to find consensus in rejecting this as impracticable: see, for example, Kindleberger and Calleo, in Calleo *et al., op. cit.* (note 16), pp. 35–7, 51–2; and Charles P. Kindleberger, 'Dominance and Leadership in the International Economy', *International Studies Quarterly*, 25:2/3 (1981), p. 253. The second is management without leadership under agreed rules. This would appear to be such a weak form of liberal system as to be indistinguishable from the liberal end of the benign mercantilist view. For discussion of it, see Cleveland, *op. cit.* (note 16); Calleo, *op. cit.* (note 21), pp. 53–6; Lewis E. Lehrman, 'The Creation of International Monetary Order', in Calleo *et al., op. cit.* (note 16); and Ruggie, *op. cit.* (note 20).

26   See John G. Ruggie, 'On the Problem of "the Global Problematique": What Roles for International Organizations?', *Alternatives*, 5:4 (1980).

27   For a useful survey of the requirements of management in a liberal economy, see Krause and Nye, *op. cit.* (note 14). On the problem of self-interest in hegemonic management, see Calleo, *op. cit.* (note 21), pp. 44–51); Calleo, *op. cit.* (note 14), p. 259; and Kindleberger, *op. cit.* (note 25, *ISQ*).

28   See note 25.

29   Calleo, *op. cit.* (note 14), pp. 246–60. J.M. Keynes foresaw the war danger that lay in the transition from a liberal to a mercantilist system, and also the political merits of a neo-mercantilism. See J.M. Keynes, 'National Self-Sufficiency, I and II', *The New Statesmen and Nation*, 4:124 and 125, 8 and 15 July 1933.

30   Gilpin, *op. cit.* (note 11), p. 259.

31   On the thesis that hegemonic states tend automatically to decline, see Wallerstein, *op. cit.* (note 3), pp. 410–12; Knorr, Murdock, Gilpin and Meltzer, in Knorr and Trager, *op. cit.* (note 14), pp. 1–8, 58–60, 67–8, 70–2, 215; C.F. Bergsten, Robert Keohane and J.S. Nye, 'International Politics and International Economics: a framework for analysis', *International Organization*, 29:1 (1975), pp. 11–18; Keohane, *op. cit.* (note 25); Krasner, *op. cit.* (note 25), p. 320; Kindleberger, *op. cit.* (note 25, *ISQ*), pp. 250–3; Gilpin, *op. cit.* (note 11), p. 258; and Calleo and

Rowland, *op. cit.* (note 2), pp. 85–117, 196–7. Some of the arguments used here apply also to the more general problem of domestic adaptation to a liberal world economy which was made on pp. 139–43. These problems affect all participating states, but their impact on the hegemonic state has more serious implications for the stability of the system overall. See, in addition, on the adaptation problem, William Diebold Jr, 'Adaptation to Structural Change', *International Affairs*, 54 :4 (1978).

32 The problem of findings a successor poses obvious difficulties for any cyclic theory of liberal decline. It may be that a inverted perspective on the problem is more useful, in which the availability of a hegemonic leader is seen not only as a precondition for a liberal system, but also as an exceptional condition in the international system. Only when a single state rises to a dominant position do the necessary security and other conditions for a liberal economy occur. The liberal system *requires* general security before it can, ostensibly, generate it. Since the balance of power should normally prevent a hegemon from emerging the sequence of Britain and the United States comprises an unusual coincidence. Britain emerged as a hegemon because of its early lead in the system-transforming process of industrialisation, and the United States because of the general collapse of other power centres resulting from the Second World War. Hirsch and Doyle, *op. cit.* (note 14), pp. 34–43, lean in this direction when they argue that the post-1945 liberal system was based on 'special, rather than general' supporting conditions, (p. 34). So also does Evans, *op. cit.* (note 21), p. viii, when he argues that mercantilism is the norm in modern world economic history. If this view is taken, then the argument against a liberal system would have to be modified to state that hegemonic collapse would be inevitable, but not necessarily cyclic. See also Ruggie, *op. cit.* (note 20), for the argument that a form of liberal system can be maintained without a hegemonic leader.

33 Richard J. Barnet, 'The Illusion of Security', in Charles R. Beitz and Theodore Herman (eds), *Peace and War* (San Francisco, W.H. Free-man, 1973), pp. 285–7; and Franz Schurmann, *the Logic of World Power* (New York, Pantheon, 1974), pp. xxvi–xxvii, 40–68; both explore domestic structures as part of the national security problem of the United States.

34 For an example of the intellectual squeeze created by accepting mercantilism and liberalism as irreconcilable opposites, see Robert Gilpin, *War and Change in World Politics* (Cambridge, Cambridge University Press, 1981), pp. 219–23.

35 Calleo and Rowland, *op. cit.* (note 2), pp. 140–2, 252–9, argue for a version of this middle ground system, as, in a very different way, does John Ruggie, *op. cit.* (note 20). Ruggie argues that the post-war liberal system has many features of a middle-ground option – he labels it 'embedded liberalism' – and that consequently it should not be strictly compared in terms of its likely evolution to the British-dominated liberal regime of the nineteenth century.

6 The Defence Dilemma

In the previous two chapters we explored various aspects of the international system which bear on the problem of national security. From that discussion, it became clear not only that level 3 sets several major conditions for national security, but also that it is an active and changing component in its own right. In this and the next chapter we shall stay on the system level, and turn our attention to some of the more specific interaction dynamics which take place among states. These dynamics affect their security affairs both as to position (are they secure, and do they feel so?) and as to policy (what policies are required to pursue or maintain national security?). Having examined the pieces and the board, in other words, we shall now look at some patterns in the process of play.

Much of the emphasis here will be on military matters, reflecting the traditional dominance which these exercise in national security thinking, and the purpose of the exercise is to complete the groundwork for our consideration of national security policy in chapter 8. In the international system, as Robert Osgood points out, 'the primary instrument of order – armed force – is also the primary threat to security'.[1] This paradox underpins the widely-held view that military power lies at the heart of the national security problem. States in an anarchy require it both for their own security and for purposes of system management. But once acquired, it generates a counter-security dynamic of its own which threatens both individual states and the system as a whole. Osgood argues that 'force must be as essential to international politics in an anarchy as elections are to domestic politics in an organized democracy'.[2] Hedley Bull supports this view from a different angle by arguing that 'the international order is notoriously lacking in mechanisms of peaceful change, notoriously dependent on war as the agent of just change'.[3] Michael Howard draws the bottom line on the matter, arguing that 'force is an ineluctable element in international relations, not because of any inherent tendency on the part of man to use it, but because the

156

_*possibility* of its use exists. It has thus to be deterred, controlled, and if all else fails, used with discrimination and restraint.'[4] He goes on to identify one of the basic engines of the whole military problem in international relations, which is that 'those who renounce the use of force find themselves at the mercy of those who do not'.[5]

The deployment of military instruments by states gives rise to the problem of war, and war has become a major area of study, indeed almost a field in its own right. The study of war has produced some classic works in international relations,[6] and war relates intimately to the problem of national security. The whole question of what causes conflict between states is as germane to the study of security as it is to the study of war. Other than explanations based on human nature, the favoured sources of conflict and war are the nature of the state, and the pattern or structure of relations among states.[7] These explanations at levels 2 and 3 can be combined into two general types: those which emphasise direct competition and hostility among states as the prime source of conflict, and those which emphasise the conflict-producing behaviours of states, or patterns of relations in the system, which do not reflect intentional action.

The first type reflects the Realist view of the international system as a struggle for power. Actors are assumed to be opportunist and the immature anarchy features of the system are stressed. Causes are sought in domestic features like fascism, communism or capitalism, in historical grievances, in the character of leaders, and in patterns of power distribution which provide opportunity and/or provoke revisionism. We shall refer to this type of explanation for conflict as the *power struggle*. The second type reflects a more moderate view of the international system as a struggle for security. Actors are assumed to be self-concerned, but still generally well-intentioned, and the prospects for a mature international anarchy are given prominence. Causes are sought in the structural dynamics of states and the system, such as fragmented and incremental decision-making procedures, misunderstandings and misperceptions, arms racing, and the sheer complexity of interest and attitudes in a system of complex interdependence. We shall refer to this mode of analysis as the *security struggle*. These two struggles are central to any understanding of the national security problem. Their dynamics, and the *power-security dilemma* which their interaction creates, are the subject of the next chapter.[8] There is a related dilemma which possesses a distinct logic of its own. This we shall call the *defence dilemma*, and we shall consider it first.[9] These two dilemmas, and the interaction between them, express the essence of the military dimension of the national security problem.

The Defence Dilemma Defined

The defence dilemma arises not from the dynamics of relations among states, although these do contribute to it, but from the nature and dynamics of military means as they are developed and deployed by states. To a very considerable extent the development of military means follows a logic which is separate from the patterns of amity and enmity among states. Although such patterns may accelerate military developments, as during war, or strongly affect particular cases, as in the Anglo-German naval race prior to 1914, they do not fundamentally determine the scientific, technological and organisational imperatives which drive the creation of ever-more powerful military means. Problems in state relations provide the demand which stimulates military improvement, and this we shall deal with when we look at the power-security dilemma. But the forces which produce military improvement, particularly in technological terms, are quite separate, and require that we deal with the defence dilemma as a phenomenon in its own right. The defence dilemma arises from inconsistencies and contradictions that exist between military defence and national security. Armed forces are justified principally by their necessity for national security, and it is often assumed, particularly for reasons of political expediency, that military might is positively correlated with national security. Since neither concept is amenable to quantification, the proposition cannot be tested, but we can, none the less, point out ways in which defence and security fail to coincide.

The defence dilemma can come in several forms. In the milder cases defence measures are inappropriate or irrelevant to security. The most compelling illustration of this comes from the discussion of economic interdependence in the previous chapter. Where states have major economic and political stakes in the maintenance of an international economy, many of their core interests cannot be effectively protected by military power. The European states, for example, can use military means neither to enhance their benefits from, nor protect their vulnerabilities to, contact with the Japanese economy. A more serious case of a mild defence dilemma arises when defence by military means becomes impossible because offensive weapons have a marked advantage of some sort over the defensive weapons available against them. The developments of aircraft and missiles, and then of nuclear weapons, have given a massive impetus to the offensive strike which has been a feature of this century ever since the end of the First World War, and which has seriously undermined the traditional ability of the territorial state to protect itself against military attack.[10] These weapons meant that the state could be severely damaged or punished without being defeated in a full-scale war, and consequently that traditional defence postures no longer carried the same security significance as previously. They provided the truth for Baldwin's prescient, if premature, comment that 'the bomber would always get through' and, in so doing, seriously undermined defence as the basic idea on which security policy could be based.

The most serious defence dilemmas occur when military measures actually contradict security, in that military preparations in the name of defence themselves pose serious threats to the state. These threats can take the form of economic damage, or social and political dislocation, caused by military mobilisation beyond the state's needs or capabilities. More seriously, they can take the form of unacceptable damage, either self-inflicted, or risked as part of an explicit policy involving relations with other states. An example of self-inflicted damage would be a ballistic missile defence (BMD) system which itself involved low-altitude nuclear bursts over the territory to be defended. Such a system might defend specified targets, such as missile silos, only at the cost of inflicting substantial radiation damage on softer targets, like cities.

The whole system of nuclear deterrence is the clearest example of a defence dilemma arising from the risk assumed in an overall defence policy. Deterrence connects a serious contradiction between defence and security to a simpler form of defence dilemma in which traditional defence has become impossible because of advances in strike weapons technology. When the simpler dilemma applies between two states armed with nuclear weapons and disposed to treat each other as enemies, their only logical military option is to rest their 'defence' on policies of assured retaliation. Under such circumstances, a convincing case can be made that the interests of both are served by remaining vulnerable to the other's strike (to ensure that incentives to strike first remain minimal on both sides) – the famous policy of 'mutually assured destruction', or MAD. Whatever its merits, and under nuclear conditions they are considerable, deterrence policy basically proposes to defend the state by a strategy which threatens to destroy it. The war-preventing objective of deterrence policy is linked by a horrible logic to credible threats of apocalyptic destruction. Not surprisingly, many people see themselves as potential victims of this arrangement and find it unacceptable, as well as absurd, thus raising the disharmony between individual and national security discussed in chapter 1. With nuclear weapons, one's perception of security no longer depends, as traditionally, on which end of the weapon one is facing. The defence dilemma arises because technological developments have inflated military means to such an extent that a general threat of destruction is the only militarily logical means of providing national defence. Given the uncertainties involved in the possession and control of such weapons, many individuals conclude that the weapons themselves, and the system of relations they create, detract from, rather more than they offer to, the pursuit of security. One such is Richard Barnet, who argues that

There is no objective, including the survival of the United States as a political entity, that merits destroying millions or jeopardizing the future of man. The pretence that it is legitimate to threaten nuclear war for political ends creates an international climate of fear in which Americans will continue to have less security, not more.[11]

Since force, as we have argued, appears to be a necessary feature of an anarchic international system, which itself appears to be a durable and persistent structure, the defence dilemma poses a substantial conundrum for national security policy over the foreseeable future. For these reasons, it is worth probing into the historical momentum which underlies the defence dilemma. In particular, we need to get some sense of whether the defence dilemma can be resolved, or at least muted, in some way, or whether the forces which drive it are so deep and strong that it is likely to remain a permanent feature on the security landscape.

The Historical Development of the Defence Dilemma

For reasons argued in chapter 3, military threats traditionally take pride of place in the hierarchy of national security priorities. Political philosophies based on the state of nature image place the function of protection against violence at the very foundations of the state. In the real world, military threats pose the most direct, immediate and visible danger to state security, and military means have frequently proved useful against both military and non-military threats. The political, economic and cultural sectors of the nation's life must be strong enough to survive the rigours of competition within their own sectors and on their own terms, but none of them can reasonably be expected to be strong enough to withstand coercive pressure or violent disruption. State military forces provide protection for these sectors against 'unfair' threats of force, and, in the process, maintenance of an adequate military establishment becomes itself a national security interest.

History is full of heroic examples of military force being used to save cultural, political and economic values from violent overthrow – the Ancient Greeks turning the Persian tide at Marathon and Salamis, the Franks stemming the Moslem conquest of France at Tours (732), the raising of the Ottoman siege of Vienna (1683), and the defeat of fascism in Europe in 1945, to name just a few. The fact that these examples are offset by as many defeats and occupations – the destruction of the Incas by Spanish *conquistadores*, the obliteration of Carthage by Rome, several partitions of Poland, colonial conquests too numerous to mention – merely underlines the prudence of being well-armed. For all these reasons, military factors have dominated national security considerations and national defence has, at least until recently, been almost synonymous with national security.

National defence has its conceptual foundations in the largely bygone days when most important state interests could be protected by military force. A monarchical state with a largely self-contained, mercantilist economy, like France during the early eighteenth century, suggests an ideal type of state for national defence. Domestic security could be enforced by the army and the local nobility, and few structures existed to facilitate the political mobilisation of opposition whether internally or externally inspired. Trade was not crucial to national survival, and to a considerable extent could be protected by military means and by the structure of empire. External threats were primarily military in nature, and the available military technology meant that they were slow moving. Military strength depended largely on domestic resources and could be used to seize, as well as defend, most things held to be of national value. War was a useable, if sometimes expensive and frequently uncertain, instrument of state policy. Ideology and economic interdependence scarcely existed as issues of political significance.

The classical image of national defence thus rests on an essentially autarkic notion of the state as a unit self-contained and self-reliant in all the major political, economic and cultural elements of life. Its principal military need was to defend its domestic universe from disruption by external military attack or internal disorder. Although pristine models of this sort are rare in reality, the ideal type is a useful reference when considering national defence. Tokugawa Japan (1600–1868) illustrates an extreme case in which the Shoguns restricted contact with the outside world to a small, tightly-controlled, trade outlet. The United States during the first half of the twentieth century also fits the model in many respects: it had no neighbours of military consequence, dominated military and economic relations in its hemisphere, was nearly beyond the reach of major military action by other powers, at least on its continental territories, and enjoyed substantial economic self-reliance within its sphere.

If we ignore for the time being the realm of military aggression in the Napoleonic, Hitlerian and empire-building senses, national defence implies a self-contained, self-reliant and rather passive outlook. The state provides itself with means of defence according to the threats it perceives and the resources at its disposal, and relies on these to deter the threats, or else to meet them should they materialise. War is not desired, but neither is it feared excessively. Defences are adjusted to meet variations in tension and changes in the pattern of threat, and although conditions may necessitate defensive alliances, self-reliance in the tradition of British and American splendid isolation is the preferred mode. In the national defence orientation, the emphasis is primarily on the state and its military capabilities, taking likely rivals into account, and on the balance of power dynamics of the international system.

In Europe the supporting conditions for the idea of national defence were deteriorating rapidly by the end of the nineteenth century. Economic activity had expanded beyond national and empire boundaries to such an extent that military means could no longer protect all the main elements of the national economic interest. The First World War devalued the concept mightily. Not only did it reveal the extent of economic interdependence, but aerial bombing and maritime blockade shook the idea that the state could be protected behind the military lines. The new military technologies revealed a terrifying amplification of the hazards and uncertainties of the military instrument, and seriously devalued the notion that war could be a useful or casual tool of state policy. This explains the attraction of the collective security policy associated with the League of Nations. Collective security sought to replace national defence during the interwar years, and reflected European disillusionment with war and defence. It is significant that the United States did not participate in the League, because for the Americans the supporting conditions for national defence remained largely unimpaired.

Collective security began to gain favour over national defence during the interwar years because the experience of the First World War had gravely weakened one of the conditions on which national defence was based: that war is an acceptable instrument of policy. If war is feared as a major threat in its own right, then defence is devalued as a posture, but military insecurity is not eliminated as a problem. Most traditional military threats remained alive, and in addition all actors were threatened by war because it had become so violent and costly that it could easily destroy, or at least damage seriously, the fabric of the state. Because of the experience of the First World War, fear of war began to rival fear of defeat as the prime concern of national security policy.[12] Fear of war among the masses became politically significant enough to threaten traditional policies aimed at meeting fear of defeat. Some form of collective security arrangement was an obvious response when doubt was cast on the self-help tradition of national defence, and history offers us a number of previous examples.

War-weariness and fear of war are a recurrent phenomenon in international relations, usually appearing after a bout of prolonged, widespread and destructive warfare, like the Thirty Years War (1618–48), the French Revolutionary and Napoleonic Wars (1792–1815), the First World War, and the Second World War. In the case of the Thirty Years War, the concluding Treaties of Westphalia (1648) are normally taken to indicate the founding of the European state system, and we cannot therefore easily compare conditions then with those when the system already existed. After such wars, war-prevention assumes a high priority, and something more than a self-reliant defence policy is required. The favoured technique is to institute measures of co-operation and consultation among the larger powers, with a view to preventing war by moderating and restraining the free-for-all operation of the international anarchy. The Congress system set up in 1815, the League of Nations and the United Nations all illustrate this conceptual shift from national defence to collective security.[13] Unfortunately, none of these attempts endured as a major controlling element in international security relations.

This failure is surprising in as much as there has been a strong tendency, especially since the First World War, for the fear of war to increase. Whereas after the Napoleonic Wars the fear of war faded along with the generational memory of those who experienced it, after 1918 the fear of war was nurtured and strengthened by rapid and obvious increases in the destructiveness of new weapons. The First World War inflicted a greater shock on European civilisation than any previous upheaval, threatening not only revolutions in the social structure of states and the composition of the state system, but also posing a real prospect that European civilisation itself would be heavily damaged, if not destroyed, by a repeat performance. The war proved not only uncertain in outcome, as war had traditionally been, but unpredictable and largely uncontrollable in process as well. Once started, the war seemed to gather a momentum of its own, grinding up life and wealth at stupendous rates, making a nonsense of centuries of military doctrine and wisdom, and forcing social mobilisation on such a scale that governments could neither control all the forces they had unleashed, nor maintain the traditional separation between foreign policy and domestic mass politics. Under such conditions, the 'war to end war' propaganda which some governments had used as a mobilising tool took root in the post-war environment, feeding on new fears of apocalypse arising from the combination of gas warfare and long-range bombing aircraft. The Second World War proved the exaggeration of these fears, but ended with the appalling mushroom cloud over Hiroshima, which de-monstrated beyond doubt that the error was merely one of timing, and not of analysis. After such a demonstration, few could question the rationality of the fear that the next major war would devastate its participants to such an extent as to render meaningless any notion of national defence.

By 1945 advances in military technology had undercut the idea of national defence in several ways. The domestic sanctity of the state could be neither protected nor preserved. Total mobilisation required massive, and not necessarily reversible, changes in social values, making war more an instrument of social transformation than of preservation. In addition, new weapons dissolved the distinction between the home front and the war front, meaning that defence in the literal sense of keeping the enemy's armed forces away from one's own social fabric was no longer possible. The destructiveness of weapons reduced the idea of national defence to an absurdity, since the state would be destroyed by the measures required for its defence. As Neville Brown put it, 'for thousands of years before [1945], firepower had been so scarce a resource that the supreme test of generalship lay in conserving it for application at the crucial time and place. Suddenly, it promised to become so abundant that it would be madness ever to release more than the tiniest fraction of the total quantity available.[14] When added to the difficulties created for defence by the increasing scope of state interests, particularly economic and ideological interests which were not so amenable to protection by military means, these conditions created a demand for a broader concept than defence with which to think about protecting the state.

Because of its peculiar geographical position, the United States, as noted above, adhered longer to national defence than the European powers. It took the experience of the Second World War to break American belief in isolationist national defence, and force the country into a more outward-looking security perspective. In a sense, this put the United States nearly three decades behind Europe in the transition of attitudes from defence to security, and it gives us a fairly clear case-study of the domestic process by which defence attitudes transformed into security attitudes.[15] National defence had clearly proved totally inadequate for the United States during the 1920s and 1930s. A passive, self-protecting attitude had allowed massive threats to build up in both Europe and Asia, eventually forcing the country to fight a huge war at a dangerous starting disadvantage. The lesson here was that security policy needed to be outward- and forward-looking, with the United States playing an active global role to ensure that no such unfavourable global conditions would arise again.

The declining viability of national defence as a solution to the problem of national security thus produced very different experiences in Europe and America. Because of the marked contrast in their geostrategic attributes, the European countries and the United States faced quite different orders of threat from military action by their enemies. In Europe, the growing contradiction between national defence and national security had been made apparent by the First World War, and became increasingly obvious with new weapons developments. Not only were the European states more vulnerable to war because of their close proximity to each other, but also their limited geographic size and economic strength made them subject to devastation and depletion on a national scale even before the advent of nuclear weapons.[16] The United States had no military problems comparable to this. In modern times it has never, and still does not, face threats of invasion and occupation. Not until the advent of Soviet intercontinental ballistic missiles (ICBM) in the late 1950s did Americans confront the prospect of the large-scale military bombardment which had haunted Europe for the previous four decades. For Americans, war was always 'over there'. The Second World War demonstrated that America's ocean buffers no longer sufficed to keep the military reach of enemies at bay, a lesson immortalised in the burning symbol of Pearl Harbor.

But even though this experience caused the United States to move away from a national defence orientation, it did not compare in intensity with circumstances in Europe. For the European states, the defence dilemma simply precluded all-out war. Any serious attempt to defend Europe in the traditional military sense would almost inevitably destroy all the values for which the defence had been mounted in the first place. Ever since the First World War, it has been obvious that security in Europe could only be approached collectively, and that preventing war from occurring must be the prime objective of security. These themes underpinned the League of Nations with its hopes for collective security machinery and its attempt to abolish war. They also underlay the gathering together of the by then even weaker western European states into the North Atlantic Treaty Organisation (NATO) after the Second World War.

For the United States, the contradiction between defence and security remained much more muted than in Europe. The country was strained, but not damaged, by the Second World War, and emerged at the end of it into a position of enormous relative strength in the international system. Defence was discredited in the United States mostly because a passive outlook had allowed war to creep too close to home. The national security doctrine which replaced it had only a little of European-style collective security and anti-war emphasis, for neither of these had anything like the relevance to American experience that they had in the European context. The principal problem for American national security was to make sure that war stayed 'over there'. The national security doctrine which emerged during the late 1940s amounted more to forward defence than anything else, the prime objective being to take early preventive action to forestall a 1930s-type build-up of threats to the United States.

Despite these basic differences in American and European perceptions of the defence dilemma, at least two common themes united them. The first of these was that both identified the Soviet Union as the prime foreign threat. The second was that both, albeit in rather different ways, acknowledged that national security could only be pursued jointly with other states. In Europe, the NATO structure symbolised the inability of individual states to defend themselves, whereas American involvement all along the periphery of the Soviet sphere merely staked out the boundaries for the forward defence of the United States. The United States, despite its initial hesitancy about getting involved, needed to defend Europe in order to defend itself. Europe was unable at the time to defend itself against the Soviet Union, and more than ever needed to avoid war. The link with America seemed to solve both problems for Europe: the United States could, and would, provide defence, and the American nuclear monopoly appeared to offer a stable, one-way threat of such magnitude as to reduce the probability of war to vanishing point.

At this juncture, the issue of nuclear weapons raises some essential paradoxes in relation to the European defence dilemma. On the one hand, nuclear weapons appear to crown the demise of defence by raising prospective levels of destruction in major military engagements to heights well beyond the limits of rational policy. On the other hand, a one-way nuclear threat such as that wielded by the United States during the late 1940s offered almost perfect security against attack. Even mutual deterrence, if properly managed, offered a good prospect of avoiding war by balancing a risk of incredibly massive destruction against a very low probability that anyone would resort to war under such circumstances. This paralysing quality of nuclear deterrence alleviated much of the contradiction between defence and security, but only so long as the probability of war remained close to zero. Even a small rise in the likelihood of war under nuclear conditions would revive the defence dilemma at a pitch far higher than that reached with conventional weapons.

Since the defence dilemma was much stronger in Europe than in the United States, both relief at its solution and concern about its failure naturally ran stronger on the eastern side of the North Atlantic. This difference in perspective on defence explains the persistent tension within NATO on matters of nuclear policy. Europe wants effective defence without war, and therefore favours a posture which maximises deterrence. From the European perspective, the one-way American massive retaliation policy of the late 1940s and early 1950s was ideal, because it emphasised war prevention and enabled problematical questions of defence to be largely side-stepped. Even under conditions of mutual deterrence, it makes sense for Europe to favour doomsday-like policies of massive retaliation, because in the European context the risk of defensive war fighting in more gradual, phased, 'flexible response' policies is little different from the risk of doomsday anyway. Massive retaliation appears better tailored to keeping the probability of war close to zero.

The United States, by contrast, is more concerned with keeping war away from itself, and therefore favours flexible-response policies designed to increase its strategic options and minimise its risks in conducting the defence of its worldwide strategic perimeter. The threat to fight a phased, limited nuclear war in Europe makes eminent good sense from an American security perspective, but except in as much as the threat of it can be argued to serve deterrence, runs contrary to the most basic security need of Europe. This problem has plagued NATO ever since the Soviet Union began to erode America's nuclear monopoly, and it underlay French motives in loosening military ties with the Alliance in 1956. Flexible response policies threaten to re-open for Europe the dilemma posed by the con-tradiction between defence and security. But since Europe has chosen to solve its security problem by making itself dependent on the United States, the European states have little room for manoeuvre in relation to American policy. Without the United States, they would still face a whole complex of difficult defence and security issues, and anyway, so long as the Americans remain committed to security through forward defence, it is not at all clear that Europe could simply ask them to leave.

In summary, then, and leaving aside for the moment the particula-rities of the European and American cases, it is clear that nuclear weapons stimulated a quantum leap in the historical trend towards greater fear of war. In so doing, they exacerbated an already serious contradiction between defence and security. Particularly for the more powerful and advanced states in their relations with each other, military means in themselves now threaten to defeat the objectives of security, or else are becoming of marginal relevance to political and economic issues which pose significant threats to national security. Almost by definition, the defence dilemma occurs much more acutely in the affairs of advanced industrial powers than it does in the affairs of Third World states. Few Third World countries have experienced modern war on anything like the scale of Europe, and few of them either command or face sufficient military means to raise their fear of war to the same levels as their fear of defeat. Kolodziej and Harkavy argue that Third World states are still 'rooted in Clausewitzian thought', and are not suffering any of the doubts about the utility of force which affect the major powers of both East and West.[17] In making this argument, however, they catalogue the massive diffusion of arms to the Third World. This trend, particularly its nuclear dimension, indicates that the conditions for encouraging the defence dilemma to spread its grip are already well in the making.

The Durability of the Defence Dilemma

The growing contradiction between national defence and national security does not mean that defence can simply be phased out of the domain of security. At least three problems prevent this solution. First, as the case of Europe indicates, the conditions which have made military defence such a contradiction have not been accompanied by relief from the threats which make it necessary. The technological inflation in the power of weapons shows no sign of going into reverse, and neither the hostile relations which create the threats, nor the anarchic structure which allows them, appear likely to abate. Even though the contradiction is high, states must make provision for defence against military threats unless they wish to abdicate both their character and their status as states. So long as threats exist which do not seem amenable to removal without sacrificing core values of the state – the case of Israel comes to mind – states must continue to tread the tightrope between self-preservation and suicide.

Secondly, national defence has a strong institutional and historical momentum within the life of most states, and of all substantial powers. Even in theory, the legal monopoly over the use of force for internal and external purposes lies close to the heart of what states are. In reality, most states have deeply institutionalised armed forces, many of which will have played critical roles in the creation and preservation of the state. Heroic founding struggles, like those of the United States, the Soviet Union, the People's Republic of China, and many Third World countries, link defence and the armed forces to the essence of the national being, as do heroic defences like the Battle of Britain, the Soviet struggle in the Second World War, the Vietnamese victory over the United States, and such-like. In most states the armed forces are so deeply enmeshed in the institutional structure of the state that rapid transformations in their position and function are inconceivable short of general social revolution. The fact that states still depend on defence against many threats, both internal and external, entrenches the position of the military establishment regardless of the paradoxes which affect defence and security, and helps to perpetuate national defence assumptions and traditions.

In the larger industrial states, armaments industries add a further element of national defence institutionalisation. Europe again furnishes a good illustration of this problem. Nowhere is the impossibility of national defence, in its strict meaning, more obvious or more openly acknowledged than in Europe. The League of Nations' experiment with collective security and the NATO structure of collective defence, both testify to this fact, and yet the independent structures of national defence persist almost undiminished in their separateness. National arms industries continue to equip national armed forces with distinctive weapons systems, many of which are incompatible with those of their allies. Although NATO has achieved some small measures of defence coordination, the momentum of national defence mentality has prevented most measures of rational standardisation, let alone progress towards something like a European defence force.[18]

Thirdly, and finally, national defence cannot be disengaged from national security because the only apparent way of doing so would be to create an effective collective defence/security system. All previous attempts at this have come unstuck because the strength of the forces dividing the international system has easily exceeded the strength of those tending to unite it. Conflicts like those of the 1930s and the Cold War preclude collective security, and they show no sign of weakening as a basic feature of international relations. For this reason, and also because the anarchic system works effectively to prevent the emergence of a single militarily dominant power, a repeat of the unifying solution to the anarchy/insecurity problem which the state provided for individuals does not seem likely in the foreseeable future at the level of states and the international system.

Conclusions: The Defence Dilemma and Security

We can conclude that the defence dilemma has established itself as a durable feature of the security problem, and that even though it now operates strongly over only a limited area, the trend in conditions worldwide favours its further spread. Much energy is poured into lamenting the proliferation of weapons, but it is not at all clear that the resultant defence dilemma is a cause for regret. Indeed, the nuclear defence dilemma which lies at the heart of the present international system might well be providing a fundamentally important stepping-stone towards a more mature anarchy. F.H. Hinsley argues that the fear of nuclear war, and the consequent ending of the legitimacy of war as a major instrument of relations among the great powers, amounts to a desirable transformation in the nature of the international system.[19] The defence dilemma, in other words, has paralysed military relations among the nuclear powers, thereby forcing them to find ways other than war to manage their rivalries. On a parallel track to the same conclusion Robert Tucker argues that:

The peace of deterrence is a peace that rests on the possibility of thermonuclear war. Once men were persuaded that they could with confidence remove that possibility from their calculations, one of the principal inducements to restraint would thereby disappear. With its disappearance would also disappear one of the principal causes of such order as international society presently enjoys.[20]

In other words, the nuclear defence dilemma is providing the international system with an unprecedented service. Because war can no longer act as the midwife of major system change – except change involving the destruction of the system and most of its components – both an opportunity and a necessity to move towards the creation of a more mature anarchy have been created, at least among the great powers. Not only do they have high incentives to prevent tensions among themselves from rising to an excessive pitch, but also they must create stable foundations for relations among themselves over the long term. These relations need not, and most probably will not, end the substantial deployment of armed force by the great powers against each other. Indeed, it could be argued that the maintenance of considerable military power is a necessary condition for maintaining the restraint on war. But such forces will necessarily be oriented primarily towards preserving the paralysis because, in a nuclear armed system, a philosophy of live-and-let-live among the great powers becomes the only practical alternative to a high risk of annihilation.[21]

Defence, then, remains an important component of security even if it no longer serves as a cover-all for security policy in the way it once did. The decline of defence, and its partial shift from being most of the solution to being part of the problem, opens up many questions about the scope and boundaries of national security policy. What issues and problems should be included? And what kinds of policies are appropriate? These questions form the focus of the last two chapters.

Notes

1　Robert E. Osgood and Robert W. Tucker, *Force, Order and Justice* (Baltimore, Johns Hopkins University Press, 1967), p. 32.
2　*Ibid.*, p. 13.
3　Hedley Bull, *the Anarchical Society* (London, Macmillan, 1977), p. 189.
4　Michael Howard, *Studies in War and Peace* (London, Temple Smith, 1970), p. 11.
5　*Ibid.*, p. 17.
6　See, for example, Quincy Wright, *A Study of War* (Chicago, University of Chicago Press, 1942); and Kenneth N. Waltz, *Man, the State and War* (New York, Columbia University Press, 1959).
7　See Waltz, *ibid.*
8　The security struggle comes out of Realist thinking – see John H. Herz, *International Politics in the Atomic Age* (New York, Columbia University Press, 1959) pp. 231–43 – but is, in a sense, more in line with idealist thinking in that it puts emphasis on weapons as a source of tension. It is usually discussed in the context of the 'security dilemma', for example by Herz, and by Robert Jervis, *Perception and Misperception in International Politics* (Princeton, Princeton University Press, 1976), ch. 3; and 'Cooperation under the Security Dilemma', *World Politics*, 30:2 (1978). These writers use the term security dilemma to refer to much the same phenomenon as I refer to with the term power-security dilemma. I prefer the longer expression because it emphasises the opposed theses which constitute the dilemma. The simpler term does not do this, and tends therefore to perpetuate the blurring of the distinction between power and security. It is a main theme of this book that understanding of international relations can be improved by distinguishing the concept of security from that of power.
9　This term is used in a narrower sense by Gert Krell, 'The Development of the Concept of Security', Peace Research Institute, Frankfurt (PRIF), *Arbeitspapier* 3/1979. He uses it in the context of nuclear weapons, and alongside companion terms like 'arms race dilemmas' and 'deterrence dilemmas'. My intention is to offer it as a basic concept in security thinking which encompasses a discrete, durable and broad pheno-

menon, stretching well beyond the confines of the nuclear weapon problem.

10 For a full elaboration of this argument, see Herz, *op. cit.* (note 8), chs. 1, 6; and John H. Herz, 'The Rise and Demise of the Territorial State', *World Politics*, 9 (1957).

11 Richard J. Barnet, 'The Illusion of Security', in Charles R. Beitz and Theodore Herman (eds), *Peace and War* (San Francisco, W.H. Freeman, 1973), p. 276.

12 This distinction between the threat of war and the threat of defeat is drawn by Hedley Bull, *The Control of the Arms Race* (London, Weidenfeld & Nicolson, 1961), pp. 25–9.

13 On this theme, see Osgood and Tucker, *op. cit.* (note 1), pp. 88–120; Richard Resources, *International Relations: Peace or War?* (New York, McGraw-Hill, 1973), p. 36; and Robert Jervis, 'Security Regimes', *International Organization*, 36:2 (1982).

14 Neville Brown, *The Future Global Challenge: A Predictive Study of World Security 1977–1990* (London, RUSI, 1977), p. 153. On the development of military technology in general, see the sources listed in note 12, chapter 3.

15 See Daniel Yergin, *Shattered Peace* (Boston, Houghton-Mifflin, 1978); and Franz Schurmann, *The Logic of World Power* (New York, Pantheon, 1974), for assessments of this transformation in the United States.

16 Michael Howard, 'Military Power and International Order', *International Affairs*, 40:3 (1964), p. 403.

17 Edward A. Kolodziej and Robert Harkavy, 'Developing States and the International Security System', *Journal of International Affairs*, 34:1 (1980), p. 64.

18 On this problem see, *inter alia*, R.W. Komer, 'Ten Suggestions for Rationalizing NATO', *Survival* (March/April 1977); A.H. Cornell, 'Collaboration in Weapons and Equipment', *NATO Review*, 28:4 and 5 (1980); G.L. Tucker, 'Standardization and Joint Defence', *NATO Review*, 23:1 (1975); and Philip Taylor, 'Weapons Standardization in NATO: Collaborative Security or Economic Competition', *International Organization*, 36:1 (1982).

19 F.H. Hinsley, 'The Rise and Fall of the Modern International System', *Review of International Studies*, 8:1 (1982).

20 Osgood and Tucker, *op. cit.* (note 1), p. 352.

21 For a very useful discussion of the utility of military power in conditions of paralysis, see Robert J. Art, 'To What Ends Military Power', *International Security*, 4:4 (1980).

7 The Power-Security Dilemma

The Power and Security Struggles: Distinctions and Links

The power and security struggles can be distinguished, as noted at the beginning of the previous chapter, by the different explanations of conflict on which they are based. The distinction is an important one, and despite the fact that the security struggle originates from Realist writers, it correlates closely with the difference in view between Realists and idealists which has long divided the field of international relations. But idealists have mostly chosen not to orient their thinking around the idea of security, preferring instead the broader and more popular idea of peace. Just as Realists have subsumed security under their preferred idea of power, idealists have subsumed it under peace. In so doing, both sides have gravely weakened their analysis.

Despite the fact that idealists have neglected it, however, the security struggle fits closely with the idealist pre-disposition to see conflict more as a structural, perceptual and resolvable problem, than as the intentional and permanent feature which it is in the Realist view. At its most extreme, the choice is between two views of international relations: on the one hand, as a ceaseless struggle for survival and dominance among states motivated by the pursuit of power; and on the other hand, as a tragic struggle for security by states trapped in a system which distorts their legitimate efforts at self-protection into a seamless web of insecurity and conflict. Taken at their extremes, they represent completely different conceptualisations of how and why the international system functions as it does.[1] This fundamental distinction requires us to treat the two resultant struggles separately in relation to our central problem of national security. The two are, nonetheless, inseparably connected in a variety of ways, and for this reason they must be considered as a single dilemma.

At least three considerations link the power and security struggles together. First is the fact that both represent essentially political problems, as opposed to the military/technological problem which underlies the defence dilemma. Both the power struggle and the security struggle stem directly from the way states behave, and the dynamics of their relations with each other. Granted, these behaviours and dynamics are strongly affected by military factors, as illustrated by the strategic significance to Britain of the development of medium-range bombers and, indeed, would not exist recognisably in the absence of military forces. However, both models take as given that states possess armed forces, and go on from there to concentrate on the political dynamics which lead to conflict under those conditions.

Second is the link created by the role which defence plays in both struggles. A desire for defence can be imputed as a prime motive underlying the two, the problem being that defence can be interpreted to cover a wide range of activities. At a minimum, defence implies a responsive action which occurs only after a clear attack has started, as when military forces are moved to meet enemy forces which have crossed the border. At maximum, it can involve forward or pre-emptive action designed either to meet threats which are still remote in time, space or magnitude, or to eliminate all significant sources of opposition or threat. Maximum defence may still be seen by its perpetrators as fitting within the security struggle mould, though in practice, and as seen by others, such behaviour fits more appropriately into the power model. This link means that the two struggles can be seen in one sense as constituting the ends of a spectrum which are joined together by the range of policies which might be pursued in search of national security. The centre point on the spectrum would be where policies defined in terms of the struggle for power became indistinguishable from those defined in terms of the struggle for security.

Third, and related to the previous point, is the link created between the two in the real world by the fact that the international system as a whole can seldom be characterised purely in terms of one or the other. While some relations within it will fit the power model, others will fit the security model. While the evidence may go quite clearly one way or the other in some cases, as, for example, Nazi Germany during the later 1930s, it may be sufficiently uncertain in others so as to defy reliable interpretation. The whole rivalry between the United States and the Soviet Union since the end of the Second World War has suffered from this ambiguity. With some observers stressing the power rivalry aspects of the relationship, and others, the baseless mutual terrorising of actors locked into a security struggle. The resulting uncertainty leads to endless clashes over policy along appeasement versus containment lines, like those which typified the debate about responses to Nazi Germany in the mid-1930s. To confuse matters, there is no reason why both struggles could not be operating simultaneously within a single case. A relatively mild power rivalry could easily generate an acute and overriding security struggle – this might be one view of the Cold War as it unfolded during the 1970s and 1980s. Because the international system cannot be characterised purely in terms of either the power struggle or the security struggle, neither model can safely be used to generate assumptions which are sound enough to serve as a basis for policy.

Despite the conceptual clarity of the distinction between the two models taken in the abstract, they are frequently difficult to distinguish from one another in practice. Two useful approaches to this confusion are, first, to look at the nature of the actors in the system in terms of the traditional distinction between status quo and revisionist states; and second, to examine the nature of weapons and the military balance. Both of these approaches offer insights into the power and security struggles which help to explain why what appears to be so clear in theory becomes so murky in practice. These approaches illuminate why the power-security dilemma is such a central component of the national security problem. The dilemma is between two choices or perspectives each of which implies a deeply-rooted and persistent source of threat. Revisionism and the arms dynamic constitute the principal mechanisms of these threats, and by examining them in some detail we can understand more about how the power-security dilemma works overall.

Revisionism versus Status Quo

The process of distinguishing between status quo and revisionist (or, in Morgenthau's terms, 'imperialist') powers has a long tradition in the study of international relations. It goes back at least to the seminal work of E.H. Carr, and played a central role in Hans Morgenthau's writing, which provided a backbone for the influential school of post-war Realists.[2] This strong link with Realism under-lines the fact that this approach has its roots in the power model of international relations. By implication, an implacable, zero-sum struggle exists between status quo and revisionist powers, and that struggle both determines and dominates the issue of security in the system. If this model presents an accurate picture, if revisionist states do push insistently against the dominance of status quo powers, then the power struggle emerges as the central challenge to national security. The security struggle model loses much of its interest if this is the case. Although it would retain interest as an additional mechanism to add onto the power struggle, it would lose most of its utility as an alternative way of viewing the problem of conflict in the international system as a whole. The security struggle comes into its own as an explanation for conflict in a system in which all of the major powers are essentially status quo in outlook. If some major powers are revisionist then no further explanation for conflict is required.[3]

Unfortunately, the idea of revisionism, much helped by Hitler, has come to carry a negative connotation similar to that which we explored in relation to anarchy. In other words, revisionist states are identified as the problem instead of being seen as one component in a problem of larger dimensions. If there were no revisionist states, there would be no power struggle. Some kind of natural harmony of the status quo would reign, and national security policy-makers would need only concern themselves with the relatively muted structural problems of the security struggle. Klaus Knorr provides a good example of this mentality by defining a use of force as 'aggressive' when 'military power is employed towards altering the relevant status quo by force or its threat'.[4] This tendency to sanctify the status quo relates strongly, of course, to the fact that most of the literature on international relations which this book addresses, and is part of, has been written within the confines of two pre-eminent status quo powers, Britain and the United States. As such, a bias towards the status quo is part of the ethnocentrism problem which Ken Booth has explored in relation to Strategic Studies.[5] In addition, a strong status quo attracts favour on the technical grounds that system management is thought to be easier when power is concentrated,[6] a point which connects clearly to the arguments about hegemonic management in chapter 5.

But as Carr points out with such force, the status quo does not represent a neutral position: it constitutes a set of interests which have acquired, and seek to maintain, an advantageous position in the system.[7] 'Every doctrine of a natural harmony of interests, identifies the good of the whole with the security of those in possession.'[8] From this perspective, the clash between status quo and revisionist powers ceases to be a moral problem in absolute terms. Although participants in the struggle may choose to see it in that way, as exemplified in the anti-imperialist and anti-communist rhetoric of the Cold War, from a more detached, systemic perspective, the rivalry between status quo and revisionist powers can be seen as a way of describing political orientations towards an existing pattern of relations. Status quo states benefit from, and support, the existing pattern, while revisionist ones feel alienated from it, and oppose its continuation. Moral judgements can be made on the respective cases, but these should be kept separate from assessment of the general propensity of the anarchic system to produce tension between status quo and revisionist powers. That propensity defines an important aspect of the national security problem for all states. The system will normally tend to be divided on some grounds between status quo and revisionist interests. If revisionist powers are assumed to be morally wrong, or aggressive by definition, then they simply get dismissed as 'the problem', without having their case considered as a legitimate and persistent part of the security dynamic of the system as a whole. The point is that revisionist states also have legitimate national security problems. For them, the prevailing system is a threat to their security. They are as much a part of the anarchy as the status quo states, and it helps to set aside moral judgements on particular cases in order to get a clearer view of the security dynamics of the system as a whole.[9]

If we accept that there are both status quo and revisionist perspectives on security, then it is useful to begin an inquiry into them by searching first for common ground. In other words, are there any minimum national security objectives which can be identified as common to all states whether status quo or revisionist in their attitudes towards the prevailing system? The answer to this question is undoubtedly yes, in as much as we can assume that the vast majority of states will give a high priority to protecting all, or at least part, of the domains, rights and powers which they hold. In other words, all states will tend to have a core of status quo objectives in relation to themselves which serve as a bottom line for security policy regardless of their attitude to the rest of the system. Exceptions occur when states become willing to dissolve themselves into a larger entity, as was done in the creation of the United States, Germany and Italy, or when they become willing to give up colonial possessions, as the European states did after the Second World War, or when they wish to divest themselves of a troublesome province, as Britain may one day do in relation to Northern Ireland. But these exceptions reflect identifiable special conditions which do not detract from the utility of the general rule. The logic of this bottom line is clear and compelling, for even the most rabid revisionist state cannot pursue its larger objectives if it cannot secure its home base. At a minimum, we can say that all states will seek to maintain their territory and their economic, political and social sectors so that they are viable in their own right, and so that changes are not imposed on them by the use or threat of force, or by political or economic threats.

Where status quo and revisionist states differ primarily is in their outlook on relations with the rest of the system. As we have seen, the compulsion to interact with the rest of the system has grown in intensity as the system has become increasingly dense. Much interaction has been forced, like the colonial 'opening up' of the Americas, Africa and Asia. Much has stemmed from the dynamics of the international economy. And much has occurred through the instrument of communications media and technology, which have made it increasingly difficult not to know what is going on all over the planet. The spreading webs of economic, political and environmental interdependence have made it more difficult for any state to separate its domestic affairs from its relations with the rest of the system. Even very large and relatively self-contained states like the Soviet Union and China have found it impossible to insulate themselves from the system for any great length of time. Because of this trend, relations with the rest of the system have become increasingly important to the maintenance of domestic welfare, stability and security in all states. Increasing interdependence naturally highlights the differences between status quo and revisionist perspectives on the system as a whole.

Status quo states are those whose domestic values and structures are, on the whole, supported by the pattern of relations in the system. This does not necessarily mean that they are in harmony with the rest of the system, for the relationship may be exploitative, as argued about centre-periphery relations in chapter 5. Nor does it necessarily mean that the state as a whole benefits in some clearly defined economic or political terms. A state may be status quo because the international system supports a pattern of relations which serves the interests of an élite which controls the government. Thus, a country like Zaire (at least up to 1982) might be classed as status quo in relation to its alignment with western interests, even though political and economic arguments could be made that this alignment did not serve the interests of the country and people as a whole. The important point about status quo states is that their dominant domestic structures are compatible with (and thereby dependent on) the dominant pattern of relations in the system.

Such compatibility ties into the point made in chapter 5 about the constraints on domestic political choice which result from partici- pation in (addiction to) a liberal international economy. This compatibility may arise because the status quo state in question is playing the role of hegemon, and has thus organised international relations to suit its own interests, as the United States did to a considerable extent after the Second World War. The leading status quo power may adopt styles of leadership ranging from the domineering and aggressive to the consensual, co-operative and contractual. Hirsch and Doyle hint in this direction with their characterisation of leadership as 'co-operative', 'hegemonic' or 'imperial',[10] and such variations offer interesting possibilities for refining hypotheses about relations between status quo and revisionist powers.

Status quo states can also be differentiated according to the power hierarchy among them. Depending on its power, a state which is in sympathy with the system may become an associate, a client or a vassal of the hegemon. In contemporary terms, one might see Japan and the major western European states as associates of the United States, countries like South Korea, and recently Egypt as clients, and countries like South Vietnam (before 1973) and Cuba (before Castro) as vassals. Status quo states thus tend to view security in terms both of preserving the system, and of maintaining their position within it. As Carr notes, security is the 'watchword' of the status quo powers,[11] usually expressed in terms of preserving stability. This could mean attempting to suppress all change in order to capture a current advantage in perpetuity, but as Carr argued, no power has the resources to make such a policy lastingly successful.[12] Richard Barnet also observes that 'To set as a national security goal the enforcement of "stability" in a world in convulsion, a world in which radical change is as inevitable as it is necessary, is as practical as King Canute's attempt to command the tides.'[13] A more likely approach is to try to maintain the existing *pattern* of relations, in terms of the distribution of power, wealth, productive capacity, knowledge, status and ideology. This could be done by using a present advantage to create conditions for superior adaptation and development in the future. The status quo thus becomes dynamic, in as much as it rides the wave of change rather than resisting it, but static in its attempt to hold on to the existing pattern of relations.[14] But as argued in chapter 5, serious doubts exist about the ability of status quo hegemons to succeed in this act in perpetuity.

The Nature of Revisionism

The basic condition for revisionism, as argued by Arnold Wolfers, is that the state is 'denied the enjoyment of any of its national core values'.[15] Revisionist states, in other words, are those which find their domestic structures significantly out of tune with the prevailing pattern of relations, and which therefore feel threatened by, or at least hard done by, the existing status quo. Because of this, revisionist states tend to view security in terms of changing the system, and improving their position within it. Although they may, for tactical reasons, give temporary or specifically limited support to policies of stability (for purposes like covering for a period of weakness, preventing all-destroying events like nuclear war, curbing unnecessary arms racing, or gaining some desired trade items), they have no long-term or general commitment to it. Whereas stability is the preferred security solution for status quo states, it defines the essence of the problem for revisionists. That said, it is obvious that system change in general is largely an independent variable. A host of factors ranging from technology to religion may push the system into directions not controlled, not anticipated, and not desired by either status quo or revisionist states.

Whereas the status quo tends to be more or less uniformly defined in terms of a particular system structure and its associated ideology, revisionism can come in a wide variety of styles. There is a tendency, following on from the cruder Realist models of power politics, to see revisionism simply in power terms, rather along the lines of pecking orders among chickens or animal hierarchies in which the dominant male retains its rights to the female herd by defeating challengers in trials of strength. In other words, the status quo power dominates the system and gains advantage from it on the grounds of previously demonstrated superior power. Challengers test their strength against the holder until one is able to unseat it and reap the fruits of the system to its own benefit. This power model does capture some important elements of revisionism, but it over-simplifies motives, and virtually ignores the varieties of revisionism which can occur lower down in the hierarchy of powers. Since membership of the international system has expanded greatly since 1945, there is now much more room for revisionism in the less desirable parts of the power hierarchy.

Revisionists can be differentiated along a number of dimensions. The most obvious is power, for it clearly makes a big difference to the system whether the revisionist forces are strong or weak. Albania, for example, is highly revisionist, but so weak that its opinion counts for little. While weak revisionists may have low influence in their own right, they can make a substantial impact if their revisionism can be aligned with that of a larger power. This is a point which Waltz misses in his eagerness to argue the merits of a bipolar system structure. While he is right to say that lesser states make little difference to the balance of power in a bipolar system,[16] he ignores the impact which they can make as the spoils of the political competition between the super-powers. Thus small powers, like Cuba, Iran and Vietnam, can make a substantial impact on the system by symbolising the fortunes of a struggle much larger than themselves. Weak revisionists also cannot be entirely discounted because, as the case of the Middle East oil states shows, they may quite rapidly acquire elements of strength which greatly increase their power within the system. Level of power may correlate with whether or not the revisionist is active or passive in pursuit of its case. China and Japan, for example, cannot pursue their territorial claims against the Soviet Union because they lack the military means to induce Soviet compliance. But relative powerlessness does not necessarily muzzle the revisionist urge, as demonstrated by states like Tanzania, Cuba and Libya which have in their very different ways pursued their views to notable effect. As these cases illustrate, the intensity with which revisionist views are held can, to some extent, compensate for deficiencies of power.

Perhaps the most important dimension of revisionism, however, relates to the motives, or the type of objectives, held by the revisionist state. As with most political struggles, motives can partly be interpreted as a power struggle between ins and outs. But real political differences usually play a central role, and Anatol Rapoport offers a useful distinction here between conflicts which are issue-oriented (those which can be solved without changing the basic structure of relations), and those which are structure-oriented (that is, they cannot be solved without changing the structure of relations).[17] We can build on this idea to suggest a three-tier distinction in revisionist objectives, which we can label *orthodox, radical* and *revolutionary*.

Orthodox revisionism involves no major challenge to the principles of the status quo, and can perhaps best be seen as a struggle occurring within the status quo aimed at producing a redistribution of power, status, influence and/or resources. The challenges of Imperial Germany and Imperial Japan to the status quo can be seen in this light, as can lesser cases like the expansion of Prussia during the eighteenth century, the Bolivian claim against Chile for a corridor to the sea, and the Argentine claim against Britain over the Falkland Islands. Territorial and colonial issues frequently reflect orthodox revisionist objectives, and these can occur on anything from a local scale, like the dispute between India and Pakistan over Kashmir, to a global scale, like the First World War. Orthodox revisionism can thus be found at relatively unimportant (in system terms) local levels, or it can represent a major struggle for the dominant place in the system. The important thing about it is that it constitutes only a struggle over power within the prevailing framework of ideas and relations. As in the numerous wars among the European monarchies prior to the French Revolution, excluding those concerned with the Christian schism, the issue is simply power, and the organising principles of the system remain unaltered regardless of the outcome. The importance of distinguishing orthodox from other types of revisionism is that it offers more scope for accommodation and peaceful settlement. Real shifts in power need not necessarily result in conflict to effect appropriate shifts in status and influence, as illustrated by the passing of the torch from Britain to America as hegemon in the international economy.

At the opposite extreme lies revolutionary revisionism. This involves not only a struggle for power within the system, but also a basic challenge to the organising principles of the system itself. The Soviet Union has presented this sort of challenge to the capitalist West since 1917, just as Republican France challenged monarchical Europe more than a century previously. The rise of a strong revolutionary revisionist threatens not only the distribution of power, but also the domestic values and structures of all the states associated with the prevailing status quo. Monarchies justly quaked before the prospect of triumphant republicanism, just as capitalist states fear the spread of communist power and influence. In both cases, a victory for the revisionists threatens major political transformations like those imposed by the Soviet Union on eastern Europe after the Second World War, or of the same magnitude as those imposed by the West on Germany and Japan in the purging of fascism. There may well also be economic dimensions to revisionism. If the status quo is liberal, revolutionary revisionists will almost invariably cultivate mercantilism. If the status quo is mercantilist, economic issues may be of low salience, or revisionism may express itself in empire-building. A liberal revisionist threat to a mercantilist status quo is possible, but less likely given the need for co-operation in a liberal system.

A revolutionary revisionist challenge means that the relatively neat divide among state interests gets seriously blurred by the transnational intrusions of political ideology. An orthodox revisionist challenge tends to emphasise nationalist interests, and so fits conveniently into the power-driven, state-centric model of the Realists. A revolutionary challenge projects political ideology into the international arena, thereby cutting across nationalist lines, and carrying the struggle into the domestic arena as well. This makes the conflict much more intractable, and amplifies it into every corner of the system where a local political development can be either interpreted in terms of, or else subverted to, the alignments of the central confrontation. After the French Revolution, domestic republicans became as much of a security threat as foreign ones, just as domestic communists have appeared to be, and in some cases have been, a fifth column against the establishment in the capitalist West.

Similarly, communists in power in Cuba make a far bigger impact on American interests than would a nationalist government, because of the way they reflect, and impinge upon, the fortunes of the larger struggle between the United States and the Soviet Union.

Revolutionary revisionism also creates an acute security problem for the revisionist state itself. Whereas an orthodox revisionist can, to a certain extent, remain quietly within the system until the time is ripe for it to launch its challenge, a revolutionary revisionist is branded by its internal structure for what it is, and is thus exposed to repressive action from the holders of the status quo. The invasions and general harassment of the Soviet Union after its Revolution in 1917 illustrate this problem graphically. In assessing the overall security picture in a system in which a significant revolutionary revisionist power exists, we must therefore look not only at the threat which it poses to the status quo powers, but also at the threat which they pose to it. Especially in its early days, the revolutionary revisionist is likely to be relatively weak and vulnerable. It is likely to be exceedingly aware of the differences between itself and the rest of the system, and to be acutely sensitive to maintaining its own basic security against what appears to be, and may in fact be, a generally hostile system. Because it is a revolutionary revisionist, it must expect the status quo powers to be deeply opposed to it.

At least two developments can follow from this situation which have major significance for the overall security picture. The first is that the revolutionary state may feel compelled to conclude that its only long-term hope for security lies in converting the rest of the system to its ideology. The second is that it may adopt a highly militarised posture primarily for its own defence, in the expectation that the status quo powers are likely to attack it long before it can itself acquire sufficient power to challenge them other than in the political arena. Such developments feed neatly into the pattern of an intense power-security dilemma.

The important point here is that where a revolutionary revisionist exists, *both sides* feel highly insecure. The political difference between them amplifies the simple power struggle by adding an insidious ideological dimension to the normal push-and-shove of military and economic power. This amplification effect may open a gulf of hostility and fear between the two sides much deeper than that justified by either their intentions towards each other, or the condition of the power balance between them. If this problem is best illustrated by the case of the Soviet Union, its opposite, in which the status quo misguidedly treat a revolutionary revisionist as an orthodox oné, is illustrated by the case of Nazi Germany. It is an irony of our present history that the failure of policy in the German case should have so directly led to the opposite failures in the Soviet one. The inability to recognise a power struggle in the first case has produced, by way of over-reaction, an intense power-security dilemma in the second.

Radical revisionists fall between orthodox and revolutionary ones. Their objectives extend beyond the simple self-promotion of the orthodox, but fall short of the transformational ambitions of the revolutionary. Radical revisionists seek to reform the system. They want to keep much of the existing structure intact, but to make significant adjustments to its operation. Both self-improvement and ideological motives may underlie this type of revisionism, and yet it may pose no central threat to the basic distribution of power and status in the system.

The best example of radical revisionism can be found in the Group of 77, or its leading exponents such as Tanzania, Algeria, India and Jugoslavia. These countries, and others in the Group of 77, occupied the international agenda of the 1970s with their call for a New International Economic Order (NIEO). The NIEO typifies a radical revisionist approach. It did not call for the overthrow of the existing order either in terms of power structure or basic principles, though extremists within the status quo might have viewed it in that light. Instead, it envisaged reforms to the system which would reduce the inequities in centre-periphery relations by allowing a more even distribution of benefits and the creation of stronger states in the periphery. Whether or not the reforms would have produced the effects desired by their proposers, and whether or not the existing system can be so reformed without undermining its basic productive dynamism, are irrelevant to our present discussion.[18] The important point is that grounds for reformist revisionism exist in the international arena just as much as they do in the domestic one. The example used here is distorted in terms of the normal conventions of revisionism, because the backers of the NIEO represent a weak rather than a strong power base in the system. One could speculate about the character of a powerful radical revisionist; or perhaps there is something in the hypothesis that radical revisionism most naturally appeals to weaker actors in the system. Because there is a possibility of negotiation in relation to it, radical revisionism offers opportunities in an interdependent system where even the weak can create some leverage by threats of disruptive behaviour.

The existence of these varieties of revisionism creates a much more complicated pattern of alignments in the international system than that implied by a simple dichotomy between status quo and revisionist states. The status quo powers may be divided against themselves along orthodox revisionist lines.[19] At the same time, they

may also be challenged by both radical and revolutionary revisionists, like the West facing both the Group of 77 and the Soviet
Union. Possibilities for innumerable, apparently bizarre, alignments
exist in this *mélange*, and help to explain the constant embarrassment
of those wedded to more strictly polarised views in the face of
developments like the Sino-Soviet split and the Nazi-Soviet Pact. A
revisionist state may be so only in relation to certain areas or issues,
and may behave more like a status quo power elsewhere. The Soviet
Union, for example, may be pegged in general as a revolutionary
revisionist. But from eastern Europe it looks like a status quo power,
and it takes a status quo position on issues like the law of the sea
because of its great power naval interests. Much of the confusion
about Nazi Germany during the 1930s arose from uncertainty about
whether Hitler's revisionism was local and orthodox, or global and
revolutionary. Competing revolutionary revisionists have to decide
whether to join forces against the status quo (the Nazi-Soviet Pact),
or give first priority to the dispute between them by seeking alignment
with the status quo (the Sino-Soviet split). Similarly, the status quo
powers may seek alignment with one revisionist (the Soviet Union),
in order to quash another (Nazi Germany). Radical revisionists may
see the dispute between status quo and revolutionary powers as a
blessing for their cause because of the increased leverage it provides
them against the status quo powers, or they may see it as a disaster,
wiping out the credibility of their middle ground and forcing them to
choose sides.

The great complexity and uncertainty of alignments which this
analysis reveals explain a good measure of the overlap and confusion
between the security and power struggles. Not only do several types
of revisionism compete among themselves and with the status quo,
but also locally focused revisionisms intermingle with and distort
those based on more global ambitions. Further complexities arise
from the style of status quo leadership. Is the revisionist challenge
being made against a co-operative, hegemonic or imperial status
quo? And what difference does this variable make to the pattern of
relations?

We find ourselves, then, back to the notion of interlocking security
complexes, though by a quite different route from that which took us
there in chapter 4. As the idea of security complexes emphasises, no
single, direct, simple power struggle exists. Instead, complicated
tangles of interests underlie a shifting and unpredictable pattern of
alignments. The business of correctly identifying revisionist actors,
the importance of which is rightly stressed by Morgenthau,[20] is
revealed to be no simple matter when the exigencies of a complex
pattern may require alignment with obvious opponents. In the light

of the outcome of the Second World War, for example, one might ask whether the status quo West made the correct choice in either moral or power logic terms in aligning with the Soviet Union against Nazi Germany.

This complexity explains why the dynamics of the power and security struggles become so entangled. Uncertainty as to the nature of other actors arises both from the intrinsic difficulty of judging their true intentions, and from the peculiarities of alignment which the system generates. This uncertainty is compounded by the general hazard of life in an armed anarchy, and is the driving force behind the confusion of the power-security dilemma. As we have seen, the security struggle, which is a natural dynamic of an armed anarchy, can easily create the self-fulfiling prophecy of a power struggle. Conversely, an actual power challenge may well be disguised in its early stages as a manifestation of the security struggle. Under such conditions, no actor can rely on absolute distinctions between the power and security models in relation to the formulation of its policy. Consequently, all find themselves forced to play with caution, suspecting power motives everywhere, a stance which has the collective result of intensifying the power-security dilemma throughout the system. This uncertainty and insecurity make a powerful input into the domestic politics of national security which we shall examine in the next chapter.

The Arms Dynamic

So far we have discussed the national security problem without addressing directly one of its most obvious components: weapons and the military balance. We have looked at military threats as a general category and dealt with the particular problem of the defence dilemma. Weapons themselves, however, have a number of independent characteristics which bear significantly on the workings of the power and security struggles. As noted above, both these struggles, though they are essentially political in nature, stem from the given condition that states in an anarchy will be armed and responsible for their own defence. Consequently, it comes as no surprise that variations in the character of the weapons, and the dynamics of their production and development, not only influence the two struggles, but constitute a major linking factor which fuses them into a single power-security dilemma.

The argument here will be that weapons possess an independent, or at least a semi-independent, dynamic of their own. This dynamic feeds into both the power and security struggles, providing a conspicuous common element which masks the motivational difference separating them. This argument ties into the traditional distinction between capabilities, particularly military power, and intentions. A threat normally consists of capabilities and intentions in combination. The existence of either is therefore sufficient cause for alarm, and since military capability tends to be visible and durable, whereas intentions are intangible and changeable, more attention gets paid to the former than to the latter. As a rule, intentions are simply assumed to be the worst case that is compatible with known or suspected military capability.

If military capability is subject to a dynamic which is wholly, or at least in good part, *separate* from the intentions which govern the power and security struggles, then military factors could be expected to complicate and confuse the security signals which states try to send to each other. Behaviour resulting largely from the semi-independent weapons dynamic, such as the replacement of an old generation of weapons with a new one, can look very much the same regardless of whether the surrounding motives belong to the power or the security struggle. Because the military idiom is similar, the political differences are hard to read. An arms race, in other words, can reflect either a power struggle or a security struggle, and still look much the same.

The key point in this analysis is that if the character of weapons remained constant, everything we have so far said about the power and security struggles would still be valid. In other words, power struggles could still occur, with revisionists challenging each other and the status quo powers in much the same way as we have come to regard as familiar. Similarly, the logic of the security struggle would still hold, with uncertainty, and the desire to hedge bets, continuing to produce upward spirals of suspicion, hostility and competitive armament. The dynamic of both struggles would be muted because uncertainty over the military implications of new weapons would no longer spur fear and competition, but the power-security dilemma would continue to feature as the central focus of the national security problem. The fact that the dilemma depends only on the existence of force, and not, except within very broad limits, on the nature of the weapons and forces involved, points to the evolution of weapons as the independent, disruptive variable on which we need to focus.

It can be argued that the pressure of the power-security dilemma does make an impact on weapons development, both in terms of accelerating the process in general and in terms of encouraging particular developments. Thus, for example, the Anglo-American atomic bomb programme early in the Second World War was pushed by the fear that the Germans would develop such a weapon first, possibly with decisive military effect. The development of aircraft, after some initial years of disinterest, has been much accelerated by the pressures of military rivalry, and the design of the Dreadnought battleship in the early years of the century was affected by the growing Anglo-German naval race.

But although the pressures of rivalry and insecurity clearly influence weapons development, they do not constitute the basic drive behind the process. That drive comes from the much broader evolution of humanity's command over science and technology, a process deeply and self-sustainingly rooted in human society. The general advance in knowledge about the physical universe makes possible continuous improvements in weapons.[21] Thus, breakthroughs in atomic physics during the 1920s and 1930s revealed the possibility of nuclear weapons to the scientists concerned, and led to the famous letter in which they informed President Roosevelt of the matter in 1939. The development of aircraft was made possible by the construction of reliable internal combustion engines, a development which itself came about as a result of many decades of expanding knowledge in mechanical engineering and other fields. The development of Dreadnoughts only became possible because of advances in metallurgical knowledge which opened the way to the development of heavy guns, armour plate and large steel hulls. Only three decades prior to the 1906 launching of the *Dreadnought*, HMS *Devastation* (1872) had marked the first major abandonment of sail for steam. Only two decades prior to that, in the early 1850s, wooden ships of the line similar to those which fought at Trafalgar (1805) still provided the backbone of naval power.

One might seek for the causes of this general technological advance in such areas as the natural accumulation of experience over time, the increasing pool of human intelligence available in succeeding generations, better political organisation and larger economic surplus. Whatever the explanation, it is clear that advances in weapons are closely associated with the general advance in civil technical capability, which in turn rests on a much broader and more compelling base than the dilemmas of international relations. On the assumption that technological advance is now a permanent feature of human society, the evolution of weapons becomes a constant problem. Just as iron swords must at first have appeared magical in power to those whose metallurgical knowledge confined their experience to softer copper and bronze weapons, so new technical innovations from Greek fire to the atomic bomb have made their impact on military affairs up to the present, and as yet unknown devices will do so in the future. We must expect military innovation to occur, and we must allow that it is likely to have an independent impact on the power-security dilemma. The prospect of a militarily significant technological breakthrough thus stands as a constant problem. It is a lure in the context of the power struggle because of the possibility of achieving a decisive shift in the balance of military capability, and it amplifies the security struggle by inserting another fear into the host of uncertainties which states already face in their relations with each other.

So close are the links between civil and military technology and knowledge, that this problem would still exist even if much less effort was devoted explicitly to the development and production of weapons than is now the case. In the absence of instruments specifically designed as weapons, industrial society would still produce a huge range of items which could serve, or be adapted, as weapons should one group decide to use them against another. At the bottom end of the scale, this is demonstrated by the use of petrol bombs, acid and fertiliser-based explosives by dissident crowds or organisations with restricted access to conventional weapons. At the top end, lies the military potential of some civil nuclear power cycles, where fuel processing and reprocessing produce fissile material of weapons grade. In between lie endless numbers of military options in a disarmed world, ranging from the dropping of industrial poisons from large civil airliners to the manipulation of climate.

To make matters worse, we appear to be in the midst of an extended period of unprecedented and rapid technological development. The industrial revolution has been with us for more than two centuries, and shows no sign either of slackening its invasion of all human societies or of losing its innovative dynamism. As a consequence, the evolution of weapons is riding on the crest of an exceptionally large and fast moving wave. Whereas military-technological breakthroughs and surprises were by no means unknown in the pre-industrial past – the breaching of feudal fortifications by early cannon, and the dominance of the English (originally Welsh) longbow during the Hundred Years War, being examples – these did not come at anything like the pace or intensity we have been experiencing since the middle of the nineteenth century. Compare, for example, the basic similarity of ships of the line during the three centuries between the early years of the sixteenth century and the early years of the nineteenth, with the multiple transformations in naval power – from battleship, to aircraft carrier, to nuclear submarine – of the last hundred years. We live, then, in an age in which the constant problem of weapons innovation operates at a high intensity. This problem seriously aggravates the power-security dilemma, and cannot be wholly avoided even by general and complete disarmament. One of its more dangerous, although potentially useful, side-effects, is the defence dilemma.

The constant problem of weapons leads us to that characteristic phenomenon of international relations which is known, often misleadingly, as the arms race. If one state is armed, others must arm themselves also. Once underway, this process of armament can be driven by the power struggle, the security struggle, and/or the innovation cycle of weapons. It properly becomes a race only when two or more countries explicitly accumulate weapons in relation to each other, as in the classic model of the Anglo-German naval race prior to 1914. A too frequently ignored point is that the process of armament in the system does not, and cannot, have a normal condition that is static. Because of the need to replace worn out weapons, and, more importantly, because of the need to update weapons which have been made obsolete by the general advance in science and technology, the arms process has to move in order to stand still. Because it moves even when at rest, and because that movement is very similar to the movement in an arms race, it is easy to confuse the dynamic which stems from the technology with that which stems from the relations among states. The technological factors create uncertainties which exacerbate the power-security dilemma and the relational tensions create motives for accelerating the cycle of technological development. The result, once again, is that what can be clearly distinguished on a conceptual level becomes hopelessly tangled in practice.

This complexity can be made easier to understand if we assume a hypothetical situation in which weapons are a constant factor – that is, they exist, but no technological improvement in them occurs. In such a case, arms racing would still exist as a phenomenon, but in a simplified form. It would be possible for the whole arms process to reach a normal, static condition in which force levels remained constant and the only movement was the replacement of worn-out weapons with new ones of the same design. Arms racing would then be easy to identify, though the motivational confusion between the power and security struggles would persist. The conditions of the race would be very largely quantitative, each side striving to procure more of weapons similar in kind. As suggested by the history of the three centuries rule of sail at sea, such a technological stasis would increase the military value of leadership, organisation, morale and tactical innovation, and would raise the value of military experience and tradition. Military uncertainties would come more from the possibility of Napoleon-like leaders, capable of using old weapons in new and more effective ways, than from the fear of new weapons which has dominated the present century.

When we introduce technological innovation into this model as an independent, or semi-independent, variable, the picture changes radically. The possibility of stability disappears, to be replaced by an open-ended process of upgrading and modernising weapons. To stand still, or in other words to retain possession of armed forces regarded as modern, and likely to be effective against other armed forces, states must keep pace with a cycle of military modernisation which is driven by the pace of the overall advance in science and technology. Whereas with technological stasis, quality resided primarily in leadership, organisation and innovative tactics, with technological innovation, past experience is no guide to future military operations, and attention shifts to the weapons themselves. A qualitative dimension is thereby introduced into the arms process in two senses in which it did not intrude before.

First, weapons quality must be maintained in relation to the general norms prevailing in the system. There is no point in building fine Dreadnoughts and superb Zeppelins if your neighbours are building nuclear submarines and long-range ballistic missiles. This general level of quality must be maintained even when no particular race is in progress between identifiable rivals. Where technological innovation is the norm, a sense of arms race exists which would not occur if there were technological stasis. Under these conditions arms race can mean simply the race to keep up with the pace of technological change. Although such a race depends on the existence of an anarchic international system, it does not necessarily involve the dynamics of a particular rivalry. It is something which all actors must engage in regardless of the pattern of their political relations. Differences in success or ability to stay close to the leading edge become a way of differentiating among states as powers.

Secondly, weapons quality has to be judged in relation to the particular rivals which any state faces. For states locked into an arms race, regardless of motives, weapons quality becomes another dimension in which racing can occur. Not only quantity of weapons counts, but also their quality. If one Dreadnought was equal to three battleships of the previous type, then fewer ships would be needed, or else a great advantage gained, until the other side could match the technological leap. These calculations are relatively easy when one is comparing weapons designed to fight others of their own kind, as with Dreadnoughts and tanks. But they become more ambiguous and complicated when the qualitative factor in racing applies either to dissimilar weapons intended to fight each other, such as tanks and anti-tank systems, or to similar weapons not intended to fight each other, like submarine-launched ballistic missiles (SLBMs). Qualitative comparisons, then, have to be made across whole sets of weapons and defences – the SLBMs themselves and their carrier submarines versus anti-ballistic missile weapons, hardening, and a wide array of possible anti-submarine weapons – resulting in much more uncertain calculations. A qualitative arms race contains much greater dangers than a quantitative one because of the risk that some new development will suddenly upset the existing balance of force. Because of this risk, qualitative races encourage the participants to push the cycle of technological innovation in the hope that security of a kind can be found in permanent occupancy of the leading edge.

These two aspects of the qualitative dimension – the general one of keeping up with technological advance, and the specific one of matching, or out-performing, an opponent – overlap to some extent, and can easily be confused completely. It is not difficult to see how the general process would stimulate the dynamics of the power-security dilemma which, in turn, would produce arms races of the more specific kind. Thus, although two quite distinct processes are involved, the label of arms race is used to cover the whole amalgam, becoming ambiguous and confusing as a consequence. If the arms race is the whole process, then there is no cure for it short of either the cessation of technological innovation in general, which is impossible short of the destruction of human society, or the detaching of military affairs from the technological imperative, which is also effectively impossible. We are left with the arms race as a permanent and incurable condition. If the arms race refers only to the process of competitive accumulation of weapons by rival states in relation to each other, we have a more tractable phenomenon. For this reason it is useful to keep the distinction between these two sides of the qualitative dimension in mind, despite the difficulties of distinguishing between them in practice. Since two different processes are involved, any policy which assumes the phenomenon to be unitary will be weakly founded.

By confining the term arms race to the latter, more specific phenomenon, we can derive three more precise categories with which to describe the whole arms dynamic in a universe of technological innovation. The first category we can label *arms maintenance*. This covers situations in which states seek to maintain their existing force levels by replacing worn-out weapons, and by updating and modernising their weapons in line with the general pace of advance in technology. No particular attempt is being made to change force levels relative to other states, though of course absolute levels of force will tend to increase with improved technologies. In the absence of an independent technological variable, arms maintenance would be a static and relatively safe process. With technological innovation, however, it can easily cease being neutral, and become transformed into a provocative process quite capable of stimulating an arms race. This could happen either because the modernisation process produces an imbalance in an existing relationship, or because it introduces a new kind of weapon into the picture. An example of the first would be the introduction of multiple, independently-targetable re-entry vehicles (MIRVs) onto American ICBMs during the 1960s. While in one sense just a modernisation, these MIRVs greatly multiplied the strike capability of the American ICBM force in relation to the Soviet Union, thereby stimulating a Soviet effort to catch up. The introduction of the Dreadnought in 1906, though similarly a modernisation in one sense, also had the makings of an arms race-provoking event. An example of the second would be the introduction of a cost-effective ballistic missile defence (BMD) system by either the United States or the Soviet Union. A new weapon like this, though also reflecting the general advance of technology, would deeply disturb the existing structure of deterrence, and would require a major, focused response by the other side.

These kinds of arms-maintenance-stimulating-arms-race events can also happen in low-arms areas, where weapons are introduced from outside rather than manufactured by the states concerned. The introduction of advanced aircraft into a country like Pakistan to replace less sophisticated models can only be seen as a substantial threat by India requiring an arms racing response in kind. Since imports can occur quickly, and since quite small numbers of advanced weapons can make a big difference to an overall balance based on relatively low levels of force, many Third World areas are particularly vulnerable to this escalation effect. This is a major mechanism underlying the modern power-security dilemma, and, by stimulating fears, it can transform mild power struggles into much deeper antagonisms.

The second category we can label an *arms build-up*. This represents a rather uncommon selection of cases, but is none the less worth distinguishing from the other two for reasons both of logical neatness and practical analysis of events. An arms build-up occurs when a state sets about increasing its military forces relative to others, but not so specifically in relation to another state or group of states that we can identify the process as a race. This normally occurs when some circumstance which has resulted in abnormally low levels of arms ceases to apply. The ending of British hegemony in the Persian Gulf in the late 1960s triggered off a considerable arms build-up in that region which was clearly much more than mere arms maintenance, but clearly not an arms race. An arms build-up has considerable potential for turning into an arms race, as the one around the Gulf eventually did, and as did the German rearmament during the 1930s. But there is no reason why this need be the case. The build-up could just as easily phase into the normal cycle of arms maintenance at some level of equilibrium insufficient to provoke a race. Japan is a contemporary example of a state that could undertake an arms build-up should it decide to end its low arms policy.

The third category comprises the more tightly defined version of the arms race discussed above. In an arms race, the increase in military power arises not only from the technological dynamic of arms maintenance, but also reflects competition among two or more specified states. This competition results from the operation of the power and/or security struggle, so that the participants increase their military strength in relation to each other on the basis of political and military assumptions about each other as sources of threat. The British policy of 1912 in which Dreadnought construction was set at a ratio of 8 : 5 in relation to the German construction programme, with a ratio of two keels to one for any additions to the German programme, provides a clear example of the arms race dynamic, as do contemporary concerns about comparative strategic nuclear strength between the super-powers. Within this definition, there is still room for an enormous variety of arms race styles and types. A full investigation of these is beyond the scope of this book, but it is worth suggesting a few points about the major variables involved.

Obviously, arms races will not all be of the same intensity. Like any other form of competition, they will range on a spectrum from very mild at one end, to highly intense at the other. A mild arms race might be hard to distinguish from the process of arms maintenance. In such a race, military expenditure could remain at a constant and moderate proportion of GNP, perhaps even declining from this on occasion. A high intensity race, by contrast, would look more like a mobilisation for war, with military expenditure either rising as a proportion of GNP, or else hovering around some high proportion, as in the case of Israel.[22] Although arms races can be compared on this general basis,[23] it is useful also to look deeper into the nature of the objectives and the nature of the weapons which underlie levels of intensity. In these two factors we can find some indication of the full richness and diversity of arms races as a phenomenon.

The analogy of a race conjures up images of a track event in which two or more runners start from a fixed line and strive to reach a finishing tape first. This image is in some ways unfortunate, for it draws attention away from the more mixed condition and objectives which are likely to attend an arms race. In an arms race, the competitors are unlikely to start from the same line, and they may well not wish to win or lose in the unconditional sense of the 100 metre sprint. If we assume a two-party arms race (which is unlikely to occur, given that most states relate to a larger pattern of security complexes), and that the states do not start the race with equal armaments (which is normal in modern arms racing history), and that the weaker state initiates the race (in the real world, the question of initiation may be very difficult to answer clearly), then we can derive a model for arms race objectives. In an arms race, at least one party must want to change its relative military capability, otherwise the process is arms maintenance, not racing. Assuming that the initiator state (I) is behind, and wants to change, it can have three objectives: it may hold just one of these, or it may hold all three as a phased plan, or it may hold a lower one, and then take up the others if opportunity seems to warrant a change of mind. It can seek a partial catch-up with the respondent state (R), trying to improve its position without changing the direction of the balance between them. It can seek parity, causing an evening out, but not a reversal, of the balance. Or it can seek superiority, a reversal in direction of the existing balance.

In the face of these challenges, R has five options. It can attempt to increase its lead, hoping thereby to demonstrate to I the futility of the challenge. It can simply maintain its lead, matching I's build-up, and assuming that I will weary of its labour. It can allow I to achieve a partial catch-up, so that the distance between them is narrowed, but the direction of the balance remains the same. In this case, R would be adjusting to a real increase in I's weight in the system. It can allow I to achieve parity, a much larger adjustment. Or it can allow I to win the race, and accept for itself a diminished stature either in its local security complex, or in the system as a whole.[24] If we arrange these objectives into a matrix, some of them appear as conflicts which are unresolvable short of changes in objectives by one side or the other. Some of them do not clash, and indicate that a race need not necessarily ensue. Some combinations are most unlikely ever to occur.

The disputes summarised in Figure 7.1 get more serious as we move towards the top right corner of the matrix, and more resolvable as we move towards the lower left corner. This exercise obviously begs a number of important questions, and is far removed from an operational state. The objectives are assumed to be known to both sides, and to be honest neither of which may be the case. One or both sides may not have their objectives formulated explicitly even to themselves, or if they are clear, they may be kept secret from the other side. Attempts by one deliberately to mislead the other as to its objectives may occur. Even attempts at full and honest communication by both sides are unlikely to prevent misunderstanding and suspicion. Furthermore, the matrix infers that real military strength can be measured with considerable accuracy, which is unfortunately not the case, and it ignores differences in arms racing style resulting from the kinds of weapons involved.

Figure 7.1 *Possible objectives in a two-party arms race*

		Initiator		
	Increase lead	U	U	U
	Maintain existing lead	U	U	U
Respondent	Allow gain short of parity	R	U	U
	Allow gain to parity	R	R	U
	Accept inferiority	R	R	R
		Partial Catch-Up	Parity	Superiority

U = Unresolvable objectives.
R = Resolvable objectives.
/ = Unlikely situation.

Nevertheless, the matrix serves to indicate that a more tractable range of objectives exists for arms racing than would at first appear to be the case in the light of a strict race analogy. It illustrates a set of resolvable combinations, and in so doing moderates the notion of a race as being a stark zero-sum game. The matrix also leads us back to our larger concern with the security and power struggles. The more extreme objectives on both sides fit easily into the assumptions of the power struggle, with its emphasis on intense zero-sum competition. If a power struggle is operating, then the arms race it generates is most unlikely to be resolved short of one side reducing its objectives. The band of resolvable combinations fits more easily into the assumptions of the security struggle. In a security struggle, neither side wishes to threaten the other, but each sees the other as a threat. The mutual, but incorrect, imputation of extreme objectives can lead to an arms race which is indistinguishable from one attending a power struggle, except that it is amenable to resolution if the falseness of the imputed objectives can be demonstrated. In either the power struggle or the security struggle case the independent cycle of weapons improvement can act both to spur the racing dynamic and to complicate the calculation of relative strength.

One further twist in the structure of arms racing motives needs to be examined before we look at the nature of armaments themselves. We have so far assumed that arms racing motives are externally oriented. In other words, a state engages in an arms race either because it feels menaced by another state, or because it wishes to increase its ability to menace others. This assumption is encouraged by the race analogy, with its image of competitors forcing the pace of each other's behaviour. It is also supported by the many case-studies of arms races in which each side explicitly justifies its own behaviour by reference to that of another state. Thus, the British built Dreadnoughts in pace with German construction, Pakistan and India justify arms acquisitions in relation to each other, Israel argues for its military needs in terms of surrounding Arab strength, and the United States points to Soviet ICBM numbers in making the case for its MX missile system.

It is, however, quite possible for this dynamic of external competition to become institutionalised internally in the competing states to such an extent that the pace and progress of the arms race can no longer be explained by the logic of reciprocal external stimulus. Once an arms race begins, states naturally make internal adjustments to facilitate the required behaviour. Attitudes need to be focused against the opponent in order to generate political support for increased militarisation, and both the economy and the military establishment need to be geared up for their role. These adjustments can easily take on a momentum of their own, becoming an internal institutionalisation of arms race behaviour which is significantly detached from reference to what the other side is actually doing. Attitudes can harden to a point at which the opposition is simply assumed to be pernicious, all of its behaviours being interpreted in the worst possible light in such a way as to make the initial assumption self-maintaining.[25]

Even more important than attitudes, however, is the institutionalisation of militarisation. The large production and administrative bodies necessary to pursue an arms race naturally tend to take on a life and momentum of their own:[26] and since their survival and welfare as organisations depend on the continuance of the arms race, they become a significant political force in its favour. Many studies of the arms industry and the so-called military-industrial complex (MIC) make this case in detail, so there is no need to pursue it here.[27] One point is particularly important to our argument, however, and that is the way in which this process can lead to a long-term acceleration in the cycle of weapons innovation. A modern arms race naturally pushes the rate of innovation because of the strong imperative to keep pace on qualitative grounds. The side with the more effective innovation will tend to lead the race, resting its security to some extent on its ability to keep one jump ahead. Because there is a general imperative to push qualitative innovation, the focus of the competition can easily shift from responding to what your opponent is doing, to a more internalised and eternal competition with the frontiers of the technically possible. The reference point for continued innovation and competition thus becomes not the external activities of one's rival, but the constant challenge from the expanding frontier of knowledge.

This process is particularly visible in the United States, where the intermediary forms of competing companies within the arms industry make it explicit. These companies compete with each other to offer ever more advanced weapons to the government, and their competition has become a main part of the dynamic in what is ostensibly an arms race between the United States and the Soviet Union. The external arms race provides the justification for keeping the arms companies in being, and for pursuing the ever-receding technological leading edge. But while the Soviet Union provides a general challenge, in almost no field does its technological quality pose any threat to the United States. Here the Americans compete with themselves, and in so doing tend both to accelerate the pace of the arms race and to lock the pattern of the race into a mould which is extremely difficult to break. The American cycle of technological innovation in weaponry proceeds with reference to the Soviet Union as a threat, but largely independently of it as a technological competitor. The Soviets respond as best they can, generally by building larger quantities of lower quality equipment.[28] But since the primary motor of innovation is almost wholly contained within the United States, the arms race does not proceed according to the logic of Soviet-American relations alone, but increasingly responds to the technological dynamic of weapons innovation. In this way, the internalisation of the weapons dynamic creates a dangerous short circuit between the process of arms maintenance and the process of arms racing. If these two become hard to distinguish, as they do under these conditions, then the weapons dynamic can intrude into, and even dominate, the process of arms racing, making it much more dangerous, intractable and unstoppable than it would otherwise be. As argued above, one of the most distressing aspects of the weapons dynamic is that, when unleashed, it greatly exacerbates the power-security dilemma. Where an internalised arms race exists, the weapons dynamic shifts into top gear, with effects that are so familiar that they require no illustration other than the US $500 billion which the world was spending annually on military strength by the end of the 1970s.[29]

Another major variable in determining the character and variety of arms races is the nature of the weapons involved. In the preceding discussion, we have treated weapons as an aggregate phenomenon to which we could apply general notions like quality, quantity, cost, military power and technological innovation. But on a more detailed level, weapons comprise an enormously diverse category, the members of which display such great differences among themselves that their individual characteristics must also count as a distinct feature of arms races. It seems reasonable to assume, for example, that, other things being equal, an arms race centred on naval weapons will differ in significant ways from one involving ground forces. More obviously, a race involving nuclear weapons will differ from one confined to conventional machines, and, across time, a race in the technical conditions of the fifteenth century, like those involving the giant cannon of that time, will differ from one in the rather more dynamic technological climate of the twentieth century. Many variables can be identified which could serve as the basis for inquiry along these lines. Weapons differ as to the medium in which they operate, and therefore as to the kind of effect they have in practice, and as to the kind of threat they pose in the context of an arms race. Navies, for example, pose a more specialised, and, on the whole, less potent threat than do armies. Although you can damage a country with a navy, you cannot occupy it, an argument used often by the British to justify their benign role in the European balance of power. Britain, with a strong navy and a weak army, could not threaten to invade any continental power. In the years before the First World War, the British argued that Germany, with both a strong army and a strong navy, threatened everyone, particularly themselves. One might expect, on this basis, that arms races centred on land power would tend to be more acute than those focused more on air and sea power.

Weapons differ along many performance dimensions, such as destructive power (Second World War V-2 rockets versus the MIRVed, nuclear-armed ICBMs of three decades later), range (B-52s versus B-17s), speed (nuclear submarines versus earlier diesel-electric models), and accuracy (laser-guided bombs versus traditional free-fall models). They also vary as to cost, the rapidity of their research-development-production-deployment-obsolescence cycle, the kinds of resources (type and quantity) they require in relation to the overall productive capacity of society, and their overall success as a design in comparison with others of their class. Any or all of these variables might make a significant impact on the character of an arms race involving them. Most obvious, for example, is the much debated proposition that when weapons become sufficiently destructive, as nuclear weapons have done, the standard logic of the arms race (that is, racing to achieve goals like parity, superiority or relative improvement in military strength) becomes meaningless. Past a certain (ill-defined) point, increases in capability make no significant difference because targets can only be destroyed once. Under these circumstances, ideas like 'sufficiency' and 'minimum deterrent' emerge, and give a character to the arms race that would not occur in races with lesser weapons. Many other more subtle influences on the character of arms races could probably be found along this line of inquiry, but space forbids further exploration here. In a related vein, as noted above, it could be added that the character of an arms race will vary according to whether the weapons concerned are to be pitted against each other, like Dreadnoughts, tanks and tactical aircraft, or relate to each other only via complicated military systems composed of many weapons, like SLBM. The sense of race will be much clearer in the former case, and comparative military evaluations will be very difficult in the latter. These considerations underline the point made in chapter 4 about the hazards of comparing phenomena like arms races across historical periods. At the very least, such comparisons should specify the role of weapons variables in the cases concerned.

One notable attempt to explore the weapons variable has been made by Robert Jervis.[30] By focusing on whether weapons are offensive or defensive in character, he produces some useful insights into the impact of weapons variables on arms racing and the security dilemma. Jervis concludes his piece with a discussion of four scenarios which result from a 2×2 matrix.[31] Across the top, the variable is whether offensive or defensive weapons have the advantage at the time under consideration. War-proven examples here would be the First World War (defensive-dominant), and the Second World War (offensive-dominant). Down the side, the variables are, first, that offensive weapons (and therefore postures) *cannot* be distinguished from defensive ones, and second, that they *can* be distinguished. Although there are some well-tried difficulties in distinguishing between offensive and defensive weapons – as illustrated both by pre-1914 assumptions that the offensive was dominant, as it had been in 1870, and by the lengthy, and eventually fruitless, debates of the 1932 Disarmament Conference on the subject – Jervis's scheme suggests some powerful insights into the security implications of weapons variables.

In brief, his argument is that when offensive weapons are dominant, and the difference between offensive and defensive weapons cannot be distinguished, incentives to acquire offensive weapons will be high all round, and the situation will be very unstable, with the power-security dilemma operating at full pitch. When the offensive weapons are dominant, but the difference can be distinguished, the situation is less tense, and aggressive states can be identified as such by the weapons they procure. The spoiler here is that if the offensive advantage is great, a passive defence option will not suffice, and even status quo states will be obliged to procure offensive weapons. When the defence has the advantage and the difference cannot be distinguished, the power-security dilemma operates, but is moderated by the fact that arms acquisitions produce more security for their owners than insecurity for others. When the defence has the advantage and the difference can be distinguished, the situation is very stable, with aggressors giving themselves away, and the uncertainties which produce the security struggle kept to a minimum.

This kind of analysis points to the importance of the weapons variable as a factor in the international security environment. At a minimum, it offers a basis for assessing particular situations, and for understanding the implications of the endless variations in weaponry which are generated by the advance of technology. At a maximum, it suggests criteria for arms control and the management of the whole arms maintenance process.

Arms Control and Disarmament

Any discussion of weapons and arms racing as part of the national security problem begs for a balancing exploration of what can and should be done about it. Such work normally comes under the heading of arms control and disarmament (ACD), and an enormous literature exists on every conceivable theoretical and practical aspect of it.[31] Limitations of space preclude any significant summary of this literature here. But the argument made so far in this book does bear on ACD, and some comment is necessary. Both opponents and advocates of ACD can agree on one fact: that neither efforts made towards ACD, nor the results from those efforts, have come anywhere close to matching the widespread hopes which supported them. In other words, ACD is widely regarded as the cure to the problem posed by war and weapons, despite the fact that its practical impact has been marginal. Three explanations for this poor record can be derived from our analysis of the security problem and are significant for the discussion of national security as a policy problem in the next chapter.

The first explanation, as argued in part above, and by implication in chapters 1, 3, 4, and 6, is that disarmament, especially on the scale of general and complete disarmament (GCD), is fundamentally incompatible with the whole structure of the international anarchy. The control of armed forces is basic to the constitution of sovereign states, both for domestic purposes, and in their relations with each other.[33] Since humanity has not yet devised political systems good enough to allow it to abandon the use of force, and does not appear to be close to doing so, military power cannot be eliminated even under a GCD scheme. A strong central authority would be required to police a GCD regime, and it would have to be armed as a check against cheating. Since the potential benefits from cheating rise as the general level of arms drops,[34] such a central authority would need to amount to a world government. Neither the force nor the political consensus for a development along these lines is anywhere in sight, and consequently GCD, whatever its merits, is not a feasible policy in relation to present security problems. Furthermore, so long as the structure of the system continues to be anarchic, and especially when the distribution of benefits within it is as uneven as it now is, the prospect of rivalry between status quo and revisionist interests will continue to justify the possession of military power. Such rivalries, and the prospect of them, are a permanent and primary obstacle to disarmament. The status quo interests will not lightly surrender their advantages, and the revisionist ones having less to lose are even less likely to give up their claims. *Both* the power and the security struggles operate to bedevil the security of states in the international system, and there are no safe gounds for assuming, as a basis for policy, that one has to deal only with the more tractable problems of the security struggle.

The second explanation arises from the constant problem of the weapons innovation cycle. The continuous developments of new weapons, or the potential for them, cannot be separated from the broad process of technological advance. Because of this, both arms control and disarmament must run in order to stand still. Since the problem is not fixed, there is no fixed solution to it. Compounding this difficulty is the fact that if a demand for weapons exists, as we have argued it will, then the nature of armaments will ensure that the demand is for the best that can be produced given limits of resources. This double pressure for improved weapons works continuously and powerfully against any attempts at ACD. Arms control, in particular, has to be based on the specific technological conditions which exist in any given period, and these are likely to be short-lived.[35] An agreement to limit numbers of battleships will be meaningful in one decade and irrelevant in the next; and agreements to limit missile numbers, like SALT I, can be quickly undone by developments in warhead design (MIRV) and advances in BMD.

Arms control efforts may succeed in moderating and channeling the weapons dynamic, but they offer little hope of stopping it, and themselves require constant and difficult revision. They also run the continuous risk of being absorbed into the arms race, a criticism commonly levelled at the whole SALT effort.[36] New arms developments get justified as bargaining chips for prospective arms control negotiations, thereby reducing the whole arms control approach to a closed cycle of futility, and demonstrating the political power of an arms race process that has become internalised. Put simply, the problem is that the weapons dynamic is a large and exceptionally powerful process. Arms control efforts are severely limited in scope by the political constraints of the international anarchy, and will continue to be so if that system remains in being. An effective political base for arms control and disarmament could only be created by a major transformation in the system. No such transformation is in sight, and consequently arms control will continue to be decidedly inadequate, if not quite hopeless, in relation to its task. Its advocates, despite the moral force and sound common sense of their position, will not be able to escape from being in a position of trying to bail out a leaky boat with a teaspoon.

A third explanation for the difficulties of ACD arises from the lack of any convincingly stable configurations in the distribution of military power. Unless some arrangement exists within which all can feel secure, there will be strong incentives to continue in a competitive mode in which security is obtained at the expense of others – that is to say, by succeeding in the endless scramble for relative strength. The principal contenders for this stable configuration have been a variety of ideas all tied together by the underlying concept of evenness. These include balance, equality, equivalence and parity. All of them benefit from the inherent logic, obvious fairness, and conceptual clarity which attach to the idea of evenness, and the power of this appeal manifests itself clearly in exercises like SALT. Evenness of some description appears to have an overwhelmingly strong case on moral, political and rational grounds as the solution to the problems of insecurity which arise from the endless cycles of the weapons dynamic. Unfortunately, however, solutions based on evenness cannot provide a stable stopping place for military relations, and proposals which assume that they can will be misguided and ineffective. Even more unfortunately, alternative ideas are non-existent, which leaves only a return to the dangers of free competition in the market-place of military security.

Ideas like parity (which we shall use henceforth to designate the whole range of solutions deriving from evenness) can be faulted on two grounds in the context of military security relations. First, even if the principle was sound, the necessary conditions for parity cannot be calculated. And second, the underlying principle of parity is flawed, because evenness does not lead to stability in military relations. The problem of calculation is long-established and familiar to all those who have tried to make assessments about the state of any peacetime military balance. The sad fact is that war is the only true test of a military balance, a point demonstrated most recently by the defeat of the United States in Vietnam. Trying to assess a military balance in peacetime is impossible. Comparative lists of weapons and manpower can usually be obtained with a moderate degree of reliability,[37] but simply taken at face-value, these mislead more than they enlighten. Dozens, possibly hundreds, of subtle qualitative variables influence the potential utility of military instruments. These include quality of leadership, morale, reliability of machinery, effectiveness of command, control, communications and intelligence (C^3I), geostrategic factors, luck, possession of the initiative, choice of tactics, the preparedness of the opposition, mobilisation rates, the effectiveness of supply systems and the nature of opposing forces.

An illustration of the uncertainty attaching to military comparisons is that, despite the enormous amount of study devoted to the military balance in Europe, nobody has any clear idea of whether the Russians could break through to the Atlantic coast or not. The lists of forces suggest that perhaps they could, and several authors have caught the public eye by writing appropriate scenarios.[38] But any one of hundreds of variables could intervene to change the balance. Short of an actual test in war, nobody can predict the outcome, and therefore no reliable assessment of parity can be calculated in peacetime.

Parity in hardware and manpower does not necessarily, or even usually, equal parity in military capability, as indicated on numerous occasions by the Israelis. It cannot therefore be used as a basis for equal feelings of security which would be necessary for any long-term stability. This general problem of measurement is compounded first by the relentless push of the weapons dynamic, which constantly feeds new imponderables into the equation, and second, by the multisided nature of military balances. India worries about Pakistan and China, just as the Soviet Union worries about the West and China, and as Germany traditionally worried about France and Russia. Because military force can be projected in more than one direction, it becomes nearly impossible to isolate and stabilise any single pair of states. Pakistan looks at India, just as the West looks at the Soviet Union, and sees the whole strength of its opponent in relation to its own. India and the Soviet Union, by contrast, compare their strength with that of their combined enemies. No meaningful calculation of parity can be achieved under these conditions.

The principle of parity itself can be faulted on two grounds as a basis for stabilising security relations. The first fault relates to the arguments just made about calculation, and is that even if parity of military forces could be reliably and visibly achieved, the nature of military action is such that equality of security would not result. All other things being equal, military action rewards those who strike first. The aggressor gets to choose the time, place and conditions for his attack, and if offensive weapons are dominant, as they generally have been since the Second World War, he may be able to achieve a significant reduction in his opponent's force by mounting a Pearl Harbor-type counter-force strike. This first strike factor undermines any simple notion of parity based on a balance of military instruments. Indeed, it seems quite possible that an explicit and visible parity would amplify its effect. Where force calculations are uncertain, ambiguity acts as a restraint on the first strike option, but if the balance is known, the calculation can be made with greater certainty.

The second fault is more subtle, and hinges on the instability of relative status in a regime of parity. A case can be made that relations between two states will be most stable when the disparity in power between them is large. The greater power will feel no vital threat and the smaller will, of necessity, learn to accommodate itself. When the difference in power is large, both sides are secure in the knowledge that their relative status will not change quickly. Although the lesser power may not like it, and although the situation generates incentives to arms race, in the short term a large disparity in power is relatively stable (assuming, almost by definition, that the dominant power is status quo). By contrast, a situation of parity leaves neither side secure in the knowledge of a comfortable margin of strength, and provides incentives to make an effort to tip the balance. When powers are equal, a small increase by one serves to change their relative status from equals, to superior and inferior, in a way which does not occur when relative status is protected by larger differentials in power.[39] Arms races become much more sensitive when the race is close, because a prospect of winning or losing presents itself. Status instability in an arms race is not a new phenomenon. The Duke of Buckingham, in a letter to Sir Thomas Osborn in 1672, argued that: 'We ought not to suffer any other Nation to be our *Equals* at *Sea*, because when they are once our *Equals*, it is but an even *Lay*, whether they or we shall be the *Superiors*.'[40] The same problem occurred in 1906, when the launching of the HMS *Dreadnought* precipitated a fierce stage in the Anglo-German naval race by giving the Germans a chance to compete on fairly even terms in the new class of vessel.

Similarly, the United States has found its decline from superiority over the Soviet Union very difficult to live with. Parity and its relatives sound good enough, especially when bolstered by the idea of nuclear sufficiency, but its cost is a recurrent *Angst* that the Soviet Union is getting ahead – in other words, that the status between the two is undergoing a basic change. The American case is interesting, because it demonstrates the force of status instability even against the massive counterweight of nuclear sufficiency. The culmination of the defence dilemma in nuclear deterrence offers the prospect of restoring utility to parity in the form of mutual nuclear sufficiency. The existence of nuclear forces sufficient for mutually assured destruction (MAD) creates a form of parity which appears to obviate the problems of superiority and inferiority, and circumvents the problem of force level calculations.[41] It does not, however, constitute a stable resting place, and it requires force levels much higher than those desired by most proponents of ACD. The maintenance of MAD is notoriously at the mercy of the arms dynamic, and is haunted by the fear that technological developments will break its logic by restoring first strike capability to one side. The dismal saga of the SALT negotiations illustrates not only both of these problems, but also the difficulty over status instability, and the general uncertainty over how to calculate an appropriate force level for sufficiency.[42] Even with nuclear sufficiency, therefore, parity does not offer a good prospect for ACD proposals. Although it is the best option available, it cannot escape from the logic of high force levels and perpetual technological pressure.

We can conclude from this discussion that the arms dynamic is an exceptionally durable feature of international relations. It is sustained by two powerful and deeply-rooted factors – the drive of technology, and the demand for weapons created by the structure of the international system – neither of which can be effectively reached by the politically-hobbled forces which back ACD. The arms dynamic does not appear to be one of that class of processes which, like the conversion of ice to water and back again, can easily be made to reverse itself. It cannot simply be turned around and made to wind down by reversal of the same process which made it wind up – not, at least, without winding back most of human history at the same time. In this sense, the arms dynamic is more like the burning of wood, the hardening of cement, or the mixing of paint, all processes which are easy to work in one direction, but impossible to reverse.[43] This is not to say that the process is beyond influence, only that it cannot be made to disappear, as some would hope, by finding a way to put it into reverse gear.[44] ACD attempts can usefully affect the process at the margins, but for all three of the reasons reviewed here – the character of the international anarchy, the pressure of technological innovation, and the inadequacy of parity as stable configuration for the arms dynamic – ACD proposals seem very unlikely to provide a solution either to the arms dynamic or to the power-security dilemma.[45]

Conclusions: The Power-Security Dilemma and the Defence Dilemma

We can conclude from this discussion that the power-security dilemma is an exceptionally durable feature of international relations. As we have seen, it is sustained not only by the tensions between status quo and revisionist interests, but also by the massive momentum of the arms dynamic. These two factors ensure that, for purposes of policy-making, the dynamics of the power struggle remain effectively indistinguishable from those of the security struggle. Because the power and security struggles cannot be distinguished reliably, national security policy cannot rest on the relatively clear and straightforward principles that can be derived from either in isolation. The dynamics of both struggles must be assumed to be in play, leading, in consequence, to the self-maintaining problems and policies with which we are all too familiar. The cycle of arms innovation and improvement will continue, inflaming in the process the dynamics of the power-security dilemma. These in turn will stimulate demand for weapons, thereby justifying and accelerating the arms dynamic.

The principal relief in this gloomy picture derives from the fact that the arms dynamic feeds the defence dilemma as well as the power-security one. Both dilemmas cannot continue to get worse without, in the process, strengthening a contradiction which is already very much in evidence between them. This contradiction arises from the independence of the arms dynamic which underlies and connects them both. As the defence dilemma spreads and intensifies, it erodes the traditional conditions which have allowed, and even encouraged, the struggle for power to occur. When the costs and risks of armed struggle rise to the point where massive destruction is certain to be inflicted on both victor and vanquished, then armed struggle ceases to be a useful way of pursuing competitive political objectives. Military forces still need to be maintained and upgraded in order to preserve the paralysis, but notions of inferiority and superiority no longer have the same clear political implications that they had as recently as the Second World War. Once this threshold is passed, military force ceases to be a competitive variable in the sense implied by our discussion on arms racing, and becomes more of a constant which rests on the notion of sufficiency. Sufficiency, however, still has to be maintained in the light of technical advance. The same logic of sufficiency should also mute the security struggle, although it would not remove the uncertainties and fears associated with maintaining one's forces at a reliable level of sufficiency in the face of constant pressures from technological change and the force levels of others.

In the present international system, this contradiction has already made a considerable impact on military relations among the major powers, and is most fully developed between the members of NATO and the Warsaw Pact. Many areas still exist, however, where the defence dilemma is weak enough to allow both local conflicts and external interventions by the powers to occur more or less under the old rules. Here, the power-security dilemma operates undiminished, and war remains a feasible instrument of policy. Even between the super-powers, the condition of paralysis is so new and unfamiliar that much behaviour reflecting the old rules still persists. One still gets the sense from statements on both sides that nuclear superiority has some political meaning equivalent to the traditional power significance of having more Dreadnoughts or more army divisions. While superiority may have some political effects, particularly in the way nuclear powers see each other and are seen by third parties, the new conditions of the defence dilemma mean that the old political and military meaning of superiority can never return. As F.H. Hinsley put it, 'These states have passed so far beyond a threshold of absolute power that changes in relative power can no longer erode their ability to uphold the equilibrium which resides in the ability of each to destroy all.'[46]

The defence dilemma certainly has not cured the present system of its security problem, and it is not intended to argue here that it can do so. It is not offered as a preferred solution, but as a visible and powerful trend in the mainstream of events which has major implications for the international security environment. Carried to its logical conclusion, the defence dilemma could produce not Armageddon, as might be feared from the unrestrained operation of a power-security dilemma pressed by an open-ended arms dynamic, but an effectively paralysed international system in which major military force played no role other than ensuring its own non-use.

The safest, and most congenial form for such an outcome would be the mature anarchy outlined in chapters 4 and 5. A system composed of large, politically strong, relatively self-reliant, relatively tolerant, and relatively evenly powered units (that is, all capable of mounting and maintaining a sufficiency of force to preserve the defence dilemma) might work quite well. It could, at best, reap the advantages of military paralysis to produce a stable set of relations in which the power-security dilemma would have minimum scope for operation, though it would still live with the background threat of obliteration and the need to keep pace with the arms dynamic. In a more multipolar system, the complexity of possible alignments would dilute the problem of status disequilibrium which is a conspicuous feature of bipolar relationships. Although a multipolar deterrence system is not without its problems, it has the advantage of preventing the excessive concentration of rivalry which continues to drive the power-security dilemma in a bipolar system, despite the moderating effects of nuclear sufficiency. Only in a more mature anarchy, where the power-security dilemma had been muted both by system norms of mutual respect, and by the intrinsic power and strength of the constituent units, would ACD policies have a chance of making a substantial impact on the management of military relations.

There is no guarantee that the system will evolve into a mature form, though, as argued above, rising defence costs and the attractions of nuclear paralysis might well tend to push it in this direction. The path, however, is hardly a safe one. Very high risks must be run to get to the point at which the defence dilemma produces paralysis, as illustrated by the courses of the First and Second World Wars, and by the evidence from current highly armed, but not paralysed, areas like the Middle East. It would seem, for example, necessary to take a benign view of some (not all) proliferation of nuclear weapons in pursuit of this scenario, a position which can hardly be described as popular, or in line with mainstream views on either ACD or national security.[47] Even within the confines of a fully-developed defence dilemma, there are still risks of accident and miscalculation which many find unacceptable, not to mention the high costs and moral effects of a permanently militarised system. Despite the many dangers and difficulties, however, this appears to be the direction in which the international system is moving. The problem for national security policy-makers is that there appear to be neither practicable alternatives to, nor ways of breaking out of, the dynamics and dilemmas outlined in this chapter.

Notes

1 These two views are set out at length in Robert Jervis, *Perception and Misperception in International Politics* (Princeton, Princeton University Press, 1976), ch. 3.
2 E.H. Carr, *The Twenty Years Crisis* (London, Macmillan, 1946, 2nd edn); Hans Morgenthau, *Politics Among Nations* (New York, Knopf, 1973, 5th edn). See also, Paul Seabury, 'The Idea of the Status Quo', in Seabury (ed.), *Balance of Power* (San Francisco, Chandler, 1965), ch.

22; and Richard W. Cottam, *Foreign Policy Motivation* (n.p., University of Pittsburgh Press, 1977), ch. 2.

3 For general analysis focused on the system dynamic of status quo versus revisionist powers, see Robert Gilpin, *War and Change in World Politics* (Cambridge, Cambridge University Press, 1981); and Richard K. Ashley, *the Political Economy of War and Peace* (London, Frances Pinter, 1980).

4 Klaus Knorr, *Power and Wealth* (London, Macmillan, 1973), p. 106.

5 Ken Booth, *Strategy and Ethnocentrism* (London, Croom Helm, 1979).

6 Carr, *op. cit.* (note 2), p. 84; Knorr, *op. cit.* (note 4), pp. 12, 195; and David Calleo, 'The Historiography of the Interwar Period: Reconsiderations', in Benjamin Rowland (ed.), *Balance of Power or Hegemony: the Interwar Monetary System* (New York, New York University Press, 1976), pp. 228–29.

7 Carr, *ibid.*, pp. 93–222.

8 *Ibid.*, p. 167.

9 Much of the argument in this section is based on Barry Buzan, 'Change and Insecurity: A Critique of Strategic Studies', in Barry Buzan and R.J. Barry Jones (eds), *Change and the Study of International Politics* (London, Frances Pinter, 1981), pp. 160–6.

10 Fred Hirsch and Michael Doyle, 'Politicization in the World Economy: Necessary Conditions for an International Economic Order', in F. Hirsch, M. Doyle and Edward L. Morse, *Alternatives to Monetary Disorder* (New York McGraw-Hill, 1977), p. 27.

11 Carr, *op. cit.* (note 2), p. 105.

12 *Ibid.*, p. 222.

13 Richard J. Barnet, 'The Illusion of Security', in Charles R. Beitz and T. Herman (eds), *Peace and War* (San Francisco, W.H. Freeman, 1973), p. 285.

14 This approach to the status quo is based on the structure of relations in the system. It implicitly rejects the approach used by Seabury, *op. cit.* (note 2), which relates the status quo to the existence of semi-constitutional international orders like those established by the Congress of Vienna and the Treaty of Versailles. While Seabury's constitutional approach has obvious merits, it forces him to conclude that the concept of the status quo is 'virtually meaningless' (p. 212) in the contemporary international system.

15 Arnold Wolfers, *Discord and Collaboration* (Baltimore, Johns Hopkins University Press, 1962), p. 18.

16 Kenneth N. Waltz, *Theory of International Politics* (Reading, Mass., Addison-Wesley, 1979), pp. 168–71.

17 Anatol Rapoport, *Conflict in Man-Made Environment* (Harmondsworth, Penguin, 1974), p. 176.

18 For some critical evaluations of the NIEO along these lines, see W.M. Corden, 'The NIEO Proposals: A Cool Look', *Thames Essay 21* (Policy Research Center, 1979); Nathaniel Leff, 'The New International Economic Order – Bad Economics, Worse Politics', *Foreign Policy*, 24 (1976), M.E. Kreinin and J.M. Finger, 'A Critical Survey of the New

International Economic Order', *Journal of World Trade Law*, 10:6 (1976).

19 An example of this argument is Mary Kaldor, *the Disintegrating West* (Harmondsworth, Penguin, 1979).

20 Moregenthau, *op. cit.* (note 2), pp. 67–8.

21 On this theme, see Maurice Pearton, *The Knowledgeable State: Diplomacy, War and Technology since 1830* (London, Burnett, 1982); and Hedley Bull, *the Control of the Arms Race* (London, Weidenfeld & Nicolson, 1961), pp. 195–201.

22 In 1981 Israel spent approximately one-third of its GNP on defence, *the Military Balance 1981–1982*, (London, IISS, 1981), p. 52.

23 See Lewis F. Richardson, *Arms and Insecurity* (Pittsburg, Boxwood Press, 1960); Ian Bellany, 'The Richardson Theory of Arms Races', *British Journal of International Studies*, 1:2 (1975); E.R. Brubaker, 'Economic Models of Arms Races', *Journal of Conflict Resolution*, 17:2 (1973).

24 These objectives are an elaboration from a simpler set given by P. Kodzic, 'Armaments and Development', in David Carlton and C. Shaerf (eds), *the Dynamics of the Arms Race* (London, Croom Helm, 1975), pp. 204–5.

25 See Robert Jervis, *Perception and Misperception in International Politics* (Princeton, Princeton University Press, 1976), esp. chs. 4, 7.

26 Anthony Downs, *Inside Bureaucracy* (Boston, Little Brown, 1967), ch. 2.

27 See, for example, Steven Rosen (ed.), *Testing the Theory of MIC* (Toronto, D.C. Heath, 1973); Carrol W. Pursell Jr (ed.), *the Military Industrial Complex* (New York, Harper & Row, 1972); Basil Collier, *Arms and the Men* (London, Hamish Hamilton, 1980); Franklin A. Long and J. Reppy (eds), *The Genesis of New Weapons* (New York, Pergamon, 1980); Robert C. Gray, 'Learning From History: Case Studies of the Weapons Acquisition Process', *World Politics*, 31:3 (1979).

28 The exception to this rule was the Soviet *coup* with Sputnik in 1957.

29 Ruth L. Sivard, *World Military and Social Expenditure* (Leesburg, Va., World Priorities, 1980), p. 6. A different consequence of arms racing at the leading edge of technology is argued by Mary Kaldor, *The Baroque Arsenal* (London, André Deutsch, 1982). She develops the thesis that such races tend to produce over-sophisticated weapons because concern with technological innovation begins to outweigh considerations of military utility.

30 Robert Jervis, 'Cooperation Under the Security Dilemma', *World Politics*, 30:2 (1978). See also Richard Rosecrance, *International Relations: Peace or War?* (New York, McGraw-Hill, 1973), pp. 65, 300.

31 Jervis, *ibid.*, pp. 211–14.

32 See, for example, John Garnett (ed.), *Theories of Peace and Security* (London, Macmillan, 1970), chs. 7–12; D.G. Brennan (ed.), *Arms Control Disarmament and National Security* (New York, Braziller, 1961); J.D. Singer, *Deterrence, Arms Control and Disarmament* (no

place, Ohio State University Press, 1962); John H. Barton, *The Politics of Peace: an evaluation of arms control* (Standford, Standford, University Press, 1981); Wolfram F. Hanreider, *Arms Control and Security* (Boulder, Co., Westview Press, 1979); Hedley Bull, *The Control of the Arms Race* (London, Weidenfeld & Nicolson, 1961). Although arms control and disarmament are often referred to in a single phrase, they represent quite different sets of assumptions about both international relations in general, and the problem of weapons and war in particular. On this distinction, see Ken Booth, 'Disarmament and Arms Control', in John Baylis *et al., Contemporary Strategy* (London, Croom Helm, 1975), ch. 5.

33   For the general argument on this case, see Hedley Bull, 'Disarmament and the International System', in Garnett, *ibid.*, ch. 8.

34   Kodzic, *op. cit.* (note 24), pp. 202–3.

35   For a useful discussion of this problem, see Bull, *op. cit.* (note 21), ch. 12.

36   See for example, Lawrence Freedman, 'The Consequences of Failure in SALT', in Christoph Bertram (ed.), 'Beyond SALT II', *Adelphi Paper*, 141, (London, IISS, 1977), pp. 35–41; and Colin Gray, 'A Problem Guide to SALT II', *Survival* (September-October 1975), p. 234.

37   See the annual publication, *The Military Balance* (London, IISS).

38   See, for example, Robert Close, *Europe Without Defence?* (New York, Pergamon Press, 1979); and Sir John Hackett *et al., The Third World War, August 1985* (London, Sidgwick & Jackson, 1978).

39   For some other angles on status instability, see Richard Rosecrance, 'Deterrence and Vulnerability in the Pre-Nuclear Era', in 'The Future of Strategic Deterrence', *Adelphi Paper*, 160 (London, IISS, 1980).

40   Quoted in Philip W. Buck, *The Politics of Mercantilism* (New York, Octagon, 1974 (1942)), pp. 116–17.

41   See Robert Jervis, 'Why Nuclear Superiority Doesn't Matter', *Political Science Quarterly*, 94:4 (1979–80).

42   On SALT, see, *inter alia*, 'Forum on SALT II', *Survival* (September-October 1979); Strobe Talbott, *Endgame: the Inside Story of SALT II* (London, Harper & Row, 1979); Thomas W. Wolfe, *The SALT Experience* (Cambridge, Mass., Ballinger, 1979). On the particular problem of parity in the SALT context, see Jervis, *op. cit.*, M.D. Salomon, 'New Concepts for Strategic Parity', *Survival* (November-December 1977); C.M. Lehman and P.C. Hughes, 'Equivalance and SALT II', *Orbis*, 20:4 (1977); Walter Slocombe, 'The Political Implications of Strategic Parity', *Adelphi Paper*, 77 (London, IISS, 1971).

43   R.J. Barry Jones, 'Concepts and Models of Change in International Relations', in Buzan and Jones, *op. cit.* (note 9), pp. 20–8.

44   For example, Mary Kaldor, 'Disarmament: The Armament Process in Reverse', in E.P. Thompson and Dan Smith, *Protest and Survive* (Harmondsworth, Penguin, 1980).

45   Space does not permit discussion of the arms trade, but the large literature on this topic suggests that this trade might also be argued to undermine the chances of ACD. Not only does the arms trade facilitate secondary arms races, and allow industrial states to maintain arms

industries beyond the size which their domestic markets could support, but also it ties commercial incentives into the arms dynamic, and thus links it to the larger dynamic of the international economy. The result of this bridge is to add commercial drives to those forces already tending to generate the proliferation of military force in the system. On the arms trade see, *inter alia*, SIPRI, *the Arms Trade with the Third World*, and *The Arms Trade Registers* (Stockholm, Almqvist & Wiksell, respectively 1969 and 1975); J. Stanley and M. Pearton, *the International Trade in Arms* (London, Chatto & Windus, 1972); C. Canizzo, *the Gun Merchants* (New York, Pergamon, 1980); Basil Collier, *Arms and the Men* (London, Hamish Hamilton, 1980); Robert E. Harkavy, *The Arms Trade and International Systems* (Cambridge, Mass., Ballinger, 1975); Stephanie G. Neuman and Robert E. Harkavy, *Arms Transfers in the Modern World* (New York, Praeger, 1979); I. Pelag, 'Arms Supply in the Third World', *Journal of Modern African Studies* (March 1977); Ulrich Albrecht *et al.*, 'Militarization, Arms Transfers and Arms Production in Peripheral Countries', *Journal of Peace Research*, 12:3 (1975).

46 F.H. Hinsley, 'The Rise and Fall of the Modern International System', *Review of International Studies*, 8:1 (1982), p. 8.

47 One courageous advocate of this view is Kenneth N. Waltz, 'The Spread of Nuclear Weapons: More May be Better', *Adelphi Paper*, 171, (London, IISS, 1981).

8 National and International Security: The Policy Problem

In the preceding chapters we have examined different aspects and levels of the national security problem at considerable length. The emphasis throughout has been on the objective dimensions of the problem at the level of individuals, states and the system as a whole. Regardless of these neat, and rather abstract inquiries, however, at the end of the day national security must still be dealt with as a policy problem. The various actors involved have to cope with the national security problem in real time, and in the light of their very different experiences and capabilities. Their policies, regardless of logic or merit, go out into the system, and in aggregate become the larger structures, processes and dynamics which we have discussed.

In the best of all possible worlds, all the actors in international relations would possess perfect information, would understand the positions and motives of others, and also the workings of the system as a whole, would be capable of making rational decisions based on this information and understanding, and would be free to make, and to implement, such decisions. Such a situation would greatly ease the job both of foreign policy decision-makers and of academic analysts. Unfortunately, we do not live in this perfect world. In the real world, policy-makers are only partially informed, do not fully understand other actors or the system, are capable of only limited rationality, and are highly constrained in what they can do. Because of these imperfections, the policy-making process itself becomes an important component in the national security problem. Many factors within it have little to do with the problem itself, but none the less have a considerable influence on policies produced in the name of national security. Because of the powerful feedback effects between policy and the problem, as illustrated by arms racing, the policy-making process becomes a major source of intervening variables in relation to the larger rationalities of the national security problem.

This whole issue of domestic variables has been extensively analysed in the large literature on foreign policy,[1] so we do not need to repeat that exercise here. Instead, we shall confine ourselves to

214

surveying the kinds of intervening variables which affect national security policy in particular, and to drawing some conclusions about how these variables affect the national security problem as a whole. We shall take three approaches to this subject, looking first at the purely logical dilemmas faced by policy-makers in making choices about ends and means, and then at the perceptual and the political factors which complicate the policy-making process. Every country has security relations whether it wants them or not. Most would like to have a coherent and reliable security policy, but, as always, such a policy is much harder to acquire than is the problem which gives rise to the need for it.

Logical Problems

The making of national security policy requires choices about both the objectives of policy (ends), and the techniques, resources, instruments and actions which will be used to implement it (means). Even if we assume that neither political nor perceptual problems interfere with the process, these choices are not straightforward. Many complex logical difficulties arise which, because they reflect the fundamental character of the national security problem itself, will always impinge on policy choices. Here we are back again to the essentially contested nature of security as a concept, which was the starting point of our inquiry.

Taken as an end, national security runs immediately into the problem that it can never be achieved. Complete security cannot be obtained in an anarchic system, and therefore to hold that goal as an aspiration is to condemn oneself to pursuit of an operationally impossible objective. If national security is a relative end, then extremely complicated and objectively unanswerable questions arise about how much security is enough, and about how to make adjustments to the ceaseless changes in the innumerable criteria by which relative security must be defined. Relative security is a permanently unsatisfactory condition. It can always be criticised as imperfect, because on logical grounds it must be so. And it can never serve as a stable resting place, because the factors which define a satisfactory relative level at any given moment are themselves ephemeral. The structure of the system and its interaction dynamics, as we have seen, complete this dilemma by ensuring that any attempt to acquire, or even move towards, complete security by any actor will stimulate reactions which raise the level of threat in proportion to the measures taken. The arms race, the Cold War and the defence dilemma give new meaning in this context to Shakespeare's observation that, 'security is mortals' chiefest enemy'.[2]

Attempts to clarify the ends of security policy naturally lead to attempts at definition, an exercise which we specifically eschewed at the beginning of this book. Wolfers warned about its ambiguity, and Charles Schultze argues explicitly that: 'The concept of national security does not lend itself to neat and precise formulation. It deals with a wide variety of risks about whose probabilities we have little knowledge and of contingencies whose nature we can only dimly perceive.'[3] Several writers have, none the less, taken this approach. Their efforts to define national security typically confuse aspirations with operational ends. Hence, they usually underplay its relativistic dimension, which is where most of its real meaning lies, and fall into the trap of emphasising the more appealing simplicities of security as an absolute condition.

A major reason for this is that such definitions are normally associated with discussion of great powers, which by definition are more able to approach perfect security than are lesser powers. This is particularly true of the United States. No country in the history of the modern state system has approached the level of relative dominance and absolute security which the United States enjoyed in the decade following 1945. The steady erosion of its relative position since then serves only to enhance the image of its former absolute superiority and high security as possibly re-attainable goals, even though at the time they were experienced in the paranoid context of the Cold War. The bias in security definitions towards great powers and absolute security also reflects first, the dominance of the Realist School in International Relations, with its emphasis on power, and second, an arcadian longing for the simpler days when defence was a clear and meaningful concept.

Examples of these attempts include the following:

Walter Lippmann: '... a nation is secure to the extent to which it is not in danger of having to sacrifice core values if it wishes to avoid war, and is able, if challenged, to maintain them by victory in such a war.'[4]

Arnold Wolfers: '... security, in an objective sense, measures the absence of threats to acquired values, in a subjective sense, the absence of fear that such values will be attacked.'[5]

Michael H.H. Louw: national security includes traditional defence policy and also 'the non-military actions of a state to ensure its total capacity to survive as a political entity in order to exert influence and to carry out its internal and international objectives'.[6]

Ian Bellany: 'Security itself is a relative freedom from war, coupled with a relatively high expectation that defeat will not be a consequence of any war that should occur.'[7]

Frank N. Trager and F.N. Simonie: 'National security is that part of government policy having as its objective the creation of national and international political conditions favourable to the protection or extension of vital national values against existing and potential adversaries.'[8]

John E. Mroz: Security is 'the *relative freedom* from harmful threats'.[9]

These definitions are not without merit, especially that of Mroz which avoids any absolutist bias, and is too vague to get bogged down in specifics. For purely semantic reasons, it is difficult to avoid the absolute sense of security. The word itself implies an absolute condition – something is either secure or insecure – and does not lend itself to the idea of a measurably-graded spectrum like that which fills the space between hot and cold. Although these definitions do a useful service in pointing out some of the criteria for national security, they do a disservice by giving the concept an appearance of firmness which it does not merit, and by focusing attention primarily onto level 2. Most of them avoid crucial questions. What are 'core values'? Are they a fixed or a floating reference point? And are they in themselves free from contradictions? Does 'victory' mean anything under contemporary conditions of warfare? Are subjective and objective aspects of security separable in any meaningful way? Is war the only form of threat relevant to national security? And what right does a state have to define its security values in terms which require it to have influence beyond its own territory, with the almost inevitable infringement of others' security interests which this implies? This last point leads us back to the discussion of objectives as between status quo and revisionist states in the last chapter, with its strong lesson that national security cannot be considered in isolation from the whole structure of the international system.

These definitions tend towards an absolute view of security, a great power orientation, and the notion that national security has some firm and readily identifiable meaning. Their bias is important because it affects a major logical divide in how the ends of national security are defined, and therefore in how policy is oriented. This divide connects particularly to the arguments made in chapter 3 about the nature of threats and vulnerabilities, and the choice between action on level 2 or level 3 as a response. If we start with the tautology that the purpose of national security policy is to make the state secure, or at least *sufficiently* secure if we reject the absolute possibility, then we are led to the question 'How?'. It is within this question that the divide on security ends occurs. The whole inquiry assumes that threats exist, that insecurity is a problem. The divide is this: security can be pursued either by taking action to reduce vulnerability, or by trying to eliminate or reduce the threats by addressing their causes at source. The first of these options we shall call the *national security strategy*, because it is based largely within the threatened state. The second we shall call the *international security strategy*, because it depends on the adjustment of relations between states.[10]

If a national security strategy is adopted, then security policy will tend to be focused on the state. Vulnerabilities can be reduced by increasing self-reliance, and countervailing forces can be built up to deal with specific threats. If the threats are military, then they can be met by strengthening one's own military forces, by seeking alliances, or by hardening the country against attack. Economic threats can be met by increasing self-reliance, diversifying sources of supply, or learning to do without. The whole range of threats surveyed in chapter 3 is relevant here, for any or all of them might have to be met in this strategy by countervailing actions based on the threatened state, and appropriate to the particular situation. Thus, for example, one of the primary British responses to German naval building programmes in the early years of this century was to increase the strength of the Royal Navy as an offset force. The British made quite clear their intention to match and exceed German construction, so that whatever the German effort, they would be allowed to make no gain beyond a ratio of forces set by, and favourable to, Britain. In this way, Britain could meet the German threat directly by taking measures within Britain which would counteract or offset the particular type of threat being developed by the Germans.

The national security strategy is not without its merits but, almost by definition, it makes less sense for lesser powers. As a rule, only great powers command sufficient resources to carry it off.[11] This great power emphasis connects the national security strategy with the biases in thinking about national security which we looked at above. Indeed, the very term 'national security' implies a self-help approach which is perhaps not surprising given its American origins. The principal advantages of a national security strategy are that threats can be met specifically as they arise, and that the measures which provide security are largely, if not wholly, under the control of the state concerned. In theory, and resources permitting, measures could be taken against all identified threats which would have the total effect of blocking or offsetting all sources of insecurity. A pleasing certainty attaches to this approach, not only because the state retains firm control over the sources of its own security, but also because it deals with the firm realities of capabilities rather than with the uncertainties of other actors intentions. For this reason, a national security strategy enables its practitioner to avoid the burden of making difficult distinctions about whether other actors are status quo or revisionist, and whether the security problem reflects a power struggle or a security one. All these distinctions can be ignored to the extent that the state can afford to protect itself against any threats. At its best, this approach would produce a security which was clearly founded, relatively straightforward in operation, and indisputably in the hands of each actor in relation to itself.

The problem with the national security strategy is that its logic is based almost wholly on level 2. Great powers will be able to make it work to some extent, but even they will not be able to ignore the powerful security logic which operates on level 3. Because the national security strategy ignores the sources of threats, it risks both an open-ended commitment to expenditure of resources and a failure to account for the security dynamics which we examined in chapters 4–7. The logic of the national security strategy by itself leads, on level 2, to a militarised and security-obsessed society, of which the best contemporary examples are Israel and the Soviet Union. On level 3, it leads to a highly charged security dilemma which will largely, perhaps completely, defeat the strategy by subjecting it to intense, negative feedback, as in an arms race. The weakness of the national security strategy by itself is that it cannot escape from the interactive consequences of its own effect on the system. Although national security measures may be argued to influence the sources of threat by having a deterrent effect on their perpetrators, any such effect must be balanced against the stimulation which the measures give to the power-security dilemma. Where a defence dilemma is also in operation, the logic of the national security strategy collapses even further, because military threats can no longer be turned aside but only deterred by threats of unacceptable retaliation. Under these conditions, as we have seen, the danger arises of a disharmony between individual and national security which can undermine the political foundations of the strategy. The national security strategy, then, falls victim both to Booth's critique of ethnocentrism, and Ashley's critique of 'technical rationality'.[12]

If the second option – an international security strategy – is adopted, security policy focuses on the sources and causes of threats, the purpose being not to block or offset the threats, but to reduce or eliminate them by political action. Thus, the British had options other than building more Dreadnoughts than the Germans. Had the British government been bent on an international security strategy, they would have given priority to reaching a naval agreement of some sort, or to changing the basis of relations with Germany so that the

Germans had lower incentives to acquire massive naval forces of their own. Some attempts at reaching a naval agreement were indeed made during the later stages of the naval race. The international security strategy has a number of advantages: it addresses the security logic of level 3 squarely, and offers a prospect of a much more efficient security policy than that available with a national security strategy. If threats have been eliminated at source, then resources do not have to be wasted in meeting each of them on its own terms. Such resource economies would have a positive feedback effect in as much as they muted the power-security dilemma, and led to a general lowering of threats all round. They make an attractive alternative to the costly and dangerous competitive security-seeking of unregulated national security strategies. In addition, an international security strategy offers options other than association with a great power to the majority of lesser states whose resources do not permit them to pursue a national security strategy on their own. One of the reasons why these lesser powers pose continuing security problems to the great powers is precisely because they are unable to pursue an effective national security strategy on their own, and therefore need to be attached to a larger power. Pressure from the defence dilemma also makes a very good case for an international security strategy, since the high risks of mutual deterrence need to be offset by sufficient management of relations to ensure that the probabilities of major conflict remain as close to zero as possible.

Unfortunately, the international security strategy is also not without its problems. The most obvious of these is that, where a power struggle is in operation, the basic conditions for an international strategy cannot be met. If states actually want to threaten each other, then there will be severe limits to the scope for threat reduction by negotiation, and those feeling threatened will be forced to adopt a national security approach. Related to this is the disadvantage that states lose considerable control over the factors which provide their security. An international security strategy depends on the management of relations among states, and these are notoriously fickle. The instability of intentions as compared with the relative durability of capabilities is one of the longest-standing axioms of international relations. If one rests one's security on restraint by others in offering threats, then one's security is at the mercy of changes of mind by others. This contrasts unfavourably with the self-reliance logic of the national security strategy, for it seems reasonable to argue that if one does not control the conditions of one's security, then one is secure only in a superficial sense. The only remedy for this problem is to follow the logic of the international security strategy to its full extent, but this would require the erosion of the state and the dissolution of the state system, an eventuality which we have already rejected as unreal for the foreseeable future. We are back again to the problem of world government. This same dilemma occurs if we follow the logic of the arms dynamic, which can also be posited as a difficulty of the international security strategy. No easy or obvious grounds for stable ACD exist, as argued in chapter 7, and the world government solution which would resolve the dilemma is not politically available.

Taken by themselves, then, neither the national security nor the international security strategies are free from serious problems as bases for policy. The difficulty is that while national security in general represents a level 2 objective (making the state secure), this objective cannot be achieved without taking action on both level 2 and level 3. Action on level 2 or level 3 alone cannot work, because of the strain on national resources in the case of level 2, and because of the threat to the basic character of the state on level 3. The solution is a policy which mixes elements of a national security strategy with elements of an international security one, but this approach also faces a serious obstacle. While it would be going too far to suggest that the two strategies are mutually exclusive, there is much between them that makes their simultaneous operation contradictory. The imperative of minimising vulnerabilities sits unhappily with the risks of international agreement, and the prospects for international agreement are weakened by the power-security dilemma effects of a national security strategy. Despite this problem, in the real world security policy must be, and indeed is, a mix, if only because the consequences of pursuing either strategy singlemindedly are so obviously disastrous.

The most common middle ground is alliance policy as part of the balance of power game, as illustrated by Britain's move from splendid isolation to the Triple Entente in the years before 1914. Alliances manipulate the distribution of power by adding national security policies together, and in this sense they represent a step away from level 2 towards level 3. But as the fractious history of NATO illustrates, alliances do not escape the severe tensions between national and international security strategies. More important, however, is that alliances represent much more a variation on the national security theme than a move towards international security. While they may serve some security needs for some states, they do not constitute an attempt to mitigate the basic dynamics of the power-security dilemma. They are more in line with the national security strategy of increasing strength and reducing vulnerability than they are with an international strategy aimed at reducing threats. At best, alliances can serve an international security strategy by creating an aggregated framework for reducing threats. Thus, NATO not only provides a structure within which western European states can reduce the threats they would otherwise exchange among themselves, but it also serves, to a limited extent, as a multi-national unit in the pursuit of accommodation with the Soviet Union.

The question that remains is, what kind of mix between level 2 and level 3 strategies is most appropriate? The trend of our argument so far is that too much emphasis gets placed on the national security strategy and not enough on the international one, so the implication is that security policy needs a stronger international emphasis. We shall return to this point in the final chapter when we consider holistic approaches to the national security problem.

The logical difficulties of choosing between national and international security strategies represent a core element in the national security policy problem, and would do so even if threats, and the means of dealing with them, were clear and understood factors in the equation. In fact, however, neither threats nor policy means are clear factors, and consequently a second, and more basic level of logical problem exists for security policy-makers. The discussion in chapters 2 and 3 sketched out much of the problem in relation to threats, vulnerabilities and policy means. Trying to assess vulnerabilities leads us back to the ambiguities inherent in applying a concept like security to intangible referent objects like the idea of the state. Threats are numerous and diverse in type and form, and consequently the security problem they create is complex, shifting and frequently unclear. Some elements of a particular threat can be relatively clear (the capability of Soviet missiles to wreak massive damage on the NATO states), while others are clouded in obscurity (the reasons for Soviet force strength and the probability that they would risk a nuclear war). Similarly, a choice of means might appear to strengthen a state's security position (the creation of a powerful German navy between 1898 and 1914), while in fact leading to an aggregate result which worsens it (stimulating a more than proportionate growth in British naval strength, and pushing Britain into an anti-German association with the two powers which had previously been its major rivals, France and Russia).

In addition, threats cannot uniformly be seen as a bad thing. Some level of external threat may be politically useful in suppressing domestic political squabbling, and maintaining the political coherence and identity of the state. While it may be argued that this effect is most useful to repressive governments, it cannot be denied that it plays a significant political role in most states. The history of American domestic politics, for example, would have been quite different in the absence of strong and widespread anti-communist sentiments. Such unities of negatives are a political fact, and even if they serve mainly the interest of élites, they still leave the puzzle for security policy of 'When is a threat not a threat?' If neither the true nature of threats, nor the likely impact of means, can be calculated reliably, then the difficulty of security policy-making is compounded enormously.

This problem gets worse as one moves away from the highly particular, day-to-day issues of national security, and towards the more general, larger-scale and longer-term perspectives which we have emphasised in the preceding chapters. It is relatively easy, though still in an absolute sense difficult, to deal with immediate matters like what to do if the Soviets invade West Germany, or OAPEC reduces oil supplies. It is much more difficult to handle security questions of a larger scope, such as how to deal with the impact of the economic system on the political one, or what to do about the arms dynamic. These questions are so complex and incalculable that they are frequently not even asked. Yet, as the argument in this book indicates, many of the larger issues have a fundamental importance to the overall problem of national security. The difficulty of linking these ideas to policy is illustrated by the theory that hegemonic powers cannot sustain the role indefinitely. If true, this theory suggests that a country like the United States cannot maintain the international position it won for itself during the Second World War. If the United States defines its security in terms of maintaining its position, then it is doomed to a steady and highly unsettling erosion of the conditions by which it defines its own sense of security. Even worse, analysis of its security problems leads to the politically unacceptable conclusion that domestic developments resulting from initial success are an important factor in the present decline. Dwindling adaptability and loss of leadership in innovation may well be at the root of a national security problem defined in terms of past conditions. But in policy terms, this constitutes an issue of such magnitude, complexity and political sensitivity that it is unlikely to figure at all in the mainstream of national security policy-making.

Another illustration of the problem of linking larger ideas to the policy level can be taken from our earlier discussion of system structure and process. Even if one finds convincing arguments like Waltz's, that bipolar systems are the safest in security terms, or like the one made in chapter 4 about the security benefits of a mature anarchy, the question is how such ideals can be addressed in policy terms. No state commands the resources to create massive systemic effects, and systemic evolution is easily dismissed as a complicated and long-term process which is effectively beyond the reach of individual policy actions. A purposeful move towards a specified system structure would involve not only an unprecedented degree of policy coordination among states, but also a massive political commitment to a largely theoretical proposition. The international economy is often thought about in macro-terms, but only in rare watersheds, like that following the Second World War, can major changes in design be implemented by conscious policy. Most of the time, the character of the economic system is determined more by the cumulative impact of many actors pursuing their own interests than it is by the impact of attempts of international economic planning. The creation of the European Community (EC) is a rare example of macro-policy in the political domain. In a fully developed version, the EC would amount to a major transformation in the international distribution of power, with profound implications for the structure of the system. Little thinking, outside the not unimportant resolution of the western European security complex which it provides, appears to have been done as to the macro-purposes of this transformation. Those who accept Waltz's argument on the virtues of bipolarity must presumably view its implications with alarm.

National security policy-makers normally have enough difficulty coping with short-term problems without having to think on the grander scales which this level involves. From their perspective, it is much easier to leave the system to take care of itself. The system as an entity is both too unmanageable for them to deal with, and beyond their national political mandate. At best it can be relegated to the background with the hope that its natural development will somehow turn out to be progressive and benign, with factors such as technology, education, experience, interdependence and environmental constraints pushing steadily towards a more sensible arrangement of international relations. Only disarmament and world government among the grander ideas have actually made it onto the security policy agenda. But neither is considered realistic, and their function is, at best, to inject a moral and idealist perspective into security policy and, at worst, to provide a smokescreen for the practice of short-term, business-as-usual, power politics.

The difficulty of creating a practicable macro-dimension to national security policy tends to confine policy-makers to a narrow, short-term focus. But even at this more restricted level, the ambiguities of ends and means cause serious difficulties. These difficulties are compounded by the lack of clear direction from a well-developed sense of larger objectives, priorities and methods. What we are discussing here fits neatly into the classic model of collective action in which the narrow pursuit of interests by individual actors does not lead to the fulfilment of the general good. No benevolent, invisible hand operates to ensure that general well-being results from the pursuit of individual interest. Indeed, the invisible hand operates to reverse effect, amplifying individual security-seeking into the generally malign result of the power-security dilemma. Because the large picture is so unclear, even short-range policy can be hard to assess. How, for instance, can policy-makers determine the appropriate range and direction for their policies? If security horizons are set too widely, then resources are wasted unnecessarily, and the countervailing operation of the power-security dilemma is intensified. If they are set too narrowly, then threats will already have become dangerously large before action is taken. The United States provides an example here, having set its security horizons too narrowly during the interwar years, and, by way of reaction, too widely during the Cold War. Can it be argued in retrospect that either isolationism in the 1930s, or the intervention in Vietnam in the 1960s and 1970s, served the larger purposes of American national security?

Logical conundrums of the kind associated with utilitarian calculus arise from this problem of range. For example, is a policy like nuclear deterrence, which serves short-term interests, but subjects the interests of future generations to grave risks, sound? Was the 1919 Treaty of Versailles a good policy in view of the undeniable short-term security benefits to France and others, as weighed against the longer-term outcome in the European security complex with which the Treaty is now associated? How do American rationalisations for intervention in Lebanon in 1958 look now in the light of the civil and foreign chaos which have reigned in that country since the mid-1970s? These questions are unfair in the sense that they apply the easy critical wisdom of hindsight to decisions made under pressure and with virtually no reliable knowledge of future effects. The purpose, however, is not to score debating points, but to illustrate how poorly the normal logic of national security works, even by its own standards. The ultimate example here must be the decision by the German and Austro-Hungarian authorities to facilitate the activities of Lenin and his Bolsheviks during the early years of the twentieth century. Few short-term security ploys aimed at weakening a rival power can have produced such disastrous long-term results as this.

Applying long-term criteria to the judgement of short-term security goals can produce alarming results. In the normal context of security analysis, invasion and occupation rank just below total destruction at the top of the hierarchy of threats to national security. Such a threat is seen to justify extreme measures like those taken by invaded and threatened countries during the Second World War. On the 'better dead than red' principle and its counterparts, occupation might even be resisted by something approaching national suicide – a prospect facing front-line states in any nuclear war in Europe. If a long historical view is taken, however, invasion and occupation might be seen as often being no bad thing. Although it might be hard for the generation which experiences it, one could argue that it is seldom worse than war unless the invader is bent on genocide.

Many historical invasions appear in retrospect to have produced a fruitful mixing of cultures. The Roman and Norman invasions of Britain are not now seen as disasters. Much of the Mediterranean world prospered under Roman rule. Japan can hardly be said to have been devastated by American occupation. Even eastern Europe has not done badly since 1945 when compared with its previous condition; certainly not so badly that annihilation would seem a reasonable alternative if a choice were offered. One might almost argue that European and Indian civilisation has been built on the fruits of invasion and cultural mixing. Such thoughts amount to heresy in relation to conventional security thinking and the political commitment to the independent state on which it rests. Until recently, they would have been rendered politically utopian both by the vested interest of the current generation, and by the immense strength of the nation-state culture. But the rise of the defence dilemma may yet propel them into the arena of political realism. One might speculate, in this context, whether Soviet hegemony over Europe would be worse than nuclear war. Extending the thought, one might ask whether a Soviet absorption of so massive and dynamic a cultural entity as western Europe would not wreak larger transformations on the Soviet system than on the European. Such speculations are unanswerable, but no more so than calculations of nuclear risk. They serve not only to illustrate the logical difficulties of security policy, but also to raise core questions about the purposes and priorities of security policy-makers.

Perceptual Problems

Logical problems are only part of the difficulty inherent in the national security policy process. In most areas they are accompanied by perceptual uncertainties. The perceptual problem is fundamental because it affects the entire information base on which the decision-making process rests. It has two components, which are the same for individuals as for states: perceptions vary according to where the observer is located in relation to the thing viewed, and according to the internal constitution of the viewer. Positional perspectives vary in time and space. Thus, the fall of the Roman empire looked quite different to a sixth-century citizen of Rome than it did to one living in

1981, and the First World War looked quite different from Japan than it did from France. Constitutional factors reflect the sensory capability, historical memory and psychological make-up of the viewer. As Robert Jervis sums it up, one tends to see what one believes.[13] Thus, external events made little impact on eighteenth-century Japan, because contact with the outside world was deliberately kept very limited. Most Third World countries find their view of the international system heavily conditioned by their colonial experience, and Marxist thinkers will see the current economic troubles of the West quite differently from those trained to more orthodox economic views. These two components of the perceptual problem apply to all the states in the international system. Each of them has a different positional perspective on the objects and events which make up the information base of the system, and the constitutional structure of each is sufficiently different from that of all the others to ensure that they see any single event or thing differently. As argued in chapter 2, states are united as a class by relatively few factors, but differentiated from each other by many. The process maintains itself as each state accumulates a distinctive history through which current events get filtered.

The mechanisms of the perceptual problems are rooted in the Byzantine complexities of human psychology, and have already been extensively explored in the context of international politics by Robert Jervis.[14] Perception is distorted initially because information is imperfect. The relevant information for security policy is enormous in extent, covering almost all areas of human activity. It changes and expands constantly. Much of it, such as the depth of political allegiance (as in the Warsaw Pact countries), the quality of military equipment under wartime conditions, the efficiency of state machineries, and the motives of actors, is inherently unknowable with any accuracy, even to the actors themselves. Even the greatest powers can gather only a small part of this information as a basis for their security policy. Such information as they get will be distorted by the selection process (less will be available from enemies than from friends), and by deliberate deception (attempts at secrecy and bluff, like Khrushchev's cultivation of a missile gap during the late 1950s). Once received, this information will be further distorted by the various processes of deletion, condensation and interpretation which are necessary to reduce it to a form concise enough to be used by those at the business end of policy-making.

Just as in the party game where a message is passed along a chain of people by word of mouth, information going into a government bureaucratic network will emerge at the other end in a scarcely recognisable form. In the process it will encounter the numerous filters of conventional wisdom, each of which will attempt to reconcile incoming data with pre-existing theories, or mental sets. Information which tends to support the conventional wisdom will be amplified and passed on, that which tends to cast doubt on it will be suppressed, devalued or diverted.[15] The aggregate effect of these distortions will be to protect the conventional wisdom against countervailing information up to the point at which the evidence against it becomes overwhelming, either because of its cumulative weight (like the failure of the Americans to win in Vietnam year after year), or because some highly visible transformational event makes the old view publically insupportable (like Hitler's occupation of the Czechoslovak rump in March 1939, which violated the nationalist principle of German expansion and destroyed what was left of the case for appeasement).

This tendency to delay and distort the rationalising effect of new information has major consequences for the national security problem. Since the international anarchy tends naturally to generate insecurity and suspicion, the perceptual factor feeds into the power-security dilemma, amplifying and perpetuating negative images. Once a pattern of hostility is established, as between the United States and the Soviet Union, each will tend to see the other as an enemy, and assume that worst interpretations of behaviour are correct. Disproportionately large amounts of information will be required to break this cycle. The process is universal, and tends to amplify itself in each of the actors individually, precisely because it influences the behaviour of the other actors in the system. As Jervis argues, the process is also inevitable, because mental sets and theories of some sort are necessary if any sense is to be made of the huge volume of incoming information in the first place.[16] Without some means of ordering and simplifying data, policy-makers would be even more confused and inconsistent than they are with them. Each event would have to be interpreted on its own merits, and no sense of pattern would exist around which to structure policy.

Some of the other perceptual problems identified by Jervis include a tendency to assume that other actors are more centrally in control of themselves than you are, and that your role in and influence on events are greater than they in fact are.[17] Others are assumed to be more centralised because one observes mainly their behavioural output. All behaviour is imputed to conscious central command and control. In observing one's own behaviour, whether individual or state, one is much more aware of the confusion, conflict and error which underlie it. If central control is assumed, then strict and conspiratorial assessments of motive are justified, but if weak central control is assumed, then a more forgiving and less threatening analysis may be appropriate. Enormous differences in analysis and inferences for western security policy will occur, depending on whether the Soviet invasion of Afghanistan is seen as one more section of a carefully laid, long-term plan for Soviet advancement towards the Arabian Sea and the Persian Gulf, or as a bungled over-reaction to events in Iran, combined with traditional Soviet paranoia about the stability of its buffer-states. As a general feature of international relations, a tendency to apply much stricter standards to the behaviour of others than to one's own, feeds directly into the mechanisms which drive and maintain the power-security dilemma.

Similar kinds of distortion in analysis can arise from assuming that one's own influence on affairs is larger than it actually is, particularly so when combined with a tendency to assume that one's influence is generally benign, and that one's own view of events is the only correct one. These perceptual biases can lead to self-righteous behaviour, and a tendency to place blame for bad outcomes on the malignant influence of others. A great power like the United States, for example, exaggerates its influence in a place like the Middle East only at the cost of underestimating the importance of the issues and alignments within the local security complex. Already, its basis for sound policy is seriously flawed because the real balance of forces in the area has been miscalculated, with the result that vital actors in the problem, like the Palestinians, are not given sufficient weight to allow for a viable solution. If it also assumes that its influence is benign, then another strand of political misunderstanding gets woven into the picture. Opposition to its actions will be interpreted as hostility, rather than being examined as a valid complaint of a party whose interests have been damaged. This type of error will be compounded and perpetuated by a tendency to assume that one's own view is correct, because such an outlook closes the policy-making process to negative feedback, and immunises it against criticism. Only massive failure of the policy will be sufficient to break into such a closed cycle and force a reconsideration. Until such an event occurs, the tendency will be for good outcomes (like the Israel-Egypt reconciliation) to be excessively attributed to American influence, and for bad outcomes (like the situation in Lebanon since 1975) to be attributed to malignant local forces or to the machinations of hostile outside powers.

These and other perceptual mechanisms clearly play an important role in the security policy-making process. They work at all levels, from the generation and influence of public opinion, through the bureaucratic labyrinths of government machinery, to the individual personalities of leaders. They operate constantly, but can be in-tensified sharply under the pressure of crisis, when time for analysis and decision shrinks, the risks and stakes attached to policy behaviour rise, and uncertainties of information inflate. An extensive literature on crises explores both the theoretical and the practical effects of these pressures on the psychology of perception and decision-making.[18]

Even under routine conditions of policy, perceptual factors can play a fundamental role. If, for example, one assumes that one's opponent sees things in basically the same way as oneself, then this can serve as a foundation for policy, because one can calculate his reactions to be roughly what one's own would be if the positions were reversed. For many years during the 1950s, 1960s and early 1970s, the conventional wisdom in the West took roughly this view of Soviet strategic doctrine. If the Soviets accepted evolving western views of nuclear deterrence, albeit with some lag because of their technological inferiority, then policies like MAD could be pursued with considerable hope that a stable balance of deterrence would result. The falseness of this assumption was revealed during the 1970s, as growing Soviet military strength made its policy more obvious, and this revelation stimulated a reassessment of western strategic doctrine. A recent article by Fritz W. Ermarth outlines the historical, geostrategic, doctrinal and military differences in perspective between the two which make it surprising, in retrospect, that any perception of parallel perspectives could have been sustained in the first place.[19]

Instances like this illustrate both the pitfalls which perceptual factors place in the path of the policy process, and the real difficulty of establishing common ground on which to base more orderly relations. Because positional and constitutional differences among states generate different interpretations of the same reality, the natural structure of the system tends to enhance misunderstanding, and feed the dynamic of the power-security dilemma. From this perspective, international relations cannot be compared to a chess game, in which a struggle for power and position proceeds according to agreed rules which establish a common perception of the significance of events. Instead, security relations are more like a chess game in which the players follow somewhat different rules. Each player believes his own rules to be universally valid, and assumes the other player to know this. Enough similarity exists between their rules to enable a game to proceed, but where differences occur, each side assumes that the other is trying to cheat. Not surprisingly, the board is often overturned in the ensuing squabble.

Logical problems in security analysis are inherent in the nature of the issues, particularly in the weak understanding of cause-effect relations and the consequent inability to make reliable predictions.

Because of the extraordinary complexity and mutability of cause-effect relations in the international system, no solution to this problem is in sight. Perceptual problems are rooted in human psychology, and although some countervailing measures can be applied, Jervis concludes that 'no formula will eliminate misperception or reveal what image is correct. Faced with ambiguous and confusing evidence, decision-makers must draw inferences that will often prove to be incorrect.'[20] Because neither problem can be removed, security analysis is plagued by questions which have either no clear answer, or several equally plausible ones. Where such questions exist, the way is clear for politicisation of the security policy process, as different interests seek to make their view prevail. We are back again to the basic character of security as an essentially contested concept.

Political Problems

The debates and disputes about security come in many familiar forms, and on many levels of specificity. At the most general level, the contest takes the form, outlined by Carr, as a see-saw struggle between idealist, security-struggle-oriented views on the one hand, and Realist, power-struggle-oriented views on the other. As we have seen, this struggle is not resolvable within the context of an anarchic system, but that does not prevent the political ascendency of one view or the other for a time. At the most specific level, the contest takes the form of disputes about particular weapons systems, like the one which began over the neutron bomb in the late 1970s. Does a weapon like the neutron bomb enhance security by filling a gap in the warfighting arsenal (defence against mass armoured assault) and reducing collateral damage when fighting on friendly ground? Or does it threaten security by easing the path up the escalation ladder to nuclear exchange, and heightening the insecurity caused by the defence dilemma?

In between these extremes lies an enormous range of actual and potential disputes. These include, among others, questions of security alignment (Should Ireland join NATO? Should China and the United States seek a formal alliance?); of national defence policy (How much should be spent, and on what?); of situational policy (how should the West respond to the Soviet occupation of Afghanistan?); and of security methods (Given a defined goal, should emphasis be placed on military means, on economic means or on political and cultural means?). Questions of method tend to dominate these debates, mostly because there is a disinclination to define objectives in any but the most general terms. What might be labelled the Humpty Dumpty syndrome – confusion over what tasks military forces are suited to, and what tasks are best performed by non-military instruments – is a particular favourite. As Trager and Simonie note, 'an over-emphasis on the technique and detail of National Security operations has obscured the purpose of maintaining a national security system in the first place'.[21]

These disputes about security questions concern not only the relations between the state and its international environment, but also relations within the state. As we have argued in most of the preceding chapters, the state is not a unitary actor. It is perhaps best viewed as a container, or an arena, within which a variety of powers and interests pursue their political life. Disputes and contradictions are thus the normal stuff of domestic politics. Individual security interests, as we saw in chapter 1, must clash to some extent with national security policy despite the necessary existence of some harmony between the two levels. More generalised domestic contradictions exist everywhere, and where they are severe, they create what has been labelled in chapter 2 as weak states. In weak states, the willingness to use force in pursuit of domestic political objectives lies close to the surface of political life, and sub-state actors become as important as the state itself as referent objects for security.

The internal political process of the state is not a routinised, mechanistic, rational policy-making device, but a dynamic, potentially unstable, and normally fractious system of relations among contending interests. As was argued in chapter 4, under the heading of security complexes, domestic disputes form the first basic level of inquiry in analysing security problems. We must, then, expect that the national security questions raised by relations between the state and its environment will feed into the pattern of domestic political alignments and disputes. The impact of security policy choices on domestic political interests is seldom neutral, and it would be foolish to assume that domestic interests would allow policy to be made according to the detached logic of international system analysis alone.

The resulting political struggle occurs within and around institutional and normative structures which are unique to each state. In other words, the political process happens everywhere, but is different in style, form, emphasis, organisation and procedure from one country to the next. This is the familiar world of comparative politics, with its emphasis on the innumerable paths to political order which have evolved to suit the conditions of different countries. Regardless of these differences, however, it is the domestic political system in each state which actually produces national security policy. Nowhere does this process allow a detached and rational formulation of security policy. Everywhere, in some form, the dynamic of competing interests intrudes into the security policy process, with the result that extraneous influences become significant determinants of the security policy which the state eventually adopts. National security policy, in other words, cannot be seen as an unadulterated response to the inputs from the international system. It is skewed and distorted by other interests, and it is worth taking a look at what these are.

To do this, we need to open up the state for examination, as we did in chapter 2, but with a more specific focus. This task could easily fill a book in itself, and our purpose here will be simply to indicate the scope and character of the problem, without exploring it in detail. Within the state exist many layers of sub-state actors, ranging from the government and its various bureaucratic organs, through the economic, political and media organisations, to the individual citizens, both as individuals, and as the amorphous entity known as public opinion. Many of these actors have some interest in national security and involve themselves in varying degrees in the security policy-making process. The problem is that most of them also have other interests as well, and these bias their security interests in a variety of ways. To illustrate this point, we shall look briefly at the cross-pressures affecting newspapers, political parties, government bureaucracies and business organisations.

Newspapers, for example, are interested in the subject matter of national security, but are constrained in what they report by their need to sell their product to readers and advertisers. Stories of scandal, malice, threat, crisis, mismanagement, conflict and death will sell more newspapers than long-winded and complicated analyses like the ones in this book. Thus, because of their dual interest, newspapers distort the public view of what is important in national security, focusing attention on short-term issues and military means, while largely ignoring longer-range and more abstract issues. Where newspapers are controlled by the state, the bias will be towards the official interpretations of events.

Political parties suffer from some of the same dual interest pressures as the media. Security policy must be one of their areas of interest, but only one of many, and they must strive to attract a mass following. Complex, or highly unorthodox positions on security policy will not serve their political needs and will open them up to attacks from their opponents. Because security policy is so contestable, it can become a useful club with which opposing parties can beat each other regardless of circumstances. Whatever one side advocates, the other can make a plausible case against on grounds of waste, cost, militarism, risk or ideology. Such attacks may occur regardless of what the parties do when in office. In Britain, pro-military Conservatives cut the navy on economic grounds, while ostensibly anti-military Labour governments allow major nuclear warhead programmes to proceed in secret. Posturing on security issues may have more to do with electoral needs, ideological pretensions and the rituals of party rivalry than with serious thinking about the issues themselves. Considerable domestic political mileage can be wrung from security issues on the principle that a unity of negatives is easier to create and maintain than is a unity of positives. If political cohesion cannot be built on a common ground of what people want, then it can be built on the common ground of what they can be brought to fear or hate. A unity of negatives based on making a bogey out of some foreign power can usefully cover a multitude of domestic disagreements.

More parochially, parties may support certain security policies because they provide employment in politically sensitive areas. Thus, weapons might be produced more for reasons to do with the domestic political economy than for reasons deriving from the international situation. These and other interests can all affect the way a political party deals with security policy. This is not to argue that parties have no substantive positions and beliefs on security policy, and that they are therefore totally opportunistic in relation to security issues. Rather, it is to point out that many other considerations affect their position and their ability to act, and that the effect of these is to introduce domestic political considerations into the security policy-making process. The kinds of pressures on parties will vary according to whether the country is a multi-party system or not, but even in one-party states, the party must respond to domestic political interests if it wishes to remain in office. At worst, it will require the armed forces for domestic control, and this need will distort national security policy by importing it into the domestic political arena.

Government bureaucracies of various kinds participate in security policy-making, and each of them brings to the process its own mix of interests. Some will have direct interest in the issues, like those responsible for defence, foreign policy, trade and finance. Others will have the indirect interest of being competitors in the continuous game of resource allocation, in which departments do battle with each other for shares of the budgetary pie. Thus security policy will not only be subjected to cross-cutting interests, like Treasury concerns to cut public spending, or Department of Employment concerns to maintain defence production jobs, but also it will be put through the mill of resource allocation politics, where outcomes may depend as much on political strength and skill as on the merits of the issues. Even within a single department like Defence, many institutional and bureaucratic factors can intervene to skew the logic of security policy. Service traditions and inter-service rivalries are among the more notorious sources of such influence. Different services often develop strong attachments to their own traditions and to the instruments on which those traditions rest. These attachments can lead them to resist technological developments which will undermine their traditions. Thus, the Royal Navy was reluctant to abandon wood and sail for iron and steam until the pressure of foreign developments forced it to. The transition meant the loss of an entire, centuries long tradition on which British naval superiority, and style of naval life, had rested. Armies were similarly reluctant to abandon horse cavalry.

In modern times, technological developments threaten even more fundamental changes. Navies still cling to the idea of large surface ships even though they become increasingly costly and vulnerable, because without them the entire naval tradition is jeopardised. Likewise, airforces continue to advocate manned bombers because the whole airforce tradition and glamour is based on men flying in aircraft. Missiles and automated aircraft threaten to eliminate pilots entirely, and with them, the central role and symbol of the airforce itself. In addition, the services struggle among themselves to capture functions which will strengthen their case in the scramble for resources. Armies, navies and airforces in various countries have struggled among themselves for control over strategic nuclear weapons, and the additional resources and status associated with them. In earlier periods, airforces had to fight for a separate existence, while armies and navies tried to hold on to their own air components. These organisational vested interests all feed into the security policy process and play their part in determining its outcome, especially so, in that the services are a main supplier of military advice to governments. A good case-study of the counter-rational pressures which result can be found in the resistance of the United States Air Force to the results of the Strategic Bombing Survey carried out at the end of the Second World War. The Air Force could not (and did not) accept the results of the survey without undermining a major part of the rationale for its existence. Institutional survival demanded that the facts about military effectiveness be ignored, and one consequence of this was the savage and futile aerial campaign against Vietnam two decades later.[22]

Industrial and commercial organisations also have interests in security policy, and again these interests mix with their other concerns to produce distortions in rationality. Such organisations may be more or less closely attached to the government, depending on whether the economy leans towards central planning or towards the market, and this will cause significant differences in their other concerns, particularly on matters like profit. These organisations can have an interest in security policy either because they produce goods, like military equipment, which are called for by security policy, or because they have external interests, like markets, investments, transportation routes or sources of supply which they wish to see come under the aegis of national security policy.

The arms industry is an obvious example to take here, because it ties into the discussion of arms racing in the previous chapter. Arms manufacturers in a market economy will have a number of organisational interests of their own which can affect national security policy.[23] In particular, they will have the normal concerns of business about profit, about creating a reliable demand for their product, and about participating in technological advance in their field. Unless they can ensure these things, their existence as organisations is in jeopardy. Governments, as a rule, will share some objectives with the arms industry. They will wish to ensure that good quality weapons are available for their armed forces, and that research and development is adequate to match the efforts of possible enemies. They may want to keep in being a surplus capacity in the industry in order to allow for a rapid meeting of increased demand in time of crisis or war. Where resources allow, governments will prefer to maintain as much domestic independence in arms manufacture as possible in order to minimise constraints on their freedom of action, though this logic applies mainly to larger powers capable of mounting a significant arms industry in the first place.

This common interest between governments and companies can result in at least two effects which might influence security policy. First, the desire to maintain a sufficient, or surplus, national capacity, combined with the companies' desire to assure markets and make profits, can lead to pressure either to consume more than is objectively required, or to export. For countries like Britain and France, maintenance of a substantial armaments industry requires the cultivation of exports, because domestic demand is too low to support such industry by itself. Larger producers like the United States could maintain their industries on domestic demand, but exports offer a way to reduce costs to the government (by increasing economies of scale in production), to ease the problem of keeping the industry in regular work, to maintain surplus capacity, and to increase profits for the companies. An interest in the arms trade, once established, can impinge on security policy in a number of ways. It creates ties to the buyers which affect national security alignments, like those between the United States and Iran under the Shah. It stimulates secondary arms races among purchasers, like those in the Middle East, which can in turn affect the general security of the system. It can create a vested interest in maintaining exports by not being too concerned about the stimulation of rivalries and conflict elsewhere. Similar arguments could be applied to the nuclear power industry, which also illustrates how economic and security dynamics can interact to distort national security policy-making.[24] Economic imperatives work to spread nuclear materials, knowledge and technology to countries like India, Pakistan, South Africa, Iraq and others whose interest in nuclear weapons is only thinly disguised.

The second effect concerns the process of technological improvement. Both governments and companies share this interest, but for different reasons. Governments are concerned at least to maintain the quality of their military equipment to the general standard prevailing in the international system, although in some cases (war, planned attack, arms racing) they may also be interested in occupying the leading edge of technological development. Companies may be interested in technological advance for its own sake, with many individuals within them deriving their job satisfaction from pushing forward the state of the art. One has only to look at the number of books published about weapons in order to get some idea of the source and strength of this fascination with the beauty and power of military technology. Companies generally have economic incentives to drive their interest in technology. On simple grounds, better technology gives them a commercial edge in sales. More subtly, sustained pressure for technological improvement increases the pace of obsolescence. If equipment needs to be replaced or upgraded more frequently, then companies can be assured of more regular demand which solves, though at considerable cost, their problem of continuity and the governments problem of assured capacity. As we have seen, however, a sustained push behind military technology feeds quickly into the arms maintenance/arms race dynamic, leading both to the self-sustaining rivalry of military competition, and to the self-locking effect in which arms racing becomes internalised in the rivalry between arms manufacturers within a single state. This process can have major implications for national security even though it derives initially from factors internal to the state, and extraneous to the pattern of external threats which define the national security problem in the first place.

We could extend this type of analysis almost indefinitely, both by looking in more detail at a range of cases within the four general categories just reviewed, and by bringing into the picture other actors in the domestic political process, such as academia, workers' organisations, the whole range of public pressure groups, and the mostly inarticulate, but constraining force of mass public opinion. We could also bring in a variety of external participants in the domestic political process, ranging from externally-sponsored political groups, through external governments or companies with economic interests in, and leverage over, the state, to allies whose own security is explicitly tied to that of the state in question. To include these latter would complete the picture, but only at the risk of confusing the domestic level with the international security environment.

The illustrations already given are, however, sufficient to illustrate the present point, which is that the structure and character of the domestic political process constitute a major independent variable in national security policy-making. Not only does the domestic political process inject a large number of powerful cross-cutting interests into security policy, but also it subjects that policy to competition with other state policy priorities. In other words, national security policy is disconnected from the rationality of the external security problem not only by domestic intrusions into the policy process, but also by a political market in which even the distorted policy may get bumped or altered while interacting with other policies competing for state attention and resources. Thus, a policy proposal for a weapons system like a manned bomber might get almost as far as the production stage, only to be cut for reasons arising from a different universe of budgetary, economic and normative considerations. Conversely, an economic policy which might normally have been politically impossible to sell, might gain acceptance because of its association with national security interests, as in the case of the Marshall Plan in the United States in 1947.[25]

Conclusions: Policy-Making as Part of the National Security Problem

The argument in this chapter has been that the logical and perceptual problems arising from security provide much of the input into domestic policy-making. We can conclude not only that the policy process has a limited ability to solve these problems, but also that it adds its own dimension of further difficulties to the national security problem overall. The political process necessarily engages a variety of domestic interests in the formulation of security policy, with the result that the national policy which goes out into the international system is as much a product of internal factors as it is of the external ones which provide its principal justification. These arguments could easily be read as a critique of the domestic political process, and in one sense they are. Their inference is that domestic factors get in the way of a rational formulation of national security policy. By doing so, they distort, impede and confuse the process by which the state deals with threats and, by implication, they result in less rational, less effective, and possibly even counter-productive policies.

Two counter-arguments, however, weigh heavily, though not totally against this critique. The first is that no purely detached and rational policy-making process is available in the real world. The logical and perceptual impediments to rationality are to a considerable extent insurmountable, and to assume that an apolitical policy process is feasible in a quintessentially political entity like a state, is both naive and contradictory. Domestic political factors will always impinge on national security policy, if only because the whole decision-making apparatus of the state is largely set up in relation to domestic interests.

The second argument reinforces the first, on the grounds that a broad domestic interest in national security policy is justified because of the massive feedback effect which security policy can have on domestic society. Two obvious ways in which security policy can intrude into domestic society are through its costs and through its risks. These considerations alone would justify a major domestic interest in the formulation of such policy. By the late 1970s, the cost of national defence seldom dropped below 1 per cent of Gross National Product (GNP), and for larger states it was normally above 3 per cent. For the United States it was over 5 per cent, for the Soviet Union well over 10 per cent, and for Israel over 30 per cent. The absolute amounts involved are huge. Three states each spent over $50 billion in 1980, and four more spent over $10 billion each. Around forty states spent over $1 billion each. Even a country like Japan, which is normally thought to be very lightly armed, spent nearly $9 billion (0.9 per cent of its GNP).[26] These sums often amount to a sizeable proportion of public expenditure, and as disarmament enthusiasts never tire of pointing out, their opportunity costs in alternative social goods and services are very great. More schools, more hospitals, cleaner environments, more disposable income, more investment, and such-like all have to be weighed against expenditures on national security. This implies a set of choices about social priorities between security and other values, and such choices are what the domestic political process is all about. The risks in security policy are more abstract and intermittent than the costs, but pose even graver questions. Bungled policy might lead to the termination of all social values in nuclear obliteration, or to their drastic revision as a result of invasion or revolution. For these reasons, the substance of security policy is clearly a legitimate matter for domestic political concern.

On more subtle grounds, we can increase the strength of this argument by exploring the numerous ways in which security policy can influence the basic structure of political society. Most of these links are well known. Many of them come under the general heading of the militarisation of society. They include arguments about conscription, about military influence in government, about the military-industrial complex as a powerful élite interest, about the corruption of higher values by the blatant willingness to use force, about the infringement of civil liberties by the requirements of domestic security, and about the self-perpetuating logic of security demands on society which arise from the dilemmas we explored in the previous two chapters. These arguments link to those about resources above, for at some point, discussion about the allocation of resources becomes indistinguishable from debate about the value priorities at stake. Commitment to a military establishment creates a new power in domestic politics which will generate organisational imperatives of its own. These imperatives may, in the long run, result in consequences which outweigh the original purpose of having a military establishment. Military interests may lead to the self-defeating cycles of an internalised arms race, or to the militarisation of national politics which is such a problem in many weak states. As one Latin American observer put it, 'What we are doing is building up armies which weigh nothing in the international scale, but which are Juggernaughts for the internal life of each country. Each country is being occupied by its own army.'[27]

On this level, national security policy has implications which run through the entire structure of the state. An obsession with security can lead to versions of the warfare state in which all political structures and values are subordinated to the accumulation of military power. This Spartan model has echoes in places like Israel and the Soviet Union, where high levels of mobilisation, or readiness to mobilise very quickly, have become a permanent condition rather than a wartime phenomenon and permeate society with their effects. Corrupted versions of the warfare state are possible in which the military dominates the state for its own purposes, rather than in response to any pressing external threat. By turning its powers inward, a military establishment could exploit the state as a resource base for its own organisational aggrandisement.

The linkage between security and other state structures is obvious in these extreme cases, but it can also be found in more normal circumstances. One might follow Alexis de Tocqueville[28] by arguing, for example, that while the political institutions of the United States are excellently designed to contain and to manage the numerous and divergent political forces within that vast society, they are, as a direct consequence, remarkably poorly suited to the conduct of foreign and security policy. Features which serve well in the general political context, such as openness to pressure groups, intricate checks and balances, frequent elections and a politically-appointed civil service are ill-designed for the specialised needs of foreign and security policy. They impede continuity of policy where it is most vital (international negotiations, arms policy), and compel it where flexibility might serve better (anti-communism, notions of military superiority, extravagant energy consumption). They amplify the role of domestic factors and interests in the policy-making process, and restrict input from, and sensitivity to, the needs, fears and dynamics of other actors in the international system. Such criticisms are not unique to the United States, they are merely more obvious there because of the openness of the American system and the extent of its impact on the rest of the world. Most states respond more to domestic pressures and interests than to external ones, but when the United States floats the value of its currency, or subsidises the price of oil, or changes its attitude to the export of weapons, the effect in the international system is large.

To the extent that domestic forces cause these actions, foreign policy gets made without reference to the rest of the international system. If domestic factors dominate policy-making in most states, then the international system becomes one in which feedback between the units is weak. Behaviour, in other words, is internally generated, and therefore relatively insensitive to the effects which it creates in the system. We have argued that states are not, and cannot be, cool, calculating and rational actors in relation to the international dimension of the national security problem. To the extent that domestic factors dominate decision-making, their behaviour towards each other will tend to be myopic, insensitive and inconsistent. They will be attuned to others as threats and opportunities, and to themselves as possessors of rights and as victims of uncontrollable circumstances. But they will be only dimly aware of how others see them, of the extent to which others are victims of uncontrollable circumstances, of the impact which their actions make externally, and of the sensitivities which drive the domestic politics of others.

Self-centred actors are the key to turning an anarchy into a chaos. If each actor generates most of its behaviour internally, treating others primarily as sources of threat or support, then the combined effect is to maximise the power-security dilemma which encompasses them all. The internal dynamics of each will result in policies which others see as threatening and inflexible, and because the policies are internally set, they will be difficult to change. Level 2 policies will dominate by default, because that is the only level which receives serious policy-making attention. As Rosecrance puts it, 'one of the fundamental reasons for tension in the international system is the formulation of objectives and policies on a purely domestic basis'.[29] This political dominance of level 2 amplifies the singularity of positional perspective which is the natural geographical and historical heritage of each state. Each tends anyway to interpret the system from the perspective of its own position within it, and when domestic political preoccupations intrude as well, the propensity to take a parochial view grows stronger. In as much as each state is governed by parochial views, no strong common view of the system as a whole can develop among them. The absence of such a common view in turn reinforces the parochial impulse, because the system appears to be an unmanageable chaos which leaves no option but to rely on one's own resources.

If one argues that this situation is dangerous, as most of this book does, then the inescapable conclusion is that the structure of domestic politics must be altered. How such alteration should be done, given the numerous justifications for domestic political involvement in security policy, constitutes a major area for inquiry. The link between domestic political structures and security policy is both basic and unavoidable, and the national security policy problem which arises from it is a problem both for individual states and for the international system as a whole.

Notes

1   See chapter 1, note 16.
2   Macbeth, III v. The speaker is Hecate. The meaning of the quote in its original context is that an excessive feeling of security leads to carelessness in action, and is therefore a cause of weakness and vulnerability. This sense might also be applied to the national security problem, in as much as excessive military power, and its accompanying policy orientation, can lead to underestimation of other factors, as illustrated by the American performance in Vietnam.
3   Charles L. Schultze, 'The Economic Content of National Security Policy', *Foreign Affairs*, 51:3 (1973), pp. 529–30.
4   Cited in Arnold Wolfers, *Discord and Collaboration* (Baltimore, Johns Hopkins University Press, 1962), p. 150.
5   *Ibid.*
6   Michael H.H. Louw, *National Security* (Pretoria, ISS – University of Pretoria, 1978), the quote is from the introductory note titled 'The Purpose of the Symposium'.

7 Ian Bellany, 'Towards a Theory of International Security', *Political Studies*, 29:1 (1981), p. 102.

8 Frank N. Trager and Frank L. Simonie, 'An Introduction to the Study of National Security', in F.N. Trager and P.S. Kronenberg, *National Security and American Society* (Lawrence Kansas, University Press of Kansas, 1973), p. 36.

9 John E. Mroz, *Beyond Security: Private Perceptions Among Arabs and Israelis* (New York, International Peace Academy, 1980), p. 105, (emphasis in original).

10 The same problem of confusion between level 2 and level 3 arises here as was discussed in chapter 4. The term 'international security strategy' cannot be used in the sense indicated without involving both levels. The prime referent is the state, because that is the level on which policy is made. But, carried to its logical conclusion, the strategy has implications for the system as an object of security. If all states had made themselves secure by dealing with threats at their external source, then the system structure would also be secure, probably in the form of a mature anarchy. This approach needs to be distinguished from the stricter sense of international security in which the referent object is *only* the system structure. In that sense, the balance of power works to preserve the security of the anarchic structure, but without necessarily serving the security of the units at level 2.

11 Some smaller powers like Sweden, Switzerland and Jugoslavia have been able to go a long way down this path because of their position within a larger balance of power. The importance of external factors to their success is indicated by the failure of Belgium to succeed with a similar approach.

12 Ken Booth, *Strategy and Ethnocentrism* (London, Croom Helm, 1979); Richard K. Ashley, *The Political Economy of War and Peace* (London, Frances Pinter, 1980), pp. 205–30.

13 Robert Jervis, *Perception and Misperception in International Politics* (Princeton, NJ, Princeton University Press, 1976), p. 170.

14 *Ibid.* See also J.C. Farrell and A.P. Smith, *Image and Reality in World Politics* (New York, Columbia University Press, 1968).

15 Jervis, *ibid.*, chs. 4, 5, and 7. Daniel Yergin, *Shattered Peace* (Boston, Houghton Mifflin, 1978), can be read as a case-study of the establishment of a major mental set in American foreign policy-making.

16 Jervis, *ibid.*, pp. 160–2, 175–6.

17 *Ibid.*, chs. 8 and 9.

18 See, *inter alia*, Charles F. Hermann (ed.), *International Crises* (New York, Free Press, 1972); Raymond Cohen, *Threat Perception in International Crises* (Madison, University of Wisconsin Press, 1979); D. Frei (ed.), *International Crisis and Crisis Management* (Aldershot, Gower, 1978); 'Special Issue on international Crises', *International Studies Quarterly*, 21:1 (1977); Ole R. Holsti, 'The 1914 Case', *American Political Science Review*, 59 (1965); Graham T. Allison, *Essence of Decision* (Boston, Little Brown, 1971).

19 Fritz W. Ermarth, 'Contrasts in American and Soviet Strategic Thought', *International Security*, 3:2 (1978).

244   *People, States and Fear*

20 Jervis, *op. cit.* (note 13), p. 409.
21 Trager and Simonie, *op. cit.* (note 8), p. 36.
22 John K. Galbraith, *A Life in Our Times* (Boston, Houghton Mifflin, 1981), pp. 195–6, 201, 204–6, 213, 215, 225–37.
23 On the arms industry, see notes 27 and 45, chapter 7; and Anthony Sampson, *The Arms Bazaar* (London, Hodder & Stoughton, 1977); and Philip Noel-Baker, *The Private Manufacture of Armaments* (London, Gollancz, 1936).
24 For an interesting study of this, see Michael J. Brenner, *Nuclear Power and Non-Proliferation* Cambridge, Cambridge University Press, 1981).
25 L.B. Krause and J.S. Nye, 'Reflections on the Economics and Politics of International Economic Organizations', in C.F. Bergsten and L.B. Krause (eds), *World Politics and International Economics* (Washington DC, Brookings Institution, 1975), pp. 324–5.
26 Figures from *the Military Balance 1980–81* (London, IISS, 1980), pp. 96–7.
27 Edvardo Santoz, quoted in Edwin Lieuwen, *Arms and Politics in Latin America* (New York, Praeger, 1961), pp. 236–8.
28 Alexis de Tocqueville, *Democracy in America* (New York, Vintage Books, 1945), vol. I, pp. 241–4.
29 Richard Rosecrance, *International Relations: Peace of War* (New York, McGraw Hill, 1973), p. 186.

9 Conclusion: A Holistic View of Security

There is one theme which stands out as common to all the preceding chapters: that the national security problem cannot be understood without reference to factors at all three levels of analysis. Although the term 'national security' suggests a phenomenon on level 2, the connections between that level and levels 1 and 3 are too numerous and too strong to deny. The concept of security binds together individuals, states and the international system so closely that it demands to be treated in a holistic perspective. Although some sense can be made of individual security, national security and international security as ideas in their own right, a full understanding of each can only be gained if it is related to the other two. Attempts to treat security on any single level invite serious distortions of perspective.

The security of the individual, as we saw in chapter 1, is locked into an unbreakable paradox in which it is partly dependent on, and partly threatened by, the state. Individuals can be threatened by their own state in a variety of ways, and they can also be threatened through their state as a result of developments in the international system. The connections not only run from the higher levels down to the lower, but also from the lower up to the higher. As we saw in chapters 1, 2, 3, 6, and 8, pressures from individuals bear upwards strongly into national security, and through their impact on the state also influence the international system. Individuals can pose threats to the state, and if these are serious and numerous enough, they can corrode the existence of the state as a meaningful entity. Individuals constitute an important part of the amorphous referent object of national security at level 2, and as such play their role in the general process of security policy-making as well as in particular policy phenomena like the defence dilemma. The question of national security cannot be reduced to the individual level because each of the other levels has characteristics which make it more than the sum of its parts. For this reason the tension between level 1 and the other levels is a permanent feature. As we saw in chapter 8, the upward and

245

downward connections between the levels interact to sustain each other, and together form a vital component of the national security problem.

National security makes only limited sense as an idea confined to level 2. The self-help image of the state as an actor trying to use its own resources to reduce its vulnerabilities in the face of threats provides only a narrow view of the national security problem. While such a view can accommodate much, though not all, of the interaction between levels 1 and 2, it heavily discounts the vital elements of the problem which lie between levels 2 and 3. As we argued in chapter 4, the structure and character of states, and the structure and character of the international system, are the opposite ends of a single political phenomenon. To consider states as the prime focus of the national security problem is mainly useful because it concentrates attention on the principal source of policy. But the problem which that policy seeks to address can only be defined in terms of the state-system nexus as a whole. Not only does sovereignty at level 2 define the general condition of anarchy at level 3, but also the character of the units generally provides a major input into the character of the system. We argued in chapters 4, 5, 6 and 7 that patterns in the structures and dynamics at the system level defined many essentials of the national security problem, and that these patterns were largely conditioned by the character and behaviour of states. Although immature anarchy defined the national security problem, mature states were a necessary part of the solution. Although both liberal and mercantilist economic structures generated conflict and insecurity, alternative economic orders could not be created without substantial changes in the actors at level 2. And although the defence dilemma and the power-security dilemma represented system-wide phenomena, the dynamics which created them stemmed from the behaviour of states. In all of these analyses the national security problem can only be understood by reference to levels 2 and 3 combined. The security problems of states cannot be assessed without reference to the system, and the character and dynamics of the system cannot be understood without reference to states.

International security can also be understood in a narrow sense by reference to the system structure as an object of security. It is this sense which is meant when the balance of power is said to serve the security of the international anarchy. As discussed in chapter 4, the balance of power can work to preserve the anarchic structure overall, without serving the security interests of any particular state. Those meanings of national and international security which are restricted tightly to levels 2 and 3 respectively do have their uses. But as argued above, it is in the nexus between them that we find the real substance of the national security problem. Taken by themselves, they produce an image of the security problem that is so distorted as to be more misleading than helpful. In relation to the concept of security, strict observance of the levels of analysis conventions weakens analysis because the space between the levels is as important as the levels themselves. To argue that the levels should not be treated in isolation, but instead should be approached as different ends of a single phenomenon, is not to suggest that each level is merely the sum of its parts. The wholly laudable attempt to clarify the basis of theory by specifying the level of analysis should not be allowed to obscure the connections which range across the levels and bind them into a single phenomenon. The levels are worth identifying because they represent an analytical synthesis which expresses something more than the sum of its parts. To focus on the 'something more', and to discount or ignore the fact that it rests on 'the sum of the parts', is to risk a division of analysis which is at odds with the fundamental wholeness and continuity of events.

The lesson to be taken from our investigation into the different levels of the national security problem is that the concept of security can only be understood by reintegrating the levels. Although individuals, states and the international system provided valuable starting points for our inquiry, they do not, in the end, provide three distinct, separable categories of referent object for the concept of national security. We see, instead, that the full richness and meaning of the concept is to be found in the interplay among them. Major security phenomena like terrorism and deterrence, or like Jervis's 'security regime', simply cannot be understood properly without a full appreciation of their sources, effects and dynamics at and among all three levels. Only when all three levels are in play can the contradictions which connect them be exposed sufficiently to be brought into the analysis. The national security problem turns out to be a systemic security problem in which individuals, states and the system all play a part. From this reintegrated, holistic perspective the three levels appear more useful as viewing platforms from which we can observe the problem from different angles, than they appear as self-contained areas for policy or analysis.

The conclusion that national security is a problem best considered in terms of the whole system would, in some respects, be a happy note on which to draw this discussion to a close. In a fit of holistic enthusiasm, we might suggest abandoning the separate usage of individual, national and international security, or at least restricting them to narrowly specified meanings, and substituting the term *systemic security* as the label by which the problem should be identified. Systemic security carries the requisite sense of parts, and the relationship among them, forming an analytical whole. It directs our attention to the integration of the three levels which we have argued is essential for understanding contradictions which define the problem, and it draws us away from the preoccupation with level 2 which distorts so much analysis of contemporary security issues.

The temptation to end in this way reflects the nature of the approach taken to this study in the first place. The objective of the book was not to find a definition for national security, but to explore the concept in an attempt to clarify its domain, identify its contradictions, and gain some idea of its part in the overall picture of international relations. As a consequence of that mandate, we have conducted our inquiry at a rather high level of abstraction, avoiding the harsh world of specific crises and problems except as illustrations along the way. The purpose of the exercise was not to seek solutions to particular policy problems, but to alter, and hopefully to expand and enrich, the background of ideas against which particular policy problems are viewed. For that purpose, the conclusion about systemic security serves well. It captures the breadth of the analysis developed in chapters 1 to 8, and obliges those who accept it to test their views on particular issues against a coherent holistic framework which forces them to deal with the contradictions inherent in the problem. The whole approach reflects the comfortable academic belief that if one can change the way people think about something important, then reality will also be changed, and never mind questions about how many people will read the book and how long the ideas will take to work their alchemy.

But although the analysis presented here is designed primarily for conceptual purposes, there is no escaping the fact that much of it can be read with policy-making in mind. The concept of security lies at the heart of many intense and important policy problems, and we cannot entirely avoid the obligation, and indeed the temptation, to forge something practical out of this mass of ideas. Two major constraints apply to this exercise. The first is the general rule that understanding something does not necessarily increase one's ability to do anything about it. Awareness of contradictions is only a preliminary to their resolution, and as we saw in chapter 8, policy-making is a heavily politicised activity, bounded by numerous pressures and restrictions. We cannot expect the leeway for dramatic reforms to be very wide. The second constraint arises from the high level of abstraction at which we have conducted our analysis. Although well-suited to the task of shifting perceptions, this level is too general to serve as a basis for firm policy prescriptions. In order to talk sensibly about definitions of national security and the appropriate policy options associated with them, one needs to anchor one's discussion firmly onto the empirical realities of a case-study. The necessity for a case-study is underlined by the arguments from chapter 2 about the diversity of states, and the arguments from chapter 3 about the need to assess threats in terms of vulnerabilities. Such a study is beyond the scope of the present volume.

What can we say about security policy in the absence of a case-study? If, for analytical purposes, we can define the security problem as systemic, and encourage a systemic perspective, does that imply that a systemic security policy is possible? One caution against excessive optimism about the prospects for systemic security policy is that a main advantage of holistic analysis is in making explicit the contradictions with which policy must deal. Our principal argument has been on the need to treat security more broadly than is conventionally done in order to capture the full implication of these contradictions. Implicit in this argument is a fundamental criticism of security policies and perspectives which are so narrowly based that they exclude or devalue some of the important components of the problem. The most common error here is to base security analysis either on level 2 or on level 3, and this error is compounded by those who argue that the problem is to choose between the two. The problem of choosing between a level 2 or a level 3 basis for security policy is not new in international relations. We visited it briefly in chapter 8 when we discussed national versus international security strategies, and we can use it to advance a general assessment of the policy problem in the light of a systemic security perspective.

The basic issue at stake is whether national security is essentially divisible in character, or whether it is essentially indivisible. If it is divisible, then a policy emphasis on level 3 is essential. This question has dominated the policy debate about security in such a way as to distract attention from more constructive lines of inquiry by perpetuating a largely sterile polarisation of views. It lies at the heart of the traditional divide between Realist and idealist approaches to international relations. Realists broadly assume that security is divisible, and consequently place their policy emphasis on the state. They acknowledge, of course, an element of indivisibility in the balance of power as the definition of the problem at level 3, but their policy orientation is almost wholly towards level 2, with the significant, but not basic, exception of alliances. Idealists stress the indivisibility of security, and concentrate much more on policies oriented towards, or made at level 3.[1]

Both positions represent a logic which is internally correct, but too narrowly based. What makes them false is the larger logic of their separation from each other. If it is assumed that the two approaches must be separate, because their logic is mutually exclusive, then each is forced into a more extreme version of itself which appears to justify the initial assumption that they stand as alternatives. In other words, because Realist policies require the arming of the state and a power-struggle analysis of the system, they naturally clash with idealist policies based on disarmament, international co-operation, and a harmony-of-interests model of the system. If that clash is seen as so basic that it precludes a meaningful mix between them, then each alternative must carry alone the whole burden of security. To do this, the Realist policy must exaggerate the necessity for a powerful state, and the idealist one must leap all the way into utopias of general and complete disarmament and world government. When presented in those forms, they appear to confirm the idea that no common ground exists between them, so making the initial distinction self-reinforcing.

The fallacy of idealism thus lies in its excessive emphasis on indivisibility, while the fallacy of Realism lies in its excessive emphasis on divisibility. These fallacies are deeply-rooted in both the practice and the study of the national security problem. The polarisation which they generate makes the middle ground hard to occupy, as many an advocate of arms control has discovered. Broader views lack the appealing simplicity of either extreme, and failures, or short-lived successes, in middle ground policies like the SALT negotiations simply justify critics on both wings.

Acceptance of a necessary divide between idealist and Realist approaches leads to E.H. Carr's despairing logic of a pendulum relationship between them, in which a period dominated by one is followed by a period dominated by the other.[2] Thus, the Realist period before 1914 led to the idealism of the interwar years, which produced the Realism of the post-1945 era. Since, as Carr rightly argued, neither approach was adequate by itself, the pursuit of either would lead to policy failures and to political reaction, which would provide the incentive for the swing to the other. On the face of it, this logic would appear to condemn us to an unprogressive and increasingly dangerous future. Repeated trial and failure of inadequate alternate approaches can only lead to cynicism.

A slightly more progressive view can be obtained if we replace the pendulum analogy with Arnold Toynbee's image of a wheel which rotates endlessly in the same pattern, but which in doing so moves itself and its burden forward over the ground.[3] This suggests that we look for improvement in each turn of the cycle. Some elements of idealist policy, for example, have carried forward into the current Realist period. On the global level we have the United Nations and its family of functional organisations, the fragmentation of the system is alleviated by the growth of extensive institutions and linkages among the states which comprise the competing groups within the system, for example, the Council for Mutual Economic Assistance (COMECON), the Organisation for Economic Co-operation and Development (OECD), the Group of 77, the Non-aligned Movement, and a host of regional bodies. All of this might be seen as an advance on the earlier Realist period, and thus as evidence of progress within the cycle: of some dialectical mechanism by which the two extremes subtly merge into, and moderate, each other.

Some comfort can be taken from this latter view, subject to the caveats about automatic progress argued in chapter 4, but it does not address the core of the problem, which is that the polarisation between the two approaches is false in the first place. In reality, as this book has sought to demonstrate, there is no choice. On practical grounds, there is no choice, because neither alternative can possibly deliver the security objectives desired of it. The very process of choice ensures not only that policy will be self-defeating, but that subsequent policies which result from reactions to it will also be ineffective. On conceptual grounds, there is no choice because, as we have argued at length, state and system cannot be disconnected from each other in relation to security.

Instead of alternating between state and system in an endless cycle of frustration, a more appealing logic is to combine and expand the two approaches by operating security policy on all three levels simultaneously. In this way, an expanded and clarified concept of security can fill the ground between the power position of the Realists and the peace position of the idealists. At a very minimum it should help to short-circuit the tedious, and largely fruitless, zero-sum debate between them. At a maximum, it might divert some of their energy onto more constructive ground. Such thinking requires the cultivation of a more sophisticated holistic view of security than does the separate pursuit of either alternative. Simplistic notions of security as deriving either from the power of the state, or from the creation of trust and order in the system, have to be replaced by more complex appreciations of how state behaviour and system structure interact. Security is partly divisible and partly indivisible, and the problem is not to emphasise one aspect at the expense of the other, but to find a balanced and workable blend. In addition to being sensitive about the vulnerabilities of, and threats to, their own state, policy-makers must also take into account the vulnerabilities of other actors, their assessments of threat, including threat from the policy-makers' own state, and the security/insecurity dynamics of the system as a whole. All policies need to be judged not just on one level, such as whether a given weapons acquisition will strengthen the state's military capability, but in relation to the other two levels, so that feedback effects can be assessed as well.

The most difficult requirement here is that states assess and acknowledge the threats which they pose to others. As Jervis notes: 'To put oneself in another's skin is terribly hard. But the costs of acting as though the meaning of one's behaviour is self-evident are enormous.'[4] If such threats are intended, then they need to be controlled in relation to the desired effect, as in deterrence policy. If they are unintended, then their effect on the system, and by way of feedback on the state concerned, must be assessed in relation to the domestic costs of whatever reforms would be required to remove them. Such assessments might be very difficult to make, requiring acknowledgement of unpleasant facts or contradictions about one's own society. They may also reveal irreconcilable ideological differences, where there is no ground for agreement between the state perceiving a threat and the state which is allegedly generating it. Market economy states, for example, might refuse to acknowledge that their economic practices pose a threat to weak developing states, because to do so would undermine the domestic legitimacy of their own organising ideology. Communist states might similarly refuse to acknowledge the political threat they constitute to others, on the grounds that it applies only to a class, and not to the state as a whole. Despite these difficulties, even the exercise of considering one's own state as a source of threat would lead to improved understanding of security dynamics in the system as a whole. The use of security complexes as a framework for analysis offers one useful technique for avoiding the normal excesses of both ethnocentric policy and utopian prescription, and for moving towards a more holistic view of the national security problem.

The main advantage of a systemic security policy, if it could be implemented, would be that security would rest on a broader, more stable base than it does at present. A balanced set of national and international security strategies would address the power-security dilemma by restraining, if not avoiding, the pendulum swings between excessive vulnerability and excessive provocation which result from the cycle of idealist and Realist alternatives. The power struggle would be contained by the avoidance of undue weakness at the state level, and the security struggle would be discouraged by sensitivity to the feedback effects of one's own actions and by openness to joint action. This is not to say that neither struggle would operate, but merely to suggest that their intensity could be reduced. By distributing the mechanisms of security widely through all levels of the system, some of the political problems of over-concentrated responsibility for security could also be avoided.

A further advantage of a systemic security policy is that it would serve to counteract the strong bias towards the military element in security policy which occurs when policy is excessively oriented towards level 2. A systemic perspective not only requires a broader look at the whole dynamic of vulnerability and threats, but also encourages a longer-term outlook. It shifts emphasis away from the state (as both the definition of the problem, and as the source and object of policy), and towards the larger system structures and dynamics which we explored in chapters 4 to 7. Consequently, it encourages more concern about the sources of threat, rather than just with ways to fend off the threats themselves, and more awareness of the role of one's own state in generating threats. On this level, as we have seen, the national security problem defines itself as much in economic, political and social terms as in military ones. Domestic, as well as foreign factors loom large in the matter, and the military aspect of security is seen to be merely part of a bigger picture. The simple view that military power is positively correlated with national security is revealed as being of limited application, and several lines of inverse correlation are made obvious. Conversely, the equally simplistic view that weapons are the prime element in the national security problem is also revealed as deficient. Because security is much more than a problem of weapons, proposals to achieve peace through disarmament are as misguided and dangerous as those which point in the direction of warfare states. An excessively military orientation towards the security problem is misleading in *either* its Realist *or* its idealist manifestation. Much energy is wasted in the struggle between them, and because neither addresses the full scope of the problem, the success of either simply leads to more frustration, reaction and insecurity.

As we have seen, security cannot be achieved by either individuals or states acting solely on their own behalf. Some collective measures are necessary among the members of the system if each is to achieve security. Just as security cannot be created by individual actors, neither can it be created by concentrating all power and responsibility at the upper levels. When such concentration happens, as we have seen in the case of individuals and the state, the collective institution becomes a major source of threat to those smaller actors it was supposed to protect. For the same reason, states fear submergence of their own powers and authorities in larger regional or global entities. If all power were concentrated in a world government, neither nations nor individuals would control their destinies, and both would feel insecure in relation to the higher authority which bound them. The sheer scale of larger entities necessarily reduces their sensitivity to the security needs of smaller actors. The more actors at every level retain some control over their security, the more stable the system will be, for a collapse at any point will not entail a collapse of the whole security system.[5]

From this point of view, security might best be served at all levels by a multi-layered approach. This could start with territorial defence strategies, which would ensure individual and local participation in national security.[6] On top of this could come a national security policy based on devising self-help solutions to conspicuous vulnerabilities in the social, political, economic or military sectors of the state. Beyond that could exist a variety of security arrangements among groups of states. These might include alliances and defence communities, formalised security communities and zones of peace, arms control agreements, dispute settlement procedures, arms production and purchase agreements, and such-like. The top layer at the global level would be centred on an organisation like the United Nations. This could provide permanent forums for discussion and negotiation, a mechanism for generating international law, dispute settlement machinery, international inspectorates, international forces, information services and, perhaps in a more mature system, monitoring services to back up national means of surveillance and early warning, and management services in relation to civil activities with sensitive military implications, like nuclear power reactors.

A security system along these lines would distribute both power and responsibility for security very widely through all levels. It would constrain the operation of the power-security dilemma, and would avoid the threats and insecurities generated by excessive fragmentation, or excessive concentration, of security powers. Because of its tiered nature, it should also lead to a greater consistency of policy throughout the system, because single actors could not so easily control enough variables to make big changes by themselves. Greater consistency and stability in policy would remove one of the principal dynamos of the power-security dilemma, which is the inability of states to rely on what others will do.

An ideal type of systemic security system like this, of course, begs serious questions from the real world about how to create the domestic conditions in any one country, let alone all countries, which would be necessary to make it work. There are no easy answers to these questions. What justifies the exercise is not its immediate practicality, but its use as an image of what might be strived for. The policy problem outlined in chapter 8 serves in this context not only to identify part of the implementation problem, but also to suggest how a systemic perspective might begin to contribute to its solution. Prevailing images of the security problem constrain new policy approaches both because of their hold on the minds of policy-makers and because they define the political dimension of public opinion on security policy. When public opinion becomes concerned about security issues, it tends to do so in the extreme forms of the idealist or Realist view. The cry goes up either for power or for peace, and in the end neither is, or can be, delivered. So long as political opinion is dominated by images of anarchy as chaos and order as world government it will be difficult to begin the reform of policy.

The systemic security perspective provides several alternative concepts which might be useful in recasting public opinion. Security complexes provide a much more subtle and balanced image of day-to-day crises than does the conventional model of power struggles. The defence dilemma and the power-security dilemma also weigh against crude images of power struggle, and might usefully supplant the arms race as the key phrase which sets the framework for discussions about military affairs. But the most important image is that of the mature anarchy, which offers an alternative ideal image for the political economy if international relations as a whole. The international system has already developed to a point at which the internationalist ideal model has convincingly demonstrated its bankruptcy as a practical alternative. Since anarchy is generally perceived as a negative condition, cynicism is widespread and the power struggle perception is reinforced by default. The image of a mature anarchy opens a possible way forward which concedes much not only to the fears of the Realists but also to the aspirations of the idealists. Like the other images, it is simple enough in its basic idea to be easily grasped, but complex enough so that the process of working through its logic would create real change. Without such holistic images, security policy can only steer aimlessly through immediate crises without any larger sense of direction or purpose.

This completes our tour of security as a concept. We return to where we started, not to find any eternal, all-purpose definitions or foolproof policy proposals, but merely to take away a clearer understanding of the problem, and a more coherent basis on which to consider contending policy alternatives.

We conclude our inquiry by going back to some of the academic questions raised in the Introduction about the role of security as a basic concept in the field of International Relations. The holistic view of security which we have developed here serves a number of useful purposes in relation to these concerns. It helps to restore the links between Strategic Studies and International Relations, and in doing so strengthens both. An excessive emphasis on national security has tended to isolate the sub-field from its parent to their mutual detriment. It justifies the subordination of security to the specialised intricacies of military affairs, thereby down-grading the importance of the concept in the more general field of International Relations, and validating the pursuit of Strategic Studies as a separate, and largely self-contained, exercise. A holistic view of security re-establishes the concept as central to International Relations. Not only does it tie together many elements of what passes for International Relations theory, but also it connects powerfully into the whole idea of interdependence, and the related attempt to reintegrate the political and economic dimensions of the subject. The concept of security offers a way of linking together international politics and international political economy into some sort of meaningful whole, as examined in chapter 5. A whole range of phenomena which are usually studied separately and for their own sake, such as arms racing, the arms industry, international trade and investment, foreign policy-making, system dynamics and sovereignty can be connected into a meaningful pattern by the concept of security. Its centrality to the study of international relations is underlined by the fact that we can derive from it major concepts and images like the security complex, the defence and power-security dilemmas, weak states and mature anarchy. These ideas stand comparison with those that can be derived from the concept of power, and, on this evidence, security stands available as an organising idea for International Relations which is at least as effective as power in unifying the subject.

A holistic concept of security serves additionally as a useful, and much needed, introduction to Strategic Studies. It not only puts the study of military affairs into a larger context, but also reintegrates it into International Relations. The theoretical and practical links between the two fields are strong, and reasserting them would relieve Strategic Studies of the heavy normative burden of being solely responsible for security. The need for this reintegration is illustrated by the attempts of Strategic Studies to take up the economic and political dimensions of security which have become increasingly prominent since the early 1970s. Issues like oil and Islamic politics have become established parts of the strategic agenda, but they fit uneasily into the adversarial mode of analysis because they invite ambiguity as to whether or not they constitute security problems in their own right, or act simply as stimulants to the use of force. In as much as the former is true, these issues constitute a more appropriate topic for the broader field of International Relations. For such a shift to occur, however, would require a greater willingness in the field to develop thinking about the economic, social and political sectors of security, and to apply them much more than is now the case to ideas like interdependence.

As we have seen, purely military approaches cannot solve, because they do not encompass, the problem of security. But in as much as analysis of security has become identified with Strategic Studies, the field appears to be engaged in a fruitless and cynical exercise in deception. The whole idea of security is degraded by exclusive identification with manipulations in military variables, because it cannot escape from the permanently two-faced nature of weapons as sources of both threat and protection. Strategic Studies, as a consequence, could never deliver the goods with which it was entrusted, and its obvious inability to do so encouraged scepticism and distaste about the nature of its work and the concept of security. If security is placed in its proper, larger perspective, then Strategic Studies is freed to make its important, specialised contribution to the study of the national security problem, without the suspicion that it is merely a front for vested interests in the domestic game of national security policy-making. When security and insecurity are seen to rest on much more than military factors, then Strategic Studies will cease to suffer so much from distorted images and inflated expectations.

A holistic conception of security further serves as an effective antidote to the political problem of national security as an ambiguous symbol. Upon investigation, the logic of national security is seen to lead irresistibly in the direction of international security, so much so that the two cannot be separated in relation to achievement of security as a policy objective. Increased awareness of the systemic security links would make it difficult for domestic vested interests to disguise their own objectives under the cloak of national security. A broader view of security, encompassing its political and economic, as well as its military dimensions serves to raise, rather than to suppress, questions about vested interests and domestic structures. While the military dimension of security traditionally demands, and gets, a considerable measure of secrecy, the economic and political dimensions are usually more open to debate. If security is seen to rest on international as much as national factors, and national actions are seen to have a major bearing on the international dynamic of insecurity, then the political utility and mobilising potency of national security will be much diminished. Only when the focus of security is fixed on the state can such sophistries prevail easily.

The problem still remains of how to reduce the parochial distortions injected into security policy by the domestic policy-making process. More inquiry is needed into the domestic factors in the national and international security problem, as well as into the many systemic and conceptual questions about security raised in this volume. Such research would not, of course, solve the problem. But it might contribute usefully to stimulating those domestic changes which would, in the long run, lead towards a more mature, stable and secure society of states.

Notes

1 Unilateral disarmers are a notable exception to this rule.
2 E.H. Carr, *The Twenty Years Crisis* (London, Macmillan, 1946, 2nd edn) p. 93.
3 Arnold J. Toynbee, *A Study of History*, abr. D.C. Somervell (New York, Dell, 1965), vol. I, p. 296.
4 Robert Jervis, *Perception and Misperception in International Politics* (Princeton, Princeton University Press, 1976), p. 187.
5 On the stability of layered hierarchies, see H.A. Simon, 'the Architecture of Complexity', *Proceedings of the American Philosophical Society*, 106 (1962).
6 See Adam Roberts, *Nations in Arms* (London, Chatto & Windus, 1976).

Index

259